Typing
Two in One

Third Edition

Keyboarding and Document Processing

Typing
Two in One

Third Edition

Keyboarding and Document Processing

Archie Drummond

Anne Coles-Mogford

Stanley Thornes (Publishers) Ltd

First published in 1996 by:
Stanley Thornes (Publishers) Ltd
Ellenborough House
Wellington Street
CHELTENHAM
Glos. GL50 1YW
United Kingdom

British Library Cataloguing in Publication Data

A catalogue record for this book is available from the British Library

ISBN 0 7487 2437 0

97 98 99 00 01 / 10 9 8 7 6 5 4 3 2

Cover photograph by Peter Cade © Tony Stone Images

Typeset by Tech-Set, Gateshead, Tyne & Wear
Printed and bound in Hong Kong by Dah Hua Printing Company Ltd

INDEX

PREFACE

Typing Two in One, Third Edition, Keyboarding and Document Processing, is a revised and up-to-date programme for the learning and application of keyboarding skills and techniques. It is similar to the second edition in that it includes the successful and popular keyboard approach used in the second edition—apart from minor alterations and additions—and covers the elementary and intermediate levels of any typewriting syllabus.

In addition, 75% of production exercises are new and many cover topics dealing with word and data processing which will enable students to prepare more fully for the electronic office and for today's examinations in typewriting at elementary and intermediate levels, as well as for examinations in word processing.

SKILL MEASUREMENT As only the student and/or tutor will know whether, at any given time, the student should be practising for speed or accuracy, we have called the speed/accuracy material **skill measurement**, and a choice must be made as to whether the practice should aim at increasing speed or working for greater accuracy. After **skill measurement** exercise 11 (SM11), the remaining exercises are on pages 158–163.

RECORD YOUR PROGRESS Each **record your progress** exercise contains every letter of the alphabet. After **record your progress** exercise 6 (R6), the remaining exercises are on pages 164–169.

KEYBOARDING SKILLS Directions for the introduction and development of **keyboarding skills** (which include **skill measurement** and **record your progress** exercises, **techniques and reviews** and **language arts** drills) are given at the top of the first page of each unit.

PERSONAL LETTERS As some learners may not wish to have a great deal of formal tuition beyond the keyboard stage, we have presented display and personal letters immediately after the figures and symbol keys.

DATA FILES In order to develop a student's initiative in the finding and utilizing of information, eighteen exercises have details that need to be verified. The student is instructed to refer to the **data files**, each of which is given a filename and presented in alphabetical order on pages 173 and 174. Other exercises may refer to details given on previous pages in the text book, eg names and addresses, dates, etc.

WORD PROCESSING PROCEDURES Although students may not have access to word processors and computers with word processing capabilities, they should take every opportunity to familiarize themselves with the terminology. We have included word processing and data processing terminology throughout the text, and wherever we considered it appropriate, we have mentioned word processing concepts and applications that would apply to the operations being practised. We hope these points will enable students to prepare more fully for the electronic office. Further, we have suggested certain tasks that may be used as **input**, and **text-editing** changes are listed separately.

INTEGRATED PRODUCTION PROJECTS Our objective here is to simulate typical office typing, and each project is prefaced by a **typist's log sheet** which gives the name of the organization, the originator's name and department, and the date together with a brief note of the contents of the project. The details given on this **log sheet** need to be referred to constantly by the student while typing the project. Each document is given an approximate target time, the idea being that the whole project should be completed within a maximum of two or two and a half hours, and at the same time, students are encouraged to make their own decisions and establish work priorities. Further it is hoped that the thematic approach will develop the student's ability to follow through a project under simulated office conditions, as well as preparing them for examinations. For further details about folders, mailable documents, interruptions (distractions), etc, please see pages 73–74. Five integrated production projects are included in this edition.

PROOFREADING To emphasize the importance of proofreading as part of the typist's training, we have included a variety of proofreading exercises on pages 148–154.

KEYBOARDING DISK A keyboarding disk is available to train the individual to operate the keyboard in the shortest possible time. It quickly and easily develops keyboarding skills for the alphabet keys, punctuation, figures and symbols. By the end of this short course, the learner should be capable of typing at 25 words a minute for 3 minutes with not more than three errors.

DATA STORE Straightforward information about essential aspects of typing display is given in each unit, but other details will be found in the **data store**, which is displayed in alphabetical order on pages 175–198.

BUSINESS VOCABULARY In the second edition, published in 1990, we mentioned word processing, computers and the electronic office. In this edition, we have continued to widen the operator's knowledge of modern technology, which affects every aspect of office work. We have also included a number of exercises which embrace many facets of the European Union.

Typing Three

For those students who wish to progress to a more advanced stage, *Typing Three: An Advanced Course* provides a modern and up-to-date approach and follows on smoothly from *Typing Two in One, Third Edition*.

Acknowledgements

The contents of this textbook reflects the comments, suggestions and recommendations made to us by students and tutors who have used our previous textbooks, and we attach a great deal of value to their contributions which, over the years, have helped enormously in the effectiveness and popularity of our typing publications.

We also wish to thank our colleagues for their helpful advice and assistance in copying the manuscript exercises.

The IBM Personal Computer and printer have been reproduced by kind permission of IBM UK Ltd; the Apple Macintosh by kind permission of Apple Computer UK Ltd.

The authors hope that students will gain experience, satisfaction and fulfilment from working through *Typing Two in One, Third Edition*, and will find pleasure and reward from using *Typing Three: An Advanced Course*, details of which are given on the back cover of this text.

ARCHIE DRUMMOND
ANNE COLES-MOGFORD

Print carrier
Composed of ribbon cassette, daisywheel, correction tape, carrier adjust lever and printing mechanism

Paper support

Paper release lever
Used to adjust the paper position

Display
Setting indicators, printing preview and memory operation

Keyboard
Function and character keys

Margin scale
Manual margin and tab indicators

Paper bail release lever
Separates platen and paper bail to ease manual paper insertion

Power switch
Turns typewriter ON and OFF

Platen knob (cylinder knob)
Moves paper manually

Essential machine parts

superscript. In the footnote, the sign may be typed either on the same line or as a superscript, and one space is left after the sign and before the start of the typing.

It should be noted that when you use the asterisk on the keyboard (not a combination character of x and hyphen) then the sign will be a superscript and any other footnote signs used in the same exercise must be superscripts. Usually there is no ruled line before a footnote in tabulation.

Telephone index

See page 107.

Typefaces (sizes of)

See page 9.

Variable linespacer

See pages 4 and 57.

Vertical linespacing

See pages 4 and 57.

Window/aperture envelopes

A great many organizations now use envelopes from which a panel has been cut out at the front; they are known as window/aperture envelopes. The object of the window envelopes is threefold:

1   It saves time in typing the name and address on both letter and envelope.
2   It avoids the possibility of error in copying the address on the envelope.
3   It eliminates the almost impossible task of typing envelopes on certain printout machines where an envelope feeder is not fitted.

The name and address of the addressee must be typed so that when the document is folded, the position of the address will coincide with the cut-out portion on the envelope. To help the typist, the position of the cut-out is shown on the headed paper by marks in the corners of the rectangles or by a ruled box. Window envelopes usually have a transparent cover over the cut-out part; aperture envelopes do not. Any special marks (for the attention of, urgent, etc) should be typed, in the box, two spaces above the name and address and must be visible when the folded sheet is placed in the envelope.

Words and figures

1   Use words instead of figures for:
    1.1 The number one on its own.*
    1.2 Figures at the beginning of a sentence.
2   Use figures in all other cases.

* If number one is part of a list of figures, it should be typed as a figure, eg 'Follow the instructions in 1, 2 and 3'.

NOTE: These are the basic rules, but other methods may be used.

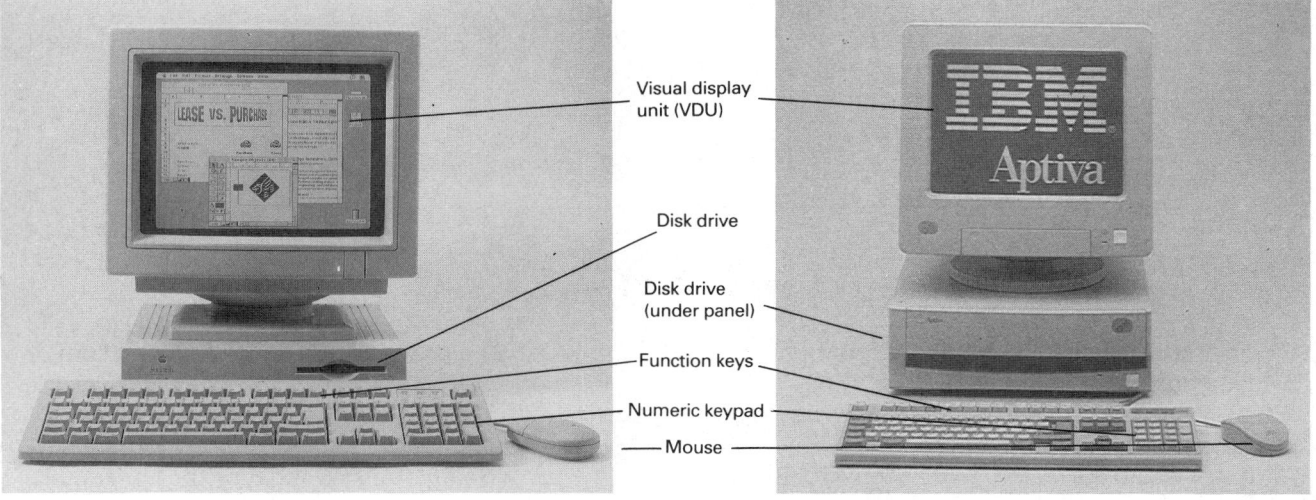

Apple Macintosh Computer   IBM Personal Computer

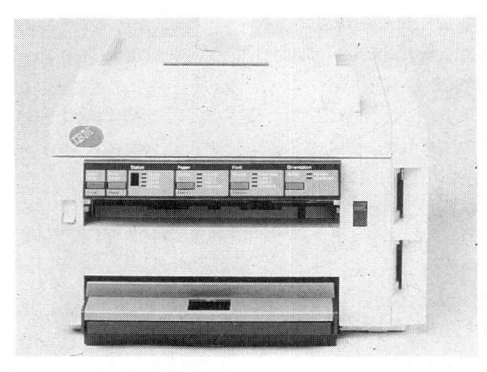

Printer

Disk drive — a diskette is inserted into the disk drive where it is rotated and a read/write head reads from or writes on to the diskette.

Function keys — special keys on the keyboard that command the machine to perform certain functions such as centring a line, emphasizing in bold type, etc.

Keyboard — the alphabetic and numeric keys are the same as any typewriter keyboard— known as the QWERTY keyboard.

Mouse — an electronic, hand-operated pointing device. The mouse can be used for positioning the cursor and for selecting menu options.

Numeric keypad — a bank of keys on the keyboard containing the figures 1–9 and 0 and arranged in a pattern similar to that of a calculator. It is usually operated by the right-hand fingers only.

Printer — the machine that produces characters on paper (hard copy). There are a variety of printers available: laser, ink jet, dot matrix and daisywheel.

Visual display unit (VDU) — a screen, similar to a television screen, on which the text is displayed (soft copy).

CRUISES - PRICES (PER PERSON)

Left margin 23(14)	27(18) Departure on or between	49(40) 9 nights		65(56) 12 nights		Right margin: 79(70) Tab stops: 47(38) 55(46) 63(54) 71(62)
		Twin	Single	Twin	Single	
	16 Oct 96	–	–	1,000	1,730	
	22 Oct 96 – 19 Nov 96	1,000	1,550	1,325	1,855	

6.1 Set left and right margins and tab stops.

6.2 Centre and type main heading.

6.3 Type first horizontal line, turn up two single spaces.

6.4 Move carriage/carrier to tab stop 47(38), and tap in one space for every two characters and spaces in the longest items in the two columns beneath '9 nights', ie Twin Single, and half the number of spaces between the two columns. This will bring you to the centre point, ie 53(44). From this point backspace once for every two characters and spaces in the heading '9 nights'. At this point 49(40) type the heading. It will then be centred over the two columns beneath.

6.5 Move to tab stop 63(54), and tap in one space for every two characters and spaces in the longest items in the two columns beneath '12 nights', ie 1,025 Single, and half the number of spaces between the two columns. This will bring you to the centre point, ie 69(60). From this point backspace once for every two characters and spaces in the heading '12 nights'. At this point 65(56) type the heading. It will then be centred over the two columns beneath.

6.6 Turn up once and type the horizontal line. Mark the top of the vertical lines, and keep a note of the scale points. Turn up twice.

6.7 Type each of the words 'Twin' and 'Single' at the tab stops.

6.8 The two lines of the heading in the first column 'Departure on or between' must be centred vertically. The number of lines of typing and blank lines taken so far in typing the column headings is four. If the words 'Departure on' are typed on the line beneath '9 nights' '12 nights' and the words 'or between' typed on the line below that, they will be centred on the headings already typed.

6.9 With the alignment scale at the base of the words '9 nights', turn up one single space. From the left margin find the centre point of the longest line in the first column. From this point backspace once for every two letters and spaces in the line 'Departure on'. At scale point 27(18) type the words 'Departure on'. Turn up one single space.

6.10 Centre the next line 'or between' in the same way, and type it at scale point 28(19), then turn up two single spaces and type the horizontal line.

6.11 Turn up two single spaces and type the column items remembering to type units under units, tens under tens, etc. Centre the hyphen where there are no figures given.

6.12 Turn up one single space before inserting the last horizontal line and mark the points at which the vertical lines will be placed.

7 Subdivided column headings–blocked style

If you use blocked-style tabulation, then it is not necessary to centre subdivided headings vertically or horizontally. Starting points for headings will be the left margin and the tab stops for each column. Each column heading will start on the same horizontal line which will be the starting point for the deepest heading.

8 Columns of figures

In columns of figures, care must be taken to see that units are typed under units, tens under tens, etc. When figures are in thousands and above, you may leave a space between hundreds and thousands, thousands and millions or you may put in a comma, eg 1,326,978; 793,220; or 1 326 978; 793 220.

9 Reference signs and footnotes

Tabular work frequently has footnotes to explain some reference to the figures or details in the table. The same points apply to these footnotes and their corresponding reference signs in the body of the tables as those already explained for manuscript work, ie the footnotes are typed underneath the table in single spacing with double spacing between each. The reference sign in the body is typed immediately after the item to which it refers and is always a

This is the symbol that we will use to draw your attention to information and instructions about word processing concepts and applications. In business today, it is important that you understand how modern machines with the QWERTY keyboard may be employed to format more easily a great variety of documents.

If you are typing on an electronic typewriter, a word processor or a computer with word processing software, study the manufacturer's handbook that accompanies your machine and practise the functions, movements and settings. You will find that there are a number of automatic operations. As it is essential for you to know the types of errors you make and how to overcome errors, **do not** employ the correction key during the keyboard-learning stage or when typing exercises from **skill measurement**, **record your progress** or **skill building pages**.

Cursor

When a VDU (visual display unit) is used in conjunction with an electronic machine, the typing appears on the VDU screen. On the screen there is a movable dot (hyphen) that indicates the typing point at which the next typed character will appear. This movable dot/hyphen is called the cursor. At the end of the typing line the cursor will return to the left margin automatically or when the return key is pressed.

Margins

To save the typist's time, electronic typewriters and word processors have pre-stored margin settings, tab settings, page length, etc, which may be changed to suit the layout required for a particular document. When any of these pre-stored settings are not appropriate for a particular exercise in this textbook, we suggest that you may wish to change the setting(s) by following the instructions given in the manufacturer's handbook.

Pitch

When only manual typewriters were marketed, the two typefaces available were 10 pitch (pica) or 12 pitch (elite). Then the golf ball electric typewriter brought dual pitch and a choice of 10 or 12 on any one typewriter. Most electronic typewriters now offer 10, 12 and 15 pitch and some of the more sophisticated machines offer proportional spacing (PS). Most word processing packages offer an almost unlimited choice of point size. The instructions and exercises in this edition of *Typing: Two in One Third Edition*, are based on 10 or 12 pitch and we use the word pitch when referring to margin settings.

Single-element typewriters

Nearly all electric and electronic typewriters have single-element heads. These typewriters have no moveable carriage, and there are no type bars. Instead they have a printing head attached to a carrier that moves across the page from left to right, stroke by stroke. When you wish to return the carrier to the left margin, you press the return key as you would with the electric typewriter. On most electronic keyboards, the automatic carrier return is employed.

The printing element is usually a daisywheel which is a rapidly spinning disk with spinning arms. On the tip of each arm there is a typeface character. The required character stops at the printing point and is stuck by a small hammer which imprints the image on the paper.

4.1 Blocked style

4.1.1 Set margins and tab stops.

4.1.2 All column headings start on the second single space after the main or subheading. However, if the table is ruled, then the column headings will start on the second single space after the first horizontal line.

4.1.3 The heading over the first column is typed at the left margin.

4.1.4 Headings in other columns start at the tab stop set for the beginning of the longest line in the column. Each line in any one heading will start at the same scale point. The £ sign is usually typed above the first figure of the £'s.

4.2 Centred style

Each line of a column heading is centred horizontally within the space allocated for the longest line in that column/heading. The whole of the heading in any one column is centred vertically in the space allocated for the deepest heading.

When typing multiple-line headings, proceed as follows:

4.2.1 Turn up two single spaces after the main/ subheading or, if a ruled table, turn up two single spaces after the first horizontal line.

4.2.2 Type the deepest heading first.

4.2.3 Move carriage/carrier to tab stop set for column with deepest heading.

4.2.4 If the longest line is the column itself, then all lines in the column heading are centred on the longest line in the column.

4.2.5 If the longest line is the column heading, then that line is typed at the tab stop and all other lines in the heading centred on it.

4.2.6 Find the centre point by tapping once for each two spaces/characters in the longest line. Make a note of this point.

4.2.7 Backspace one for each two characters/ spaces in the line to be centred. Type the line at the point reached.

4.2.8 In this way centre and type all lines in the heading.

4.2.9 Move to the next deepest heading.

4.2.10 Count the number of lines in this heading and subtract the number from the number of lines in the deepest heading just typed. Divide the result by two; eg:

Deepest heading	5 lines
Next deepest	2
Difference	3
Divide by two	$1\frac{1}{2}$—turn up one and a half spaces from first line of deepest heading.

4.2.11 Turn the cylinder towards you so that the alignment scale is at the base of the first line of the deepest heading just typed. From this point turn up one and a half spaces and start typing the next deepest heading. Use the same method as in 4.2.6 and 4.2.7.

4.2.12 Continue with other column headings in the same way.

5 Leader dots (*leader lines*)

Leader dots (full stops) are used to guide the eye along lines from one column to another. There are four methods of grouping which may be used, viz:

5.1 One dot three spaces .   .   .   .   .

5.2 Two dots three spaces ..   ..

5.3 Three dots two spaces ... ...

5.4 Continuous dots ....

5.5 Continuous dots are the simplest and are recommended unless you receive instructions to the contrary. Type leader dots lightly and evenly. When using continuous leader dots in a tabulated statement, move carriage/carrier to first tab stop and backspace one for each space between the columns **plus one**. At that point type last leader dot. Leave one space after the last typed character and then complete the leader dots.

5.6 If any item in the column takes more than one line, the leader dots should be typed only on the last line of the item.

5.7 When using grouped dots (5.2 for example) care must be taken to see that the groups of dots come underneath one another in all lines. To ensure this, you should adopt the following procedure: bring the carriage/carrier to the first tab stop set for the second column; backspace once for every space between first and second columns plus an extra two spaces. At this point set a tab stop. Backspace five from the tab stop just set, and set another tab stop. Continue in this way until you have reached the last word of the shortest line in the first column. Bring carriage/carrier back to margin and type first line, and using tab bar/key insert leader dots as and when required.

6 Subdivided column headings—centred style

Tabular statements may have subdivided columns. A column heading may be further divided into two or three separate items which are displayed beneath the main column heading as three separate columns. See the example on page 196; the following explanatory steps will give you an idea of how to proceed. Paper used is A5 landscape.

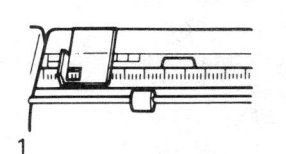

1 Paper guide

One of the marks on the paper rest shows where to set the paper guide so that the left edge of the paper will be at '0' on the paper guide scale. Check that the paper guide is set at that mark.

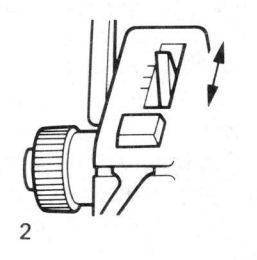

2 Linespace selector

The linespace selector has a 1, a 2 and in some cases a 3 printed on or beside it. In addition, many machines are now fitted wtih half-line spacing to give $1\frac{1}{2}$ and $2\frac{1}{2}$ linespaces. Use the manufacturer's handbook and make sure you know how to set the selector. Always adjust the selector so that it is at the required position.

3 Margins

See previous page and manufacturer's handbook.

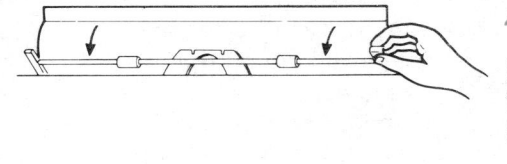

4 Paper bail

Before inserting the paper into the typewriter or printer, pull the paper bail forward, away from the cylinder, so that you may insert the paper without it bumping into the paper bail.

5 Inserting paper—typewriters and printers

5.1 Hold the sheet in your left hand. Place the paper behind the cylinder, against the raised edge of the paper guide. Turn the right cylinder knob to draw the paper into the machine. Many machines now have a special paper insertion key that should always be used when inserting the paper.

To prevent damage to the cylinder of the typewriter, use a piece of stout paper as a backing sheet.

5.2 **Check that the paper is straight**
Push the top of the paper back. If the left side of the paper, at top and bottom, fits evenly against the paper guide, your paper is straight. If it is not straight, loosen the paper (use the paper release), straighten it, and return the paper release to its normal position.

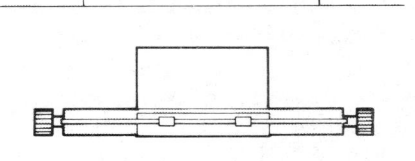

5.3 **Place the paper bail against the paper**
Slide the rubber rollers on the bail to the right or left to divide the paper into thirds. Then, position the bail back against the paper.

5.4 **Top margin**
For most exercises, it is usual to leave 25 mm (1 inch) clear at the top of the page. Many machines now have a pre-stored top margin setting; if necessary, change this so as to leave 25 mm (1 inch) clear. Where an automatic paper insertion key is not provided, turn up seven single spaces which will leave 25 mm (1 inch) clear.

Before typing the **column items**, clear tab stop already set, find centre point of column by tapping space bar once for every two characters and spaces in the heading (this will give you the centre point of the heading) then backspace one for every two characters and spaces in the longest column item. Set a tab stop at point reached. If the column items are words, this scale point will give you the starting point for each item in the column. If the column items are figures, units must be typed under units and tens under tens.

Where the **column heading** is **shorter** than the **longest item** in the column, find the centre point of the longest column item by tapping space bar once for every two characters and spaces in that item. From the point reached, backspace once for every two characters and spaces in the heading. At this point type the heading. If there is more than one line in a column heading, see instructions under **multiple-line** headings.

3 Ruling

Tabulated statements are sometimes made more effective and clearer by ruling horizontal and/or vertical lines. Although it is assumed that you have already learnt how to rule up tabulated work, the following notes will serve as a reminder.

3.1 If horizontal lines only are ruled, use the underscore and let the lines project two spaces beyond the margins on either side.

3.2 Always turn up one single space before a horizontal underscore and two single spaces after.

3.3 If both horizontal and vertical lines are required, rule these (a) either by underscore, in which case the paper has to be removed from the machine after the table has been typed, and reinserted sideways for the ruling of the vertical lines; or (b) by ink; or (c) a combination of the two, eg horizontals by underscore, verticals by ink. See that the ink ruling is the same colour as the underscore line.

3.4 The vertical lines between the columns must be ruled exactly in the middle of each blank space. It is therefore advisable to leave an odd number of spaces between the columns—one for the vertical ruling and an equal number on either side of the ruling. The points on the scale at which the vertical lines are to be ruled should be marked by light pencil marks at the top **and** bottom of the columns.

3.5 To find the point at which to mark the vertical line, proceed as follows: (It is assumed that you have left either three, five or seven spaces between columns.) (a) Move to tab stop following first vertical line. (b) If you have left three spaces between columns, backspace two

and make a pencil mark; if you have left five spaces between, backspace three; if seven spaces between, backspace four.

3.6 Move to second and other columns and repeat 3.5.
NOTE: Do not extend the vertical lines above or below the horizontals—see that they meet precisely.

3.7 **Ink** If horizontal and vertical lines are to be ruled in ink, follow the same procedures as for ruling by underscore, but in this case the beginning and end of each horizontal line must be marked in pencil, as well as the vertical lines. When the table has been completed, remove paper from machine and, with a fine nib, rule lines carefully and neatly to scale points marked. It is essential that vertical and horizontal lines meet exactly.

3.8 **Typewriter** Apart from the use of the underscore, on some typewriters provision is made for the speedy ruling of both horizontal and vertical lines. On the alignment scale/card holder you will find two small notches or round holes. Place the point of a pencil or suitable ball pen in one of these notches or holes and hold it in position against the paper with the right hand. With the left hand on the carriage release, you will obtain a continuous horizontal by running the carriage along. To avoid running the carriage too far, it is advisable to stop about two spaces before the scale point at which the horizontal line is to end, and then tap the space bar until the scale point is reached.

To make a vertical line, instead of running the carriage along, you release the cylinder ratchet by means of the interliner and turn the cylinder up with the left-hand knob. If the vertical lines extend almost to the bottom of the page, it is better to rule these by hand after the paper has been removed from the machine, to avoid the paper slipping when the cylinder is turned down for the start of the next line. After you have had some practice in ruling in this way, you will find that it saves a great deal of time, particularly if carbon copies are being taken. On your electronic typewriter there may be a function key for inserting vertical lines.

3.9 If you wish to make a very clear distinction between sections of a table, the horizontal and vertical lines can be emphasized by double or thicker ruled lines. With electronic keyboards, the **bold** function key may be used.

4 Multiple-line headings

Where column headings consist of more than one line or are of unequal depth, they are always typed in single spacing. They are never underscored in a **ruled** table.

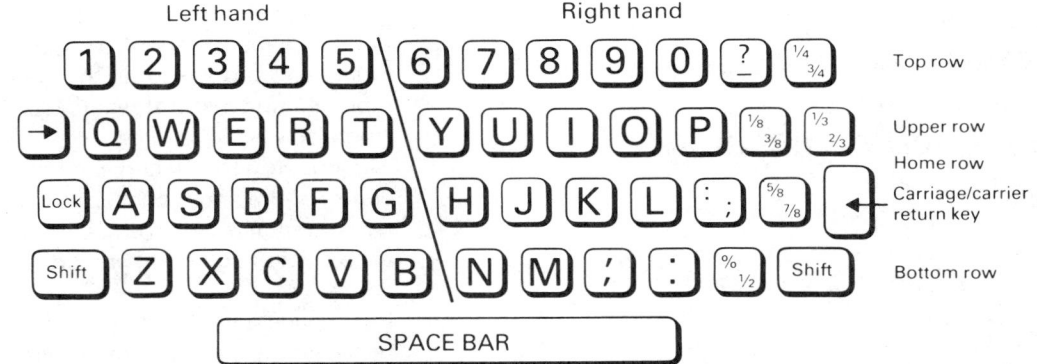

Left hand   Right hand

| 1 | 2 | 3 | 4 | 5 | \ 6 | 7 | 8 | 9 | 0 | ? | ¼ ¾ | Top row |

Back space key

| → | Q | W | E | R | T | Y | U | I | O | P | ⅛ ⅜ | ⅓ ⅔ | Upper row |

Home row

| Lock | A | S | D | F | G | H | J | K | L | : ; | ⅝ ⅞ | ← | Carriage/carrier return key |

| Shift | Z | X | C | V | B | N | M | , | . | % ½ | Shift | Bottom row |

SPACE BAR

Preliminary practice

1   Place your book on the right-hand side of your machine, or as indicated by your teacher.

2   Place your finger tips on the home keys. Left finger tips on **ASDF** and right finger tips of **JKL;** check that you place them correctly. On an electronic keyboard with raised dots on letters **F** and **J**, use the dots as a guide for finger positioning.

3   Keep your left thumb close to your left first finger.

4   Extend your right thumb so that it is slightly above the centre of the space bar.

5   Now check your **posture**.

Your head—hold it erect, facing the book.

Your shoulders—hold them back and relaxed.

Your body—centre yourself opposite the J key a hand-span away from the machine.

Your back—straight, with your body sloping slightly forward from the hips.

Arms and elbows—let them hang loosely.

Wrists—keep them low, barely clearing the machine.

Hands—close together, low, flat across the backs.

Fingers—slightly curved.

Waist—sit back in the chair.

Feet—on the floor, one foot slightly in front of the other.

6   **VDU screen**

Wherever possible:

6.1   Position the body so that you are looking straight ahead at the VDU—avoid looking at the screen sideways.

6.2   Eyes should be level with the top of the screen and between 406 mm (16 inches) and 762 mm (30 inches) from the screen.

6.3   Use adequate lighting and see that there is no glare on the screen from daylight or artificial light.

Finger movement drill

1   Without typing, practise the finger movement for the exercise you are about to type. During this preliminary practice, you may look at your fingers. You will find it helpful to say the letters to yourself. Continue the preliminary practice until your fingers 'know' where to move from the home key. Always return finger to its home key.

2   When you are confident that your fingers have acquired the correct movement, repeat this practice **without looking at your fingers**. Keep your eyes on the copy in your book and do not strike the keys. If you hesitate in making the finger movement, go back and repeat step 1.

3   Practise the finger movement for each new key until your finger moves confidently and crisply to that key.

Preliminary practice, Posture, VDU screen, Finger movement drill   **5**

Subscripts

See page 66.

Sums of money in columns

See page 61.

Sums of money in context

See page 36.

Superscripts

See page 66.

Tabulation

There are many kinds of statements and records that the typist may have to set out in tabulated form.

As you gain experience in the different forms of display, you should be able to look at a script and decide what margins are suitable. With tabulation, it is often possible to study a table and decide on a left margin. In other cases, all that will be necessary is to type out the longest line in each column, or tap out the longest line of each column (together with the spaces between columns) and see whether the table will fit in with the margins already set (within a document you are already typing) or whether a 25 mm (1 inch) left margin would be adequate.

In other situations, it will give a better result if you use the backspacing method for the horizontal centring and adopt the following procedure:

1 Main headings and columns without headings

1.1 Clear margin stops and all previous tab stops.

1.2 Insert paper with left edge at 0.

1.3 Calculate number of vertical lines in exercise and subtract this number from number of vertical lines on paper being used. Divide answer by two and add one to this figure: turn up this number from top edge of paper. Example using A5 landscape paper:

Number of vertical lines
in A5 landscape paper   35
Less number of lines in
exercise to be typed, say $\underline{22}$
Divide by two $\overline{13} \div 2 = 6$ (ignore
Plus one $\underline{1}$ fractions)
Turn up 7

1.4 Bring carriage to horizontal centre point of paper.

1.5 If **centred** style is being used, from centre point of paper backspace once for every two characters and spaces in the main heading and type heading at point reached. Turn up two single spaces.

1.6 Mark the longest line in each column. From the centre of the paper backspace once for every two characters and spaces in the longest line of each column, carrying any odd letter to the next column.

1.7 Backspace once for every two spaces to be left between the columns, including any odd number left over in step 1.6.

1.8 Set margin stop at point reached.

1.9 From left margin, tap space bar once for each letter and space in the longest line of the first column, and once for each blank space between the first and second columns. Set tab stop at point reached for start of second column.

1.10 From the first tab stop, again tap space bar once for each character and space in the longest item of the second column, and once for each blank space between second and third columns. Set tab stop at point reached for start of third column.

1.11 Continue in the same way for any additional columns.

NOTES: (a) If **blocked** style is being used, follow items 1.6–1.11 and type main heading at left margin.

(b) The number of spaces left between columns depends on the total width of the table. A minimum of three and a maximum of seven are recommended.

2 Column headings

2.1 **Blocked**   Set margins and tab stops. Turn up two single spaces after the main/subheading or, if a ruled table, turn up two single spaces after the first horizontal line. The heading over the first column is typed at the left margin. Headings in the other columns start at the tab stop set for the beginning of the longest line of each column (could be heading or column item). The £ sign is usually typed above the first figure of the £'s.

The column **items** are typed at the tab stops set for the start of the longest item. With figures, remember to type units under units and tens under tens, etc.

2.2 **Centred**   Set margins and tab stops. If the **column heading** is **longer** than the column items and if there is only one line in the heading, type it at the left margin or at the tab stop set. If there is more than one line in a column heading, see instructions under **multiple-line** column headings.

1   *MANUAL MACHINES*
    See manufacturer's handbook.

2   *ELECTRIC MACHINES*
    2.1   Preliminary practice *without returning the carriage/carrier*. Look at the carriage/carrier return key (on the right-hand side of the keyboard) and make the reach with your right-hand little finger from the semicolon to the return key and back to the semicolon.
    2.2   All fingers remain just slightly above their HOME KEY except the right-hand little finger.
    2.3   With eyes on textbook:
          2.3.1   raise the little finger of the right hand and lightly press the return key,
          2.3.2   return the little finger to the semicolon key immediately.

3   *ELECTRONIC MACHINES*
    With electronic keyboards you can, by depressing a function key, use automatic carrier/cursor return. You will notice that the carrier/cursor returns automatically at the set right margin when the line is full. This is often referred to as word wraparound. Follow the instructions given in the machine handbook or ask your tutor for advice.

Striking the keys

Manual machines—strike keys firmly and sharply.
Electric/electronic machines—stroke keys.

Prepare to type

In order to prepare yourself and your machine for typing, take the following action:
1   Electric/electronic machines—insert plug in socket and switch on machine.
2   Place book on right-hand side of machine or as instructed by your teacher.
3   Place blank typing paper on left-hand side of machine or as instructed by your teacher.
4   Set left margin at 20*.
5   Set linespace selector on '1'.
6   Set paper guide on '0'.
7   Move paper bail out of the way.
8   Insert sheet of A4 paper.
9   If necessary, straighten paper.
10   Return paper bail to normal position.
11   If necessary, turn the paper back, using right cylinder knob, until only a small portion of paper shows above paper bail.
12   Place front of keyboard level with edge of desk so that the J key is opposite the centre of your body.
13   If necessary, adjust chair height so that your forearms are on the same slope as the keyboard.
14   Place chair so that you are about a hand-span away from edge of desk.
15   Feet apart and firmly on floor.
16   See that carriage/carrier/cursor is at left margin.

Pre-stored margins

Computers, word processors and electronic typewriters may be programmed to provide whatever top, bottom and side margins you consistently require.

NOTE: Until you are instructed otherwise, all exercises should be typed line for line as in the text—use return key.

* You may use a pre-stored margin setting if you wish.

Special signs, symbols and marks

A variety of words (sign, symbol, mark) is used when referring to the characters on this page. One speaks of punctuation marks, the brace symbol and the £ sign. The word symbol is employed mainly for mathematical and scientific formulae and in computer terminology.

Degree	Small o, raised half a space.	6°
Feet	Apostrophe typed after the figure(s).	8'
Inches	Double quotation marks typed immediately after figure(s).	7"
Minus	To show subtraction—hyphen with space either side.	6 - 4 = 2
Minutes	Apostrophe typed immediately after figure(s).	10'
Multiplication	Small x with a space either side.	4 x 5
Seconds	Double quotation marks typed immediately after figure(s).	9"
To	Hyphen or dash.	21-25
Hash mark	# Should not be used for £ sign. Used for word 'number'.	#259

Constructing special signs, symbols and marks

Some characters, not provided on the keyboard, can be typed by combining two characters, ie by typing one character, backspacing and then typing the second character, or by typing one character and then the second immediately afterwards. In a few cases the interliner must be used to allow the characters to be raised or lowered.

Asterisk	Small x and hyphen.	✗
Brace	Continuous brackets typed one underneath the other.	( )
Caret	Underscore and oblique.	∠
Cedilla	Small c and comma.	ç
Cent	Small or capital C and oblique.	¢ ¢
Dagger	Capital I and hyphen.	⊥
Diaeresis	Quotation marks.	̈
Divide into	Right bracket and underscore on line above.	‾)
Division	Hyphen, backspace and type colon.	÷
Dollar	Capital S, backspace and type oblique.	$
Double dagger	Capital I raised half a space, backspace and type another capital I slightly below; or capital I and equation sign.	‡
Equation	Two hyphens—one slightly above the other.	=
Exclamation	Apostrophe, backspace and type full stop.	!
Paragraph	Small c and lowered capital I.	¶
Plus	Hyphen and lowered apostrophe.	+
Section	Two capital S's or two small s's.	§ §
Square brackets	Oblique and underscore.	⌊ ⌋
Square root	Small v and oblique, followed by underscore on line above.	√
Thousand	Capital K.	£20,000 = £20K
Umlaut	Quotation marks.	̈

On modern typewriters many of the above characters are provided. On others, it is difficult to type the division or plus as combined characters. Where this is the case, it would be wise to insert these in matching-colour ink.

When the **asterisk** has to be typed in the body of the text, it is typed as a superscript (raised character). Before typing the combination asterisk, turn the cylinder one half space towards you, type small x, backspace and type hyphen; then turn back to normal typing line. Where the asterisk is already fitted, **do not** lower the paper before typing, as the sign on the typeface is already raised.

To type a **square bracket** take the following steps:

Left bracket
1 Type oblique sign.
2 Backspace one and type underscore.
3 Turn cylinder back one full linespace and type underscore.
4 Turn cylinder up one full linespace, backspace once and continue with typing up to the right bracket.

Right bracket
1 Type oblique sign.
2 Backspace two and type underscore.
3 Turn cylinder back one full linespace and type underscore.
4 Turn cylinder up one single space, tap space bar once and continue typing.

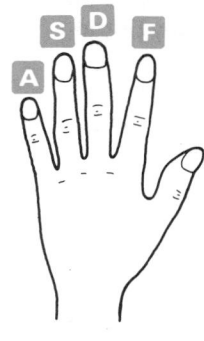

Left hand Right hand

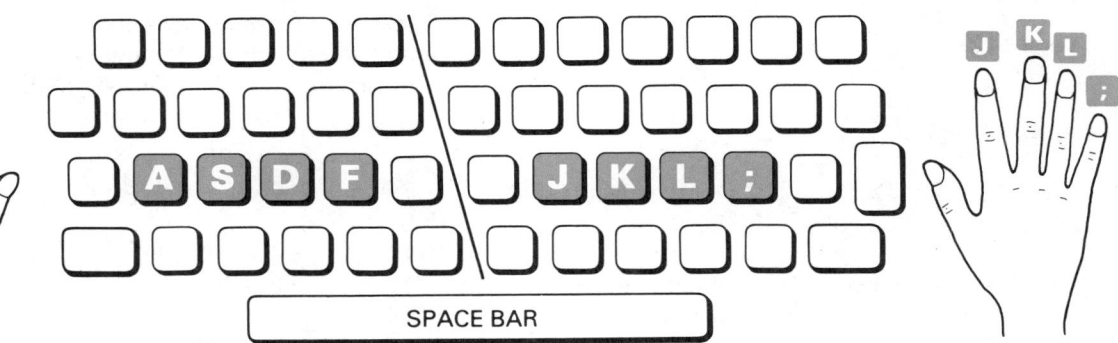

SPACE BAR

Introduction to home keys

Type the following drills.

Exercise 1

1.1 Curve fingers slightly.
1.2 Look at keyboard and place fingers on HOME KEYS
     —left hand **A S D F**, right hand **J K L ;**
1.3 Type the two lines exactly as they are—**do not look at the keyboard**.

```
f f f j j j f f f j j j f f f j j j f f f j j j f f f j j j f f f
f f f j j j f f f j j j f f f j j j f f f j j j f f f j j j f f f
```
Return carriage/carrier/cursor
Return carriage/carrier/cursor twice

1.4 Sit back, relax and look at what you have typed.

Exercise 2—operating the space bar

A clear space is left between each group of letters or words. This is done by tapping the space bar with the right thumb. Keep your other fingers on the HOME KEYS as you operate the space bar. Practise operating the space bar and returning carriage/carrier/cursor.

See that carriage/carrier/cursor is at left margin.

Exercise 3

3.1 Curve fingers slightly.
3.2 Look at the keyboard and place your left-hand fingers on **A S D F** and right-hand fingers on **J K L ;**
3.3 Type the three lines exactly as they are—**do not look at the keyboard**.

```
f f f   j j j   f f f   j j j   f j f   j f j   f f f   j j j   f f f   f j f j
f f f   j j j   f f f   j j j   f j f   j f j   f f f   j j j   f f f   f j f j
f f f   j j j   f f f   j j j   f j f   j f j   f f f   j j j   f f f   f j f j
```
Return carriage/carrier/cursor
Return carriage/carrier/cursor
Return carriage/carrier/cursor twice

3.4 Sit back, relax and look at what you have typed.

Exercise 4

Repeat exercises 1, 2 and 3.

Quotation marks

See page 112.

Roman numerals

1   Units   I (1)   X (10)   C (100)   M (1000)
     Fives   V (5)   L (50)   D (500)

2   The four *unit* symbols can be repeated to express two or three units of the *same* symbol.

Examples
1 = I	2 = II	3 = III
10 = X	20 = XX	30 = XXX
100 = C	200 = CC	300 = CCC
1000 = M	2000 = MM	3000 = MMM

3   The symbol I may be used or repeated (up to III) *after* any of the above units or fives, in which case it *adds* to the symbol in front.

Examples
I = 1	VI = 6	XI = 11	LI = 51
II = 2	VII = 7	XII = 12	LII = 52
III = 3	VIII = 8	XIII = 13	LIII = 53

CI = 101	DI = 501	MI = 1001
CII = 102	DII = 502	MII = 1002
CIII = 103	DIII = 503	MIII = 1003

4   To express 4, 9, 40, 400 and 900, take the symbol immediately *above* and put the appropriate unit symbol *in front*, which means that *it is subtracted* from the higher symbol.

4 =	5 −	1 = IV
40 =	50 −	10 = XL
400 =	500 −	100 = CD
9 =	10 −	1 = IX
90 =	100 −	10 = XC
900 =	1000 −	100 = CM.

NOTE: I can be placed *only* before V or X;
X can be placed *only* before L or C;
C can be placed *only* before D or M.

5   To express numbers other than those in point 4, take the unit of five symbol immediately *below* and *add* to it the remaining symbols by putting these *after* the unit or five symbol.

Examples
6 = 5 + 1 = VI
7 = 5 + 2 = VII
8 = 5 + 3 = VIII
14 = 10 + 4 = XIV
15 = 10 + 5 = XV
16 = 10 + 6 = XVI
17 = 10 + 7 = XVII
18 = 10 + 8 = XVIII

60 = 50 + 10 = LX
70 = 50 + 20 = LXX
80 = 50 + 30 = LXXX
600 = 500 + 100 = DC
700 = 500 + 200 = DCC
800 = 500 + 300 = DCCC

6   A horizontal line drawn over the unit symbol means that the unit is multiplied by 1000.

Example
$\overline{M}$ = 1000 × 1000 = 1,000,000.

7   To convert arabic figures into roman numerals, take each figure in turn.

Example
To convert 467, proceed as follows:
400 = 500 − 100 = CD; 60 = 50 + 10 = LX;
7 = 5 + 2 = VII; 467 = CDLXVII.

8   Used as follows:
For monarchs, form and class numbers, chapters, preface pages, tables or paragraphs. Sometimes to express the year, enumerations, subsections, etc.

Semi-blocked letters

See page 137.

Follow the routine suggested on page 6 under the heading **prepare to type**, then type each line or sentence three times, saying the letters to yourself. If time permits, complete your practice by typing each group of lines as it appears. Keep your eyes on the copy while you type and also when using the return key. The carriage/carrier/cursor must be returned **immediately** after the last character in the line has been typed. Set left margin stop at 20 (or pre-stored margin setting) use single spacing, and turn up two single spaces between exercises.

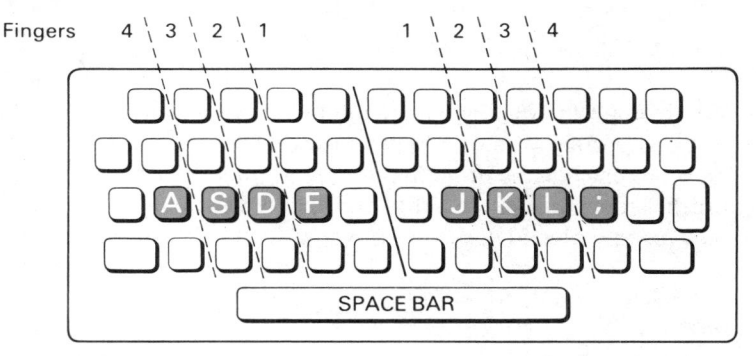

Fingers   4 \ 3 \ 2 \ 1   1 \ 2 \ 3 \ 4

Back straight   Feet firmly on floor

New keys F *and* J
Use first fingers

1   fff jjj fjf jfj fjf jfj fff jjj fjf fjfj

Turn up TWICE between exercises

New keys D *and* K
Use second fingers

2   ddd kkk dkd kdk dkd kdk ddd kkk dkd dkdk

3   fff jjj ddd kkk fkf kfk jdj djd fjk fdjk

New keys S *and* L
Use third fingers

4   sss lll sls lsl sls lsl sss lll sls slsl

5   fff jjj ddd kkk sss lll fds jkl fds jklj

New keys A *and* ;
Use little fingers

6   aaa ;;; a;a ;a; a;a ;a; aaa ;;; ;a; a;a;

7   f;f jaj d;d kak a;s lal aaa ;;; a;a a;a;

Word building

8   aaa lll all lll aaa ddd lad ddd aaa dad;

9   fff aaa ddd fad sss aaa ddd sad fad lad;

*Apply the keys
you know*

10 dad fad sad lad ask all dad fad sad lad;

11 lass fall lads fads lass fall dads fads;

ONE space after semicolon

12 all sad lads; a sad lass; a lad asks dad

13 all sad lads ask a dad; a sad lass falls

14 as a lass falls dad falls; all lads fall

*End of typing
period*

Remove paper by using paper release.
Turn off machine and remove plug from socket.
Cover machine.
Remove used and unused paper.
Leave desk tidy.

NOTE: To help you complete your keyboarding more quickly and efficiently, why not use our keyboarding software? It covers the QWERTY keyboard and a speed of 25 words a minute. For details see the Preface.

Proofreaders' marks

When amendments have to be made in typewritten or handwritten work of which a fair copy is to be typed, these may be indicated in the original copy by proofreaders' marks. To avoid confusion, the mark may also be placed in the margin against the line in which the correction is to be made. Certain examining bodies use only the stet signs, ie ⊘ in the margin, but other examining bodies may use any or all of the examples that follow.

Mark which may be in margin	Meaning	Mark in text	
lc	Lower case—small letter(s).	⎯ /	Under letter(s) to be altered or struck through letter(s).
uc or CAPS	Upper case—capital letter(s).	＝ /	Under letter(s) to be altered or struck through letter(s).
♂	Delete—take out.	/	Through letter(s) or word(s).
NP or //	New paragraph.	// or ⌐	Placed before the first word of a new paragraph.
Stet or ⊘	Let it stand, ie type the word(s) that has been crossed out and has a dotted or broken line underneath.	- - - -	Under word(s) struck out.
Run on	No new paragraph required. Carry straight on.		
⋏	Caret—insert letter, word(s) omitted	⋏	Placed where the omission occurs.
⌒	Close up—less space.	⌒	Between letters or words.
trs	Transpose, ie change order of words or letters as marked.		Between letters or words, sometimes numbered.
#	Insert space.	⋏	
‖	Straighten margin.		
ital.	Italic	⎯	(Underscore)
⊙	Insert full stop.		
;/	Insert semi-colon.		
⊙:	Insert colon.		
,/	Insert comma.		
ᵞ	Insert apostrophe.		
H	Insert hyphen.		
/−/	Insert dash.		
ᵞ ᵞ	Insert quotation marks.		
#	Insert space.		
⋏	Insert words.	⋏	
(⋏)⋏	Insert brackets.		

If a word is not clear in the text, it may be written in the margin in capitals. The word should be typed in lower case, or as indicated in the original script.

Follow **prepare to type** on page 6 and instructions given at top of page 8.

Set left margin stop at 20 (or pre-stored margin setting) use single spacing, and turn up two single spaces between exercises.

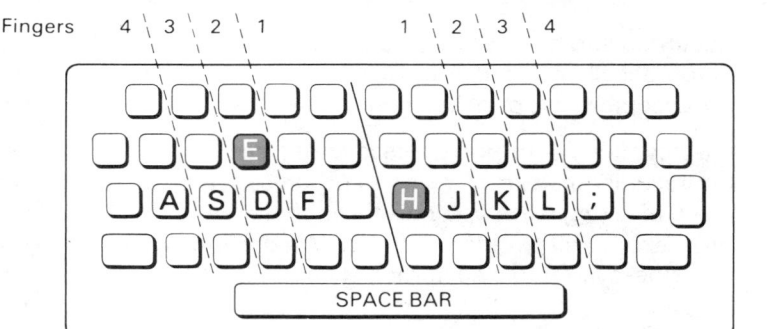

Fingers   4 3 2 1   1 2 3 4

SPACE BAR

Wrists and arms straight

Use right thumb and even strokes for space bar

Keyboarding review

1 aaa ;;; sss lll ddd kkk fff jjj asd jkl;
2 ask a lad; ask all lads; ask a sad lass;
3 all lads fall; dad falls; dad asks a lad

Turn up TWICE between exercises

New key **E**
Use D finger

4 ddd eee ded ded see ded lee ded fee ded;
5 ded sea ded lea ded led ded fed ded eke;

New key **H**
Use J finger

6 jjj hhh jhj jhj has jhj had jhj she jhj;
7 jhj has jhj had jhj she jhj ash jhj dash

Word building

8 hhh eee lll ddd held jjj aaa fff jaffas;
9 sss hhh aaa lll shall fff eee ddd feeds;

Apply the keys you know

10 see lee fee sea lea led fed eke see lee;
11 ash dash fash sash hash lash; heel shed;
12 a lass has had a salad; dad sees a lake;
13 a jaffa salad; she held a sale; he shall
14 she feeds a lad; dad has a hall; a shed;

Sizes of typefaces

10 pitch   10 characters take up 25 mm (1 inch) of space
12 pitch   12 characters take up 25 mm (1 inch) of space
15 pitch   15 characters take up 25 mm (1 inch) of space

What size of typeface are you using?

 Word processing packages offer a wide variety of fonts. A font is a complete set of characters.

documents to be photocopied and the pages automatically collated and stapled; also, some photocopiers will print in colour.

It is now fairly common practice to use the photocopier instead of taking a carbon copy(ies) or in place of taking extra originals through the word processor or electronic typewriter. When sending out a business letter to a customer, always send the original.

Photocopiers cost money—time, maintenance, electricity, better-quality paper and other supplies— therefore, only make copies that are absolutely necessary and do not 'run off' a few more just in case they might be needed!

If you are typing an original only on a manual or electric typewriter, then not taking a carbon copy does save time as any corrections are more easily made.

Postcards

See pages 105, 185.

Postscript

See page 72.

Pre-stored margins

See pages 6 and 24.

Print (typing from)

See page 128.

Proofreading

The most competent typist makes an error occasionally, but that error does not appear in the letter or document placed on the employer's desk for signature. Why? Because the typist has carefully proofread the work before it has been taken from the machine; the error has been detected and it has been corrected.

While proofreading has always been an integral part of the typist's training, it is now doubly important because if you wish to operate a word processing machine, your ability to check quickly and correct errors in typing, spelling, grammar, etc is even more meaningful. Documents prepared on a word processing machine are often used over and over again and you can well imagine the disastrous results if you typed the wrong figures, were careless in checking your finished work and your original error is then repeated hundreds of times. When checking soft copy on the VDU screen, it can be helpful to use the cursor as a guide as you move it across the screen; a less time-consuming aid is to have the base of the screen for the line you are checking and using the vertical scroll to move the text up one line at a time. Adjusting the brightness of the soft copy can also be helpful.

Follow **prepare to type** on page 6 and instructions given at top of page 8.

Set left margin stop at 20 (or pre-stored margin setting) use single spacing, and turn up two single spaces between exercises.

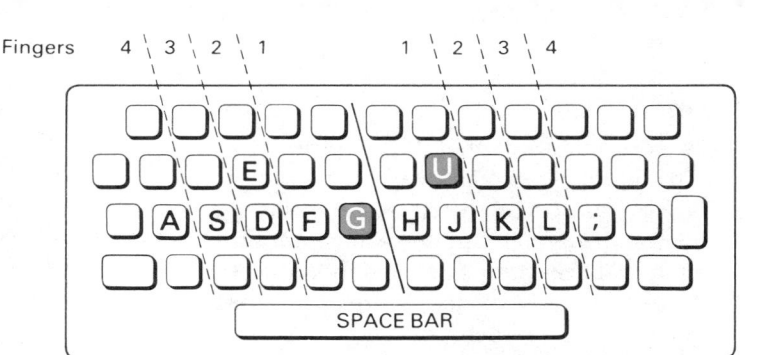

Fingers   4 3 2 1   1 2 3 4

SPACE BAR

Smooth, even strokes   Eyes on copy always

Keyboarding review

```
1  asd ;lk ded jhj def khj fed has lee had;
2  add salads; a sea lake; lads feed seals;
3  add leeks; she had leeks; he has a hall;
```

Turn up TWICE between exercises

New key **G**
Use F finger

```
4  fff ggg fgf fgf fag fgf lag fgf sag fgf;
5  fgf jag fgf gag fgf hag fgf keg fgf leg;
```

New key **U**
Use J finger

```
6  jjj uuu juj juj due juj sue juj hue juj;
7  juj sug juj jug juj dug juj hug juj lug;
```

Word building

```
8  uuu sss eee ddd use uses used useful us;
9  jjj uuu ddd ggg eee judge judges judged;
```

Apply the keys you know

```
10  fag sag lag jag gag hag keg leg egg keg;
11  dues hues jugs hugs lugs suds eggs legs;
12  he had a dull glass; a judge has a flag;
13  see she has a full jug; she used jaffas;
14  dad had a full keg; he shall guess; use;
```

Size of paper
12 pitch

When giving the measurements of paper, always state the width first.
With 12 pitch typeface there are 12 characters to 25 mm (1").
A4 paper 210 × 297 mm (8¼" × 11¾")

```
0                                                      100
|                          |                             |
|                    centre point 50                     |
|                                                        |
```

NOTE: To help you complete your keyboarding more quickly and efficiently, why not use our keyboarding software? It covers the QWERTY keyboard and a speed of 25 words a minute. For details see the Preface.

Numbers

1 Cardinal numbers

These are arabic numbers—1, 2, 3, etc.

1.1 The figure 1 is expressed either by the lower-case l or by the figure 1 if this is provided on the typewriter, but these must not be mixed, ie the same key must be used for figure 1 throughout an exercise. **Never** use capital I for the cardinal number 1.

2 Ordinal numbers

Denote order or sequence, eg 1st, 2nd or first, second.

2.1 These are not abbreviations and must not, therefore, be followed by a full stop.

2.2 Words or figures may be used: follow the script and be consistent—either words or figures.

3 Roman numerals

These are formed from seven symbols known as units and fives, viz:

3.1 Units	I (1)	X (10)	C (100)	M (1,000)
3.2 Fives		V (5)	L (50)	D (500)

4 Figures in columns

4.1 Units under units, tens under tens, etc.

4.2 Thousands, etc, should be marked either by a comma or space—be consistent.

5 Figures in continuous matter

5.1 In general, thousands and millions may be indicated by a comma or space.*

5.2 Certain examining bodies prefer a comma, rather than a space, when using full punctuation.

5.3 Always **BE CONSISTENT** when typing figures eg, type 20 000 not 20 thousand; type 300 not 3 hundred.
EXCEPTION It is acceptable to type £3 000 000 or £3m or £3 million, but it would seem preferable always to use figures.

5.4 Thousand(s) may be represented by K, eg, 24K equals 24 000.

*Because certain member countries of the EU use the comma to represent the decimal point, it would seem wise, to avoid confusion, to omit the comma from amounts of 4 or more figures. Perhaps the Community will decide on a uniform method for all members. Operators should note that, at present, certain examining bodies have set rules.

Open punctuation

See page 22.

Paper

Different qualities and weights of typing paper are available: plain bond, letterhead, bank, duplicating, etc. Most businesses use a good quality bond for their letterheads (except for airmail letters, when a light-weight paper is used) and a similar quality of plain bond paper for continuation sheets and top copies of documents.

Carbon copies are normally typed on a thin paper known as bank (flimsy); it is also available in a variety of weights and qualities. many organizations prefer an inexpensive coloured paper for carbon copies.

Paper sizes

See pages 10–13.

Paragraphs, blocked, indented, hanging

See page 135.

Personal letters

1 Personal business letters

Used when writing to an unknown person or firm about a personal business matter. The layout is similar to that of a business letter. If your home address is not printed on your stationery, type it about 13 mm ($\frac{1}{2}$ inch) from the top at the left margin, or centred on page, or in such a way that the last line ends flush with the right-hand margin. Date in usual place. Name and address of addressee may be typed in usual place or two spaces below your name at the foot of the page, and at the left margin.

2 Formal personal letters

Used when writing to someone older than yourself or to whom you owe respect. Layout as for personal business letter. Salutation is formal, eg Dear Miss Brown, Dear Mrs Taylor, Dear Mr Emery.

3 Personal letters

Used when writing to a personal friend. Your address and date as in a personal business letter. No name and address of addressee. Salutation is informal, eg Dear Mary, Dear Arthur, Dear Uncle George.

Photocopying

Because of their versatility and speed, photocopiers now have replaced duplicators. They can reduce or enlarge copy, and the more sophisticated models have collating facilities which enable lengthy

Follow **prepare to type** on page 6 and instructions given at top of page 8.

Set left margin stop at 20 (or pre-stored margin setting) use single spacing, and turn up two single spaces between exercises.

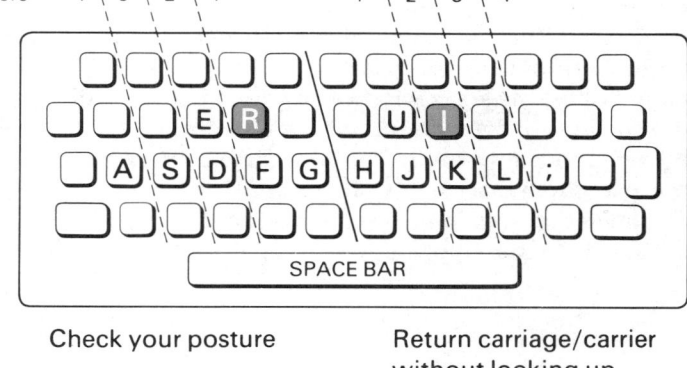

Fingers 4 3 2 1 1 2 3 4

SPACE BAR

Check your posture   Return carriage/carrier without looking up

Keyboarding review	1	fds jkl ded juj fgf jhj hag jug dug leg;
	2	a lass uses a flask; all lads had a jug;
	3	sell us a full keg; see she has a glass;

New key **R**
Use F finger

4 fff rrr frf frf jar frf far frf rag frf;
5 frf are frf ark frf red frf fur frf rug;

New key **I**
Use K finger

6 kkk iii kik kik kid kik lid kik did kik;
7 kik dig kik fig kik rig kik jig kik gig;

Word families

8 fill hill rill drill grill skill frills;
9 ark lark dark hark; air fair hair lairs;

Apply the keys you know

10 fill his flask; he is here; he had a rug
11 her red dress is here; she has fair hair
12 she likes a fair judge; he has dark hair
13 his lad fills a jug; she has rare skills
14 she is sure; ask her here; he likes figs

Size of paper
10 pitch

A4 paper 210 × 297 mm (8¼″ × 11¾″)

0   82

centre point 41

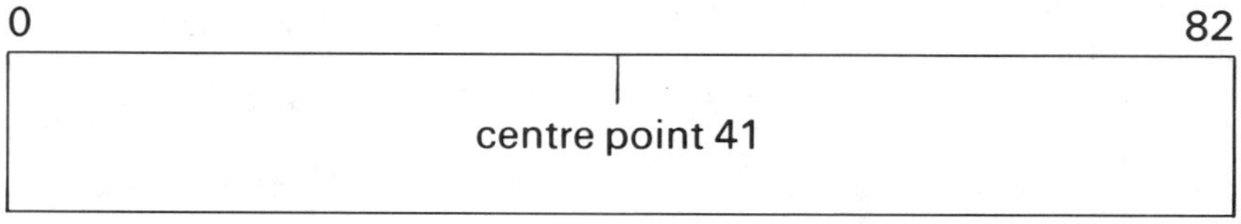

15 pitch

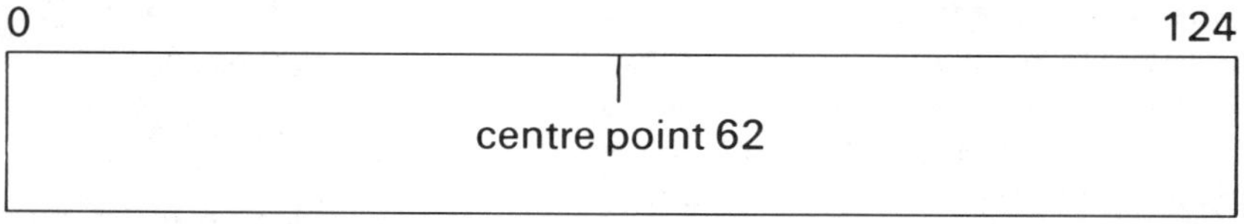

0   124

centre point 62

out invitations to weddings, coming of age parties, etc. The invitations are written in the third person with a blank space left for the insertion of names of the guests in ink. The invitation begins with the name(s) of the writer(s) whose address is placed at the bottom left margin. The date and RSVP are at the lower right margin. Invitations are not signed. The invitation should be placed in an envelope addressed to the recipient.

Itinerary

See page 124.

Labels

See envelopes page 185.

Line-end division

1   General

1.1   If possible, avoid dividing a word at the end of a line.
1.2   If it is necessary to do so in order to avoid an unsightly right-hand margin, you should not divide on more than two consecutive lines.
1.3   Divide according to syllables *provided that the pronunciation of the word is not thereby changed*.
1.4   Wherever possible, let the portion of the word left at the end of the line indicate what the word is.

2   Specific

Divide
2.1   After a prefix and before a suffix. Examples: inter-sect, absorp-tion.
2.2   *Before* the repeated consonant if the final consonant is doubled (to apply spelling rule). Example: shop-ping.
2.3   *After* the repeated consonant if the root word ends in a double consonant. Example: miss-ing.
2.4   Between the two consonants (usually) when a consonant is doubled medially. Example: bag-gage.
2.5   After a single-letter syllable in the *middle* of a word. Example: manu-script.
2.6   Between two *different* consecutive consonants in the *middle* of a word. Example: desig-nation.
2.7   After the first of three consecutive consonants in the *middle*. Example: magis-trate.
2.8   At the original point of junction in compound words and words already hyphenated. Example: fisher-man, pre-eminent.
2.9   Between two separately sounded vowels. Example: radi-ator.

Do not divide
2.10   Words of one syllable or their plurals. Examples: course, courses.
2.11   After one or before two letters only. Examples: again, aided.
2.12   Proper names. Example: Wilson.
2.13   Sums of money, sets of figures, or contracted words. Examples: £14.32, isn't, 123,456,789.
2.14   At a point which alters the pronunciation. Examples: prod-uct (*not* pro-duct), kin-dred (*not* kind-red).
2.15   The last word of a paragraph or a page.
2.16   Foreign words—unless you know the language and where to divide.

NOTE: With many electronic keyboards it is not necessary to press the return key at the end of each line to move the cursor down to the beginning of the next line. If the last word does not fit on the line, the system automatically brings the word down to the next line. This is known as wraparound or wordwrap. However, it will be necessary to press the return key for extra linespacing and after short lines, headings, etc.

It may also be possible for your machine to hyphenate a word at the end of the line, but, as the machine does not know the rules for hyphenation, it will insert the hyphen after the last character on the line, whatever it may be, and ask you to make a decision.

Manuscript (typing from)

See page 44.

Margin-release key

See page 51.

Margins (standard)

If no margin settings are given for an exercise, the following suggestions will be helpful:

	Typing line	10 point	12 point
A5 portrait	50 spaces	13–63	6–56
A4 and A5	60 spaces	22–82	12–72
Landscape	70 spaces	18–88	—not suitable
Memoranda		13–90	11–75

Measurements (typing of)

See page 53.

Minutes of a meeting

See page 102.

Modification and rearrangement of material

See page 81.

Notice of meeting

See page 100.

Follow **prepare to type** on page 6 and instructions given at top of page 8.

Set left margin stop at 20 (or pre-stored margin setting) use single spacing, and turn up two single spaces between exercises.

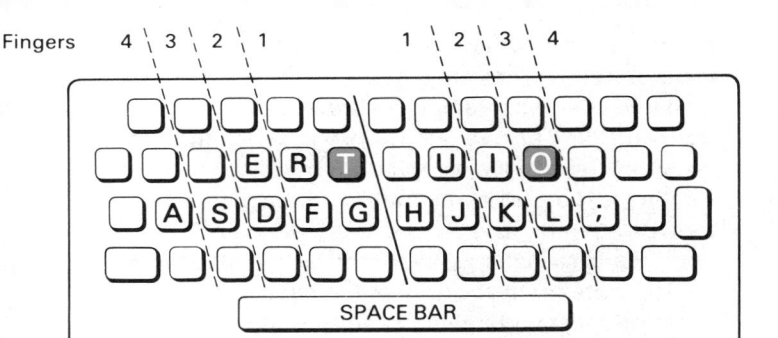

Fingers   4 \ 3 \ 2 \ 1   1 \ 2 \ 3 \ 4

SPACE BAR

Wrists and arms straight

Use right thumb and even stroke for space bar

Keyboarding review

1 fgf jhj frf juj dad kid sid did her rug;
2 his full fees; she likes a dark red rug;
3 his girl is here; he is glad she is sure

New key T
Use F finger

4 fff ttt ftf ftf fit ftf kit ftf lit ftf;
5 ftf sit ftf hit ftf sat ftf hat ftf fat;

New key O
Use L finger

6 lll ooo lol lol lot lol got lol hot lol;
7 lol rot lol dot lol jot lol tot lol sot;

Word families

8 old hold sold gold; look rook hook took;
9 let set jet get ret; rate late hate date

Homophones

Use your dictionary to check the meaning

10 sea see; here hear; tide tied; aid aide;
11 ail ale; right rite; tare tear; fir fur;

Apply the keys you know

12 get her a set; he took a full jar to her
13 he had sold the gold; at this late date;
14 that old dress looks just right for her;

Size of paper

A5 **landscape** paper measures 210 × 148 mm (8¼″ × 5⅞″), ie the width is the same as A4 but the length is half A4; therefore, the number of character spaces across a page of A5 landscape paper is 100.

0   100

centre point 50

 Spelling checker – Most word processing packages incorporate a spelling checker so that the soft copy is automatically checked for spelling errors.

When typing a draft of a document which contains a footnote(s), it is helpful to type the footnote on the next line after the reference in the text, with a horizontal line **above** and **below** it. When the final copy has to be typed, the amount of space required for the footnote(s) at the bottom of the page will then be obvious. The *Oxford Dictionary for Writers and Editors* says that copy for the printer may have the footnotes at the bottom of the page or on a separate sheet with reference figures for identification.

Form letters

See page 62.

Forms completion

See pages 59–60.

Forms of address

See pages 180, 184, 185.

Fractions

See page 36.

Full punctuation

See page 126.

Hard copy (printout)

See page 24.

Headings, blocked:

Main—See page 30.

Paragraph—See page 31.

Shoulder—See page 32.

Side—See page 82.

Sub—See page 30.

Headings, centred (with indented paragraphs)

See pages 135–136.

Horizontal and vertical display

1   Horizontal display

1.1 **Arithmetical calculation**—See page 46.

1.2 Headings and displayed items may be centred on the paper or on the typing line. In either case, find the centre point and backspace once for every two letters and spaces that the typed line will occupy (ignore any odd letter) and begin typing at the point to which you have backspaced. To centre THE TOTAL, backspace TH E*space* TO TA (ignore the L). Say the letters to yourself as you backspace.

No punctuation is inserted at the end of lines unless the last word is abbreviated and full punctuation is being used.

NOTE: When the paper is inserted so that the left edge is at 0, note the scale point at which the right edge appears; half that number is the centre of the paper. For example: A4 paper extends from 0 to 100 (elite) or 0 to 82 (pica); the centre would be 50 (elite) or 41 (pica). To find the centre point of the typing line, when the margins have already been set, add the margins together and divide by two. For example, with margins of 20 and 85 the centre point of the typing line is, $20 + 85 = 105 \div 2 = 52$ (ignore fraction left over).

1.3 **All lines centred**—See page 127.

2   Vertical display

2.1 Count the number of lines (including blank ones) that the material will occupy.

2.2 Subtract that figure from the number of line-spaces on your paper. On A4 paper there are approximately 70 single spaces; on A5 portrait paper there are 50 single spaces, and on A5 landscape paper there are 35 single spaces.

2.3 After subtracting, divide the remainder by two (ignoring any fraction) to determine on what line to begin typing. For example, to centre eight lines of double-spaced copy on A5 portrait paper:

you need 15 lines, ie 8 typed, 7 blank.

$50 - 15 = 35$ lines left over.

$35 \div 2 = 17$ (ignore $\frac{1}{2}$). Start to type the matter on the next line (18).

Inset matter (left margin)

See page 56.

Interliner lever

See page 61.

Invitations

It is customary to use formal wording when sending

Follow **prepare to type** on page 6 and
instructions given at top of page 8.

Set left margin stop at 20 (or pre-stored margin
setting) use single spacing, and turn up two
single spaces between exercises.

Follow prepare to type on page 6 and
instructions given at top of page 8.

Fingers   4 \ 3 \ 2 \ 1   1 / 2 / 3 / 4

Wrists and arms straight,   Return carriage/carrier
fingers curved   without looking up

Keyboarding review	1 ftf lol frf juj ded kik tot out rot dot;
	2 this is a red jet; the lad took the gold
	3 he asked a just fee; the old folk agree;
New key **W** *Use S finger*	4 sss www sws sws low sws sow sws row sws;
	5 sws hew sws few sws dew sws sew sws tew;
New key **N** *Use J finger*	6 jjj nnn jnj jnj fan jnj ran jnj tan jnj;
	7 jnj sin jnj kin jnj din jnj lin jnj tin;
Word families	8 end send lend tend fend rend wend trend;
	9 low sow how row tow saw law daw jaw raw;
Homophones	Use your dictionary to check the meaning
	10 sew sow; weak week; wear ware, fair fare
	11 oar ore; new knew; knead need; not knot;
Apply the keys you know	12 we saw her look at the new gate; we know
	13 he sent us a gift of red jeans last week
	14 we had left a jade silk gown and the rug

Size of paper

A5 **portrait** paper measures 148 mm (width) × 210 mm ($5\frac{7}{8}$" × $8\frac{1}{4}$"); ie
the same overall size as A5 landscape paper but with portrait paper the
shorter edge is at the top/bottom.

10 pitch	0 ——————— 59	centre point 29
12 pitch	0 ——————— 70	centre point 35
15 pitch	0 ——————— 88	centre point 44

the longest line in the left-hand figure column.

  2.2 From 50(41) tap in 7(6) and set a tab stop for the start of the items on the right half of the page.

3 Leave left and right margins of 1 inch clear which means the left margin will be set at 13(11) and a tab stop set at 89(73). To find the starting point for the money column at the far right of the page, backspace from 89(73) one for one in the longest line of the column.

4 The totals on both sides must be typed opposite each other on the same line. This may mean leaving a blank space on the shorter side, before inserting the total and the total lines.

5 The horizontal lines above and below the total itself are typed as explained on page 61.

6 Blocked or centred display may be used with open or full punctuation.

Balance sheets

The method of setting out balance sheets is the same as that already explained above, although in some instances two separate sheets are used, the heading of the balance sheet running right across the two sheets without a break—half being typed on the liabilities side and ending close to the right edge of the paper and the other half typed on the assets side starting close to the left edge of the sheet.

The side containing the larger number of items should be typed first, and, before starting to type the second sheet, you should make a light pencil mark to show the precise point at which the heading is to be continued, to ensure that the two parts of the heading are in line with one another. Also mark lightly in pencil on the second sheet the line on which the £ sign appears, the line on which the first item is to be typed and the exact position for the total, so that the two sides may coincide exactly.

Vertical balance sheets

Decide on the margins. Set left and right margin.

From the right margin backspace one for one for the longest item in the money column and set a tab stop. Where an item runs on to two lines, it is usual to indent the second line two spaces. If there are two columns of figures, leave a minimum of three spaces between each column.

Folded leaflets

See page 108.

Footnotes

1 Footnotes are used

1.1 To identify a reference or person quoted in the body of a report.

1.2 To give the source of a quotation cited in a report.

1.3 For explanations that may help or interest a reader.

2 Each footnote is

2.1 Preceded by the reference mark which corresponds to the reference in the text.

2.2 Typed in single spacing.

The reference mark in the text must be a superscript. In the footnote it is typed either on the same line or as a superscript. In the text **no** space is left between the reference mark and the previous character. In the footnote **one space** is left between the reference mark and the first word. The reference mark may be a number, asterisk, dagger or double dagger, and is placed outside the quotation mark and the punctuation mark.

It is now more popular to use one asterisk for the first footnote, two for the second and three for the third, rather than a dagger or double dagger, as the daggers are not always easy to construct on an electronic keyboard. The use of figures (in brackets) as a reference mark is favoured by printers.

In ordinary typewritten work, the footnote is usually placed at the foot of the page on which the corresponding reference appears in the body, and typed in **single** spacing. Care must be taken to leave enough space at the bottom of the page for the footnote, and, if a continuation page is needed, a clear space of 25 mm (1 inch) should be left after the last line of the footnote. It is usually separated from the main text by a horizontal line from margin to margin, and this line is typed by the underscore one single space after the last line of the text, and the footnote on the second single space below the horizontal line. If there is more than one footnote, turn up two single spaces between each. Where the typed text is short and there is plenty of white space on the sheet of paper, you may wish to make a more attractive display by leaving the clear space after the text and before the footnote, with the last line of the footnote ending 25 mm (1 inch) from the bottom of the page. Some examining bodies do not always insert a horizontal line before the footnote and, in that case, it may be wise for the examination candidate to omit the line, and we suggest that examining bodies should be asked to make the candidate's position clear. There is no horizontal line before footnotes which follow a tabulated statement.

If the typewriter has an asterisk key, the typed character will be raised half a space, but if a small x and the hyphen key are used, then it will be necessary to use the halfspace mechanism of the typewriter, or the interliner, to raise the mark above the line of typing. On word processors, there will be a superscript facility for raising characters above the typing line.

Follow **prepare to type** on page 6 and instructions given at top of page 8.

Set left margin stop at 20 (or pre-stored margin setting) use single spacing, and turn up two single spaces between exercises.

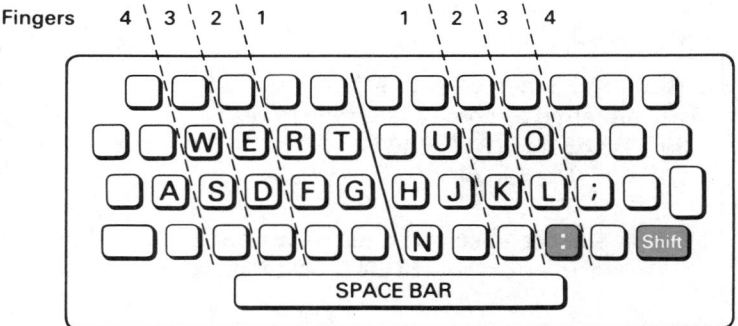

Check your posture   Eyes on copy

Keyboarding review

1 sws jnj ftf lol frf jhj won win new now;
2 we do not like those jars she got for us
3 the red dogs will go for a walk just now

Capital letters

To make capitals for letters typed by the left hand:
1 With right-hand little finger depress and hold right shift key well down.
2 Strike left-hand capital letter.
3 Remove finger from shift key and return all fingers to home keys.

New key **Right Shift**
Use right little finger

4 fF; dD; sS; aA; Ada; Sad; Dad; Fad; Wade
5 Gee; Reg; Ted; Sue; Flo; Ede; Dora; West

New key **:**
(full stop)
Use L finger

6 lll ... l.l f.l j.l Good.   Dear.   Ellis.

TWO spaces after full stop at end of sentence

7 Ask her.   Ted is sad.   Do go.   She will.

Word families

8 Wee; Weed; Feed; Reed; Seed; Deed; Greed
9 And; Sand; Wand; Rand; Send; Tend; Fend;

Homophones

Use your dictionary to check the meaning

10 altar alter; guest guessed; aught ought;
11 dear deer; aloud allowed; threw through;

Apply the keys you know

12 Ask Ed Reid if we should join the Swede.
13 She was right.   Dirk was jealous.   Fine.
14 Flora would like to go; just state when.

Typing errors

If you make a mistake, ignore it until the end of the exercise, then look at the keyboard and study the reach(es) for accurate finger movement—do not type while you look at the keyboard. *Never* overtype, ie type one character on top of another.

NOTE: To help you complete your keyboarding more quickly and efficiently, why not use our keyboarding software? It covers the QWERTY keyboard and a speed of 25 words a minute. For details see the Preface.

UNIT 8   *Keys: Right shift key, Full stop*   14

Post Office regulations

1 Post Office regulations require the address to be parallel with the longest side of the envelope.
2 Postal town should be typed in capitals on a fresh line.
3 The postcode should be typed as follows:
   3.1 It is always the last item in the address and should have a line to itself.
   3.2 If it is impossible because of lack of space to put the code on a separate line, type it two to six spaces to the right of the last line.
   3.3 Always type the code in block capitals.
   3.4 Do not use full stops or any punctuation marks between or after the characters in the code.
   3.5 Leave **one** clear space between the two halves of the code.
   3.6 **Never** underline the code.

Example Open punctuation

Messrs W H Ramsay & Co
Mortimer Street
LONDON
W1N 8BA

Full punctuation

Messrs. W. H. Ramsay & Co.,
Mortimer Street,
LONDON.
W1N 8BA

Addressing envelopes, labels, postcards, etc—See also page 42.

1 Always be sure to use an envelope sufficiently large to take the letter and any enclosure.
2 Many firms have their name and address printed in the top left corner. This ensures the safe and speedy return of the letter if, for any reason, it cannot be delivered.
3 Always type the envelope for each letter immediately after typing the letter.

4 Single spacing and blocked style are preferable on a small envelope. With larger envelopes the address may be better displayed and more easily read by being typed in double spacing.
5 On most envelopes the address should be started about one-third in from the left edge and the first line should be approximately half-way down.
6 Envelopes for overseas mail should have the town/city and country in upper case.
7 Special instructions.
   7.1 PERSONAL, CONFIDENTIAL, PRIVATE, URGENT should be typed in capitals, two spaces above the name of the addressee.
   7.2 FOR THE ATTENTION OF . . . is typed two spaces above the name and address of the addressee and may be in capitals or lower case with initial capitals when it must be underscored.
   7.3 RECORDED DELIVERY, REGISTERED MAIL and SPECIAL DELIVERY are typed in the top left corner in capitals, or immediately below the return address if there is one.
   7.4 FREEPOST and POSTE RESTANTE are typed after the name of the addressee.
   7.5 The words PAR AVION (BY AIRMAIL) are typed in the top left corner.
   7.6 Care of—typed c/o at the beginning of the line containing (a) the name or number of the house, eg Ms R Sharpe, c/o 21 Market Street, or (b) the name of the occupier, eg Ms R Sharpe, c/o Mrs U Needle, 21 Market Street.
   7.7 BY HAND is typed in the top right corner in capitals.
8 Remember to type the envelopes for any extra copies which may be sent to the other offices or persons for their information.
9 Forms of address—See page 180.

Financial statements

There are certain accounts which you may be asked to type for your employer, such as balance sheet, income and expenditure account, receipts and payments account.

Guide to typing

1 The financial statement may be divided into two sides and may have a line down the middle of the page.
2 Leave the same number of spaces to the left and right of the centre of the page—say half an inch clear on either side.
   2.1 With A5 landscape paper or A4 paper, this would mean the centre of the paper is 50(41) and, to leave half an inch clear, backspace 6(5) from 50(41) plus the number of figures in the longest item in the figure column—set a tab stop for the start of

Follow **prepare to type** on page 6 and instructions given at top of page 8.

Set left margin stop at 20 (or pre-stored margin setting) use single spacing, and turn up two single spaces between exercises.

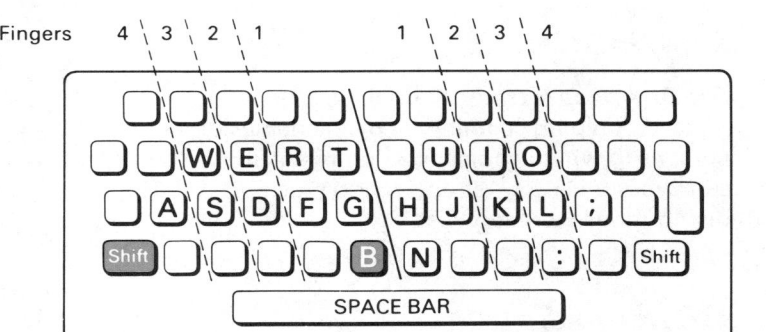

Leave TWO spaces after full stop at end of sentence

Feet firmly on floor

Keyboarding review	1	aA; sS; dD; fF; wW; eE; rR; Red; Gee; As
	2	Ask Flo. See Roger. Tell Fred. Go in.
	3	Ede had gone. Write to us. A fake jug.

Capital letters

To make capitals for letters typed by the right hand:
1 With left-hand little finger depress and hold left shift key well down.
2 Strike right-hand capital letter.
3 Remove finger from shift key and return all fingers to home keys.

New key **Left Shift**
Use left little finger

4 jJa kKa lLa jUj kIk Judd Kidd Lode Hoad;
5 Ida Ken Len Jude Owen Hilda Oakes Usual;

New key **B**
Use F finger

6 fff bbb fbf fbf bud fbf bus fbf but fbf;
7 fbf rob fbf sob fbf fob fbf hob fbf job;

Word families

8 Nib Jib Lib Job Lob Hob Hail Jail Nails;
9 Jill Hill Kill Lill Tall Ball Fall Wall;

Homophones

Use your dictionary to check the meaning

10 break brake; bare bear; blue blew; suite
11 sweet; whether weather; road rode rowed;

Apply the keys you know

12 She will be taking those salads to Jane.
13 Jill knows. Kit had to bluff Bob Green.
14 *Fred will ask us to do those jobs again.*

Typing from manuscript

You may have to type business documents from handwritten drafts. Take particular care to produce a correct copy. **Before typing**, read the manuscript through to see that you understand it. Some words or letters, not very clear in one part, may be repeated in another part more clearly.

Distribution lists

See **Business letters, 4.15**, page 179.
Instead of typing cc followed by the names of the persons to whom copies of a document should be sent, your boss may require you to type a distribution/circulation list.

Ditto marks

When the same word is repeated in consecutive lines of display matter, double quotation marks may be used under the repeated word. If there is more than one word repeated, the quotation marks must be typed under each word. The abbreviation 'do' (with the full stop in full punctuation) may be used under a group of words. When used with blocked style, the ditto marks should be blocked at the beginning of each word; with centred style, the ditto marks should be centred under the word(s). See page 124.

Document assembly

In word processing terms, this is known as boilerplating. Many documents that businesses use will contain similar information and wording and, in order to save time, form or skeleton letters (see page 62) containing the constant (unchanging) information are prepared, keyed in and stored. Space is left for the date, inside address, salutation and any other variables.

Each form letter is given a filename so that it can be retrieved easily, and a special code is placed at each point so that the machine will stop and the relevant information can be inserted at the position of the cursor. If the same letter is being sent to a number of customers, the typist keys in the names and addresses, and command keys are used to merge the two banks of information. Each customer will then receive an individually addressed and typed letter. Also, the machine, when instructed, will automatically type the name and address on a label or an envelope.

The author does not have to dictate the letter, she or he simply supplies the typist with the names and addresses of the customers and the filename of the form letter to be typed.

Standard paragraphs are also keyed in and stored. The author will supply the names and addresses and, on instruction, the machine will retrieve and assemble the paragraphs into a letter. In some cases there may be additions or deletions.

Often-used forms are also stored and are retrieved and completed as and when required.

The electronic keyboard and the VDU have made production of repetitive text very much easier and time-saving. Any variables can be inserted quickly and easily (there is no difficulty with alignment when you have a VDU) and the complete document printed out as an original – as distinct from a duplicated or printed document with the variables added.

Draft

If your employer asks you to type a draft copy of a document, it would be wise for you to enquire whether the document is likely to be radically revised or whether the draft is to show how the document will look when completed.

If the document is likely to be extensively revised after typing, then the draft should be in double or treble spacing with wide margins. On the other hand, if the draft is to show how it will look when finished, then it should be typed in the style required for the finished job.

The word DRAFT should always be typed in capitals at the top left-hand margin at least one clear space above the start of the document.

Elision

This is the omission of a letter (usually a vowel) when pronouncing a word, eg wouldn't, can't, don't. This form of abbreviation is seldom used in business correspondence unless direct speech is quoted, ie using quotation marks, or unless instructions have been given to use it.

Ellipsis

See page 98.

Enumerated items:

Arabic figures—See page 55.

Decimal—See page 103.

Letters—See page 55.

Roman, left—See page 79.

Roman, right—See page 138.

Envelopes and labels

Envelope sizes		
C5	162×229 mm ($6\frac{3}{8}'' \times 9''$)	takes A5 paper unfolded and A4 paper folded once
C6	114×162 mm ($4\frac{1}{2}'' \times 6\frac{3}{8}''$)	takes A4 paper folded twice and A5 paper folded once
DL	110×220 mm ($4\frac{1}{4}'' \times 8\frac{5}{8}''$)	takes A4 paper folded equally into three

Follow **prepare to type** on page 6 and instructions given at top of page 8.

Set left margin stop at 20 (or pre-stored margin setting) use single spacing, and turn up two single spaces between exercises.

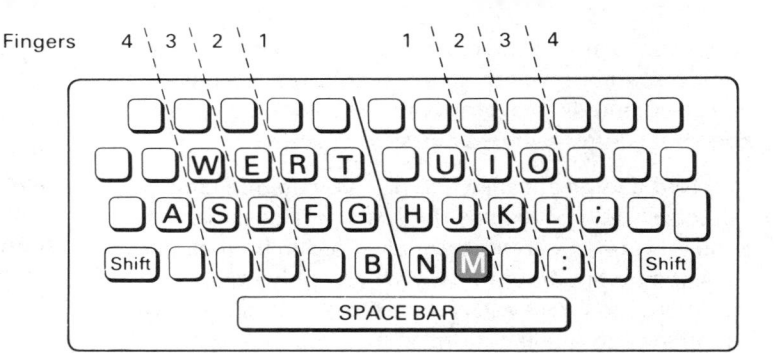

Leave TWO spaces after full stop at end of sentence

Little fingers for shift keys

Keyboarding review	1 fbf sws jnj ftf lol frf jhj Len Ken Hen Ian Win Go
	2 *Dan and Rob left. He will go just now. Ask Nell.*
	3 Lois and Earl will see June. Go with Fred Bolton.

New key M
Use J finger

4   jjj mmm jmj jmj jam jmj ham jmj dam jmj ram jmjmj;

5   jmj rum jmj hum jmj sum jmj mum jmj gum jmj strum;

Left and right shift keys

6   Ada Ben Dan East Fred Green Hilda Irwin James King

7   Lil Mark Nell Owen Rene Sara Todd Usher Wills Watt

Word families

8   arm farm harm warm alarm art hart tart darts mart;

9   game name dame fame same lame home dome some foam;

Homophones   Use your dictionary to check the meaning

10   there their; moan mown; air heir; eminent imminent

11   missed mist; mail male; aid aide; morning mourning

Practise shift keys 12   Nan Owen Miss Browne Mrs Watts Mr Usher Ms Rhodes.

Apply the keys you know

13   Most of the fame goes to John who had been working hard for his father but he has now left the works. I think he is now at home.

14   *I will see Fred tomorrow when he is in London. He will not attend the tennis meeting, but Mark will.*

NOTE: In order to avoid Repetitive Strain Injury (RSI), it is essential that you follow our instructions about posture on page 5, items 5 and 6.

qualifications you have, what your main interests are, what recreational activities and hobbies you have, etc. Sometimes this information is referred to as a personal data sheet or a curriculum vitae.

No two people are alike and no two personal data sheets should be exactly the same. It is possible that you will arrange your personal record of your career in a somewhat different way when applying for different jobs. You will always wish to emphasize the qualities and qualifications that would make you valuable in the particular job for which you are applying.

If you have worked—for a salary or as a volunteer—you should mention this. Your work need not have been closely related to the work for which you are applying, but it may indicate to your prospective employer a measure of your intelligent thinking, dependability, resourcefulness, etc. Always list temporary or part-time work (holidays and Saturdays only).

It is usual to include the name and address of one referee. See that you give the person's name—correctly spelt—his/her title (Mr/Mrs/Miss/Ms) and correct address and telephone number. **Never**, in any circumstances, give as a reference a person whose permission you have not asked in advance.

Your curriculum vitae/personal data sheet must be perfectly typed and clearly displayed with main, sub, and side/shoulder headings. The following points should be covered: your name and address; date of birth; secondary education/college/university; secretarial/office training; examinations passed; work experience (if any); special interests; name and address of a referee; date on which you are available for employment.

Cursor

On the screen of a word processor there is a moveable dot (hyphen) which indicates the typing point at which the next typed character will appear. This moveable dot/hyphen is called the cursor.

Data files

As well as being an expert typist, it is essential for you to have practice in finding and using information from various sources. Throughout this textbook, there are exercises where it is necessary for you to refer to another part of the book, or to the data files, for data to enable you to complete an exercise. The **data files** are on pages 173–174.

Dead keys

Some typewriters are provided with keys which, when depressed, do not cause the carriage/carrier to move forward the usual single character space. These are known as 'dead keys'. They are usually fitted for foreign accents so that the accent can be struck first and, without the necessity of backspacing, the letter key is then struck.

Electronic machines may have a few dead keys, eg a key for inserting vertical lines. Refer to the user's handbook for further details.

Decimals

See page 36.

Degree sign

If the typewriter does not have a special key for the degree sign, it is represented by the small o raised half a space. When typing 20 degrees, type 20° with no space between the figures and the degree sign; but when typing 20 degrees Fahrenheit or 20 degrees Celsius, type 20 °F or 20 °C—note that there is a space between the figures and the degree sign, but no space between the degree sign and the F or C. There are also other methods of display that may be used.

Display

1   Horizontal

1.1 **Block-centred**   Centre the longest line which gives the starting point for all lines.
1.2 **Centred**   All lines centred on the paper or on the typing line. To find the centre point of the typing line, add together the points at which the margins are set and divide by two.

2   Vertical

2.1 Find the number of vertical lines on the paper being used.
2.2 Count the number of lines and blank spaces between the lines, in the exercise to be typed.
2.3 Deduct 2.2 from 2.1 and divide by two (ignore fractions).
2.4 Turn up the number of linespaces arrived at in 2.3 **plus one extra**.

Distractions

See page 74.

Check your work after each exercise

After returning the carriage/carrier/cursor at the end of an exercise, check your typescript carefully and circle any errors. ALWAYS check BEFORE removing the paper from the machine.

```
                        They have to leave early.
```

1 Each incorrect character is one error.
2 Each incorrect punctuation is one error.
3 An extra space is one error.
4 Omitting a space is one error.
5 A raised/lowered capital is one error.
6 An uneven left margin is one error.
7 Omitting a word is one error.
8 Inserting an extra word is one error.
9 Inserting an extra letter is one error.
10 Omitting a letter is one error.

```
1  The(y) have to leave early.
2  They have to leave early(?)
3  They() have to leave early.
4  They have(t)o leave early.
5  (T)hey have to leave early.
6  ()They have to leave early.
7  They have() leave early.
8  They have to (to) leave early.
9  They have to leave(s) early.
10 They have to (l)ave early.
```

Half- or one-minute goals

1 Type the exercise. If any word causes you to hesitate, type that word three times.
2 Take a half- or one-minute timing.
3 If you reach the goal, or beyond, take another timing and see if you can type the same number of words but with fewer mistakes.
4 If you do not reach the goal after three attempts, you need a little more practice on the key drills. Choose the previous exercise(s) that give(s) intensive practice on the keys that caused difficulty.

NOTES:
1 There is little to be gained by typing any one drill more than three times consecutively. When you have typed it three times, go on to another drill; then, if necessary, go back to the original drill.
2 At present, techniques (operating the keys evenly, good posture, eyes on copy, returning the carriage/carrier/cursor without looking up) are very important and you should concentrate on good techniques. If your techniques are right, then accuracy will follow. However, if you have more than two errors for each minute typed, it could mean that you have not practised the new keys sufficiently and that you should go back and do further intensive practice on certain key drills.

Measure your speed

Five strokes count as one 'standard' word. In a typing line of 50 spaces there are 10 'standard' words. The figures to the right of each exercise indicate the number of 'standard' words in the complete line, and the scale below indicates the number across the page. If in the exercise below you reach the word 'we' in one minute, your speed is 10 + 6 = 16 words per minute. You will now be able to measure and record your speed on a skill measurement chart available from the publishers.

Type the following exercise as instructed under Nos 1–4 of **half- or one-minute goals**. Set left margin at 20.

Goal—8 words in half a minute   16 words in 1 minute

```
We will take her to see our new house on the north   10
                                        8
side of the new estates and we shall ask George to   20
                             16
join us at that time. (SI 1.04)                       24

  1 | 2 | 3 | 4 | 5 | 6 | 7 | 8 | 9 | 10 |
```

Clean and uncreased work

Typed work that is accurate and quickly produced can be spoilt by dirty finger marks, smudges and, particularly on the carbon copy, creases. It is important to be organized and methodical. Keep your workstation neat and tidy with everything within easy reach; this will aid you in producing neat and clean documents.

Continuous stationery

Invoice sets are usually in continuous form with perforations between the sets which may be NCR (no carbons required) paper or one-time only carbon paper. Paper for word processing printouts may also be in continuous form edged by sprocket holes for use on the tractor-feed device. The paper may be letterheads, invoice forms, payslips, etc.

Correction of errors

Correct the error as soon as you know you have made a mistake and read through the whole exercise when you have finished typing it and while the paper is still in the machine, or read it on the screen if you are using a computer, in case there is an error you had not noticed before.

There are various methods which may be used to correct errors:

1 Rubber

1.1 Turn up the paper so that the error is on top of the platen or paper table.
1.2 Press the paper tightly against the cylinder or paper table to prevent slipping.
1.3 Erase the error by rubbing gently up and down, blowing away rubber dust as you do so. (Too much pressure may cause a hole.)
1.4 If you are using a new or heavily inked ribbon, erase first with a soft rubber and then with a typewriter eraser.
1.5 Turn paper back to writing line and insert correct letter or letters.
1.6 Always use a clean rubber.

NOTE: If the typewriter has a carriage, move it to the extreme right or left to prevent rubber dust from falling into the mechanism of the machine.

2 Correction paper

These specially coated strips of paper are placed in front of the printing point over the error on the original and between the carbon paper(s) and the copy sheet(s). The incorrect character(s) is (are) typed again through the correction paper(s) which will cover up or lift off the incorrect character(s). Remove the coated strips and type the correct character(s).

3 Correction fluid

Correction fluid is produced in various shades to match the typing paper and is applied with a small brush. The incorrect letter is obliterated and when the fluid is dry, the correct letter may be typed over the top. The liquid may be spirit- or water-based. If the spirit-based liquid is used, it is necessary to add thinner to the bottle as, after a time, the original liquid tends to thicken. Spirit-based liquid dries more quickly than water-based. Avoid unsightly blobs. Use tissue paper to wipe the brush.

4 Correction ribbon

Some electric typewriters and most electronic typewriters are fitted with a correction ribbon. When making a correction with a correction ribbon, it is necessary to:

4.1 Backspace to the error.
4.2 Press the correction key—the error is then removed.
4.3 Type the correct letter(s).

5 Correction on electronic typewriters

Electronic typewriters are equipped with a memory and may have a thin window display so that automatic corrections can be made—from a few characters to ten or more lines. The correction is made by backspacing the delete key and then typing in the correct character(s). Electronic typewriters may be fitted with a relocate key which, when depressed, returns the carrier to the last character typed before the correction was made.

6 Corrections on word processors/computers

To make a correction on a word processor/computer, one would use the automatic overstrike, delete or erase functions.

Credit note

See page 65.

Curriculum vitae: a brief account of one's career

When you apply for a job, your prospective employer will require a summary of your education and training. He or she will want to know what academic qualifications you have, what specialist

Follow **prepare to type** on page 6 and instructions given at top of page 8.

Set left margin stop at 20 (or pre-stored margin setting) use single spacing, and turn up two single spaces between exercises.

Fingers 4 3 2 1   1 2 3 4

Eyes on copy   Even strokes

Keyboarding review	1	jmj fmj kmk fmf lml am; Mat Tom Ham Sam Lamb Farm;
	2	*Mrs Lamb would like to take on the job we offered.*
	3	None of them would go with Job down the long road.
New key C *Use D finger*	4	ddd ccc dcd dcd cod dcd cot dcd cob dcd cog dcdcd;
	5	dcd cut dcd cub dcd cur dcd cud dcd cab dcd cat cd
New key Y *Use J finger*	6	jjj yyy jyj jyj jay jyj hay jyj lay jyj bay jyjyj;
	7	jyj say jyj day jyj ray jyj may jyj gay jyj way jj
Word families	8	sty try fry dry cry wry dice rice mice nice trice;
	9	shy sky sly try sty slay stay fray gray dray stray
Left and right shift keys	10	He Ask Jon Sara Kite Dale Lord Ford Hall Iris Tait
	11	Ask Miss Ford if she will see Mrs Tait in an hour.
Homophones		Use your dictionary to check the meaning
	12	sealing ceiling; council counsel; cent sent scent;
	13	stationery stationary; creak creek; cereal serial;

Apply the keys you know

14   Goal—8 words in half a minute   16 words in 1 minute

NOTE: Leave TWO spaces after full stop

He is not able to find a nice jacket which^{8} he says 10
he lost on the way to your farm. *He will send you* 20
his bill in a week or so. **(SI 1.08)**   25

1 | 2 | 3 | 4 | 5 | 6 | 7 | 8 | 9 | 10 |

---

marked BY AIRMAIL (PAR AVION). Airmail postage to all EC countries is at a cheaper rate than to non-EC European countries, and dearer still to destinations outside Europe.

7.2 In a business letter the words BY AIRMAIL are typed two single spaces after the last line of the reference, or the date if it is typed at the left margin. On the envelope the words are typed in the top left-hand corner. For example:

BY AIRMAIL (PAR AVION)

    PERSONAL

    Mr Paul O'Connor
    P R O'Connor & Sons
    24 Kenmore Road
    KILLARNEY
    Co Kerry
    REPUBLIC OF IRELAND

7.3 **Letters to the United Kingdom**

    Ms A Halcrow
    12 Scotland Avenue
    PENRITH
    Cumbria
    UNITED KINGDOM
    CA11 7AA

Note For overseas mail, the name of the **town** and the name of the **country** should be in capitals.

Cards

The typist will have to type cards for a variety of purposes such as a mailing list, telephone index, credit sales index, etc.

When cards are to be filed in alphabetical order, then the filing 'word' must start near the top edge of the card, say, half an inch down. Other information on the card should be suitably displayed with at least half an inch margins all round, unless the contents are such that it is not possible to leave margins.

A fair amount of practice in typing cards is essential and a great deal of care is necessary in order to see that the card does not slip, or become out of alignment, when turned up/down. A backing sheet will help; otherwise, fold over about half an inch/one inch at the top of a sheet of A4 paper, place the card underneath the fold and feed into the machine.

Catchword

See page 98.

Chairperson's agenda

See pages 100, 101

Circular letters

Circulars, or circular letters, are letters of same contents which are sent to a number of customers or clients. The original is usually typed on a master sheet (stencil or offset litho) and a quantity is 'run off'.

Where individually typed circular letters are required, they may be prepared on a word processor or electronic typewriter and then printed.

1 Reference

In usual position.

2 Date

Typed in various ways, eg:
21 October 1996
October 1996 (month and year only)
Date as postmark. (These words are typed where you normally type the date.)

3 Name and address of addressee

3.1 Space may be left for this, and in that case the details are typed on individual sheets after they have been 'run off'. When preparing the master (or draft), turn up eight single spaces after the date (leaving seven clear) before typing the salutation.

3.2 Very often the name and address of addressee are not inserted and, if this is so, no space need be left when the master is prepared. Turn up two single spaces after the date.

4 Salutation

4.1 Dear   , the remainder of the salutation is typed in when the name and address are inserted.

4.2 Dear Sir, Dear Madam, Dear Sir(s), Dear Sir/Madam.

5 Signature

The person writing the letter may or may not sign it. If the writer is signing, type the complimentary close, etc, in the usual way. If the writer is not signing, type Yours faithfully and company's name* in the usual position, turn up two single spaces and type the name of the person writing the letter, then turn up two spaces and type the designation.

* If the company's name is not being inserted, turn up two single spaces after Yours faithfully and type the name of the writer, then turn up two spaces and type the writer's designation.

6 Tear-off portion

See page 85.

Follow **prepare to type** on page 6 and instructions given at top of page 8.

Set left margin stop at 20 (or pre-stored margin setting) use single spacing, and turn up two single spaces between exercises.

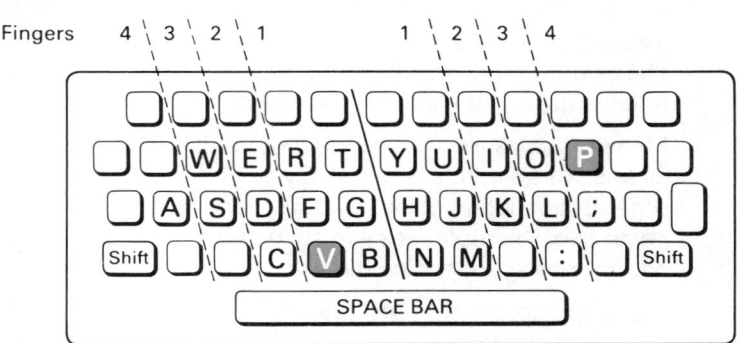

Fingers   4 \ 3 \ 2 \ 1   1 / 2 / 3 / 4

SPACE BAR

TWO spaces after full stop at end of sentence

ONE space after semicolon

Keyboarding review	1 dcd jyj dcd fbf jhj fgf lol yet coy yes call come.
	2 *Her mother had bought a new kind of jersey cloth.*
	3 He sent us a ticket for the jumble sale on Monday.
New key P *Use ; finger*	4 ;;; ppp ;p; ;p; cap ;p; lap ;p; rap ;p; jap p;p;p;
	5 ;p; pip ;p; dip ;p; sip ;p; hip ;p; lip ;p; nip p;
New key V *Use F finger*	6 fff vvv fvf fvf vow fvf van fvf vat fvf vet fvfvf;
	7 fvf eve fvf vie fvf via fvf very fvf give fvf live
Word families	8 tup cup pup sup lop pop fop hop cop top tops mops;
	9 live jive hive dive give rave pave save wave gave;
Homophones	Use your dictionary to check the meaning
	10 canvas canvass; reviews revues; patients patience;
	11 principle principal; presents presence; site sight

Apply the keys you know

NOTE: Leave TWO spaces after full stop

12 Goal—9 words in half a minute   17 words in 1 minute

She moved a pink jug away from the very back [9] shelf   10
where it had been hidden from sight[17]. *It now shows*   20
up better on that top shelf.   (SI 1.15)   26

1 | 2 | 3 | 4 | 5 | 6 | 7 | 8 | 9 | 10 |

NOTE: In order to avoid Repetitive Strain Injury (RSI), it is essential that you follow our instructions about posture on page 5, items 5 and 6.

marking the name of the recipient(s) as before. The bottom copy on which the cc/pc/bcc/bpc notes appear is the one kept for filing.

Many organizations do not now use a title such as Miss/Mrs/Mr; this is especially so within an organization when copies of documents are being sent to employees – in such cases the names would appear as follows:

bcc Harry Jones   OR   bpc HLJ
    Greta Petersen   GP
    Rose Stone   RS

ALWAYS follow the House Style.

4.17 Continuation sheets
     Blocked—See page 110.
     Semi-blocked—See page 134.

4.18 Signing letters on behalf of the writer
     4.18.1 Your employer may ask you to type and sign a letter on his behalf. The complimentary close in this case would be:

         Yours faithfully
         J R BLACK & CO LTD

         Helen M Grant

         for John Black
         Director

         or

         Yours faithfully,
         J. R. BLACK & CO. LTD.

         Helen M Grant

         Dictated by Mr. Black
         and signed in his absence

     4.18.2 Your employer may ask you to write a letter on his behalf and sign it, or circumstances may necessitate your writing on behalf of your employer, eg 'Mr Black has asked me to thank you for your letter dated 21 June, etc'. The complimentary close would be:

         Yours faithfully
         J R BLACK & CO LTD

         Helen M Grant

         Helen M Grant (Mrs)
         Secretary to J Black, Director

         or

         Yours sincerely,

         Helen M. Grant

         Mrs. Helen M. Grant
         Secretary to J. Black, Director

4.19 Titled persons   The less formal wording is now generally used, eg the salutation: Dear Lord Newton; complimentary close: I am, Sir, Yours sincerely/respectfully/faithfully, etc.

5   Folding letters

Letters and documents should be neatly folded to fit the particular size of envelope used. It is important to make sure that the envelope is of a suitable size for any enclosures that may be attached.

6   Forms of address

OPEN PUNCTUATION

6.1 Degrees and qualifications   Do not use punctuation. No spaces between the letters representing a degree or qualification, but one clear space between each group of letters, eg:
Mr (space) F (space) Eastwood (space) MA (space) BSc
Mr F Eastwood MA BSc

6.2 Courtesy titles
     6.2.1 Must always be used with a person's name, eg:
         Miss M K Green   J Bishop Esq
         Mr W P Stevens   Mrs G Hill
         Ms S G Matthews.
     6.2.2 Use either Mr or Esq when addressing a man, never both.
     6.2.3 Rev replaces Mr or Esq,
         eg Rev R S Smith
     6.2.4 Partnerships—the word Messrs is used before the name of a partnership, eg:
         Messrs Martin & Sons
         Messrs Johnson & Co
         Messrs Bowron & Jones.
     6.2.5 Courtesy titles are not used in the following cases:
         6.2.5.1 Before the name of a limited company, eg:
             P Yates & Co Ltd
             W Robertson & Sons Ltd.
         6.2.5.2 With impersonal names, eg:
             The British Non-ferrous Co.
         6.2.5.3 When the title is included in a name, eg:
             Sir John Brown & Co
             Sir Arthur Hamilton-Grey

Forms of address

FULL PUNCTUATION
See page 127.

7   Overseas mail

7.1   For quicker delivery, **all** letters to destinations outside the United Kingdom (apart from the Channel Islands and the Isle of Man) should be

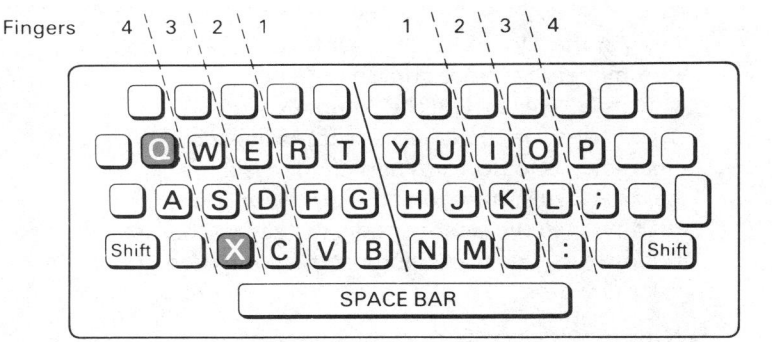

Back straight   Feet firmly on floor

Follow **prepare to type** on page 6 and instructions given at top of page 8.

Set left margin stop at 20 (or pre-stored margin setting) use single spacing, and turn up two single spaces between exercises.

Keyboarding review	1 ;p; fvf ftf jhj dpf apf kpf pot van cop map eve p;
	2 *Jack was glad my family all moved to north Avenue.*
	3 Daniel may have to give back a few paper journals.
New key X *Use S finger*	4 sss xxx sxs sxs tax sxs lax sxs pax sxs wax sxsxs;
	5 sxs sex sxs hex sxs vex sxs rex sxs cox sxs vox sx
New key Q *Use A finger*	6 aaa qqq aqa aqa quad aqa aqua aqa equal aqa quick;
	7 aqa quin aqa quit aqa quite aqa equal aqa query qa
Word families	8 qua quad squad quit quip quins quill quint quilts;
	9 fox cox mix fix nix axe lax pax wax tax taxi taxed
Homophones	Use your dictionary to check the meaning
	10 accede exceed; accept except; access excess; stake
	11 steak; checks cheques; choir quire; coarse course;
Apply the keys you know	12 Goal—9 words in half a minute 17 words in 1 minute

Joe quickly moved the gross of new boxes for which 10

you had paid and then took an extra box of the red 20

quilts and sheets you wanted. **(SI 1.15)** 25

1 | 2 | 3 | 4 | 5 | 6 | 7 | 8 | 9 | 10 |

Vertical spacing

6 single lines = 25 mm (1 inch)
Number of single-spaced lines in full length of:
A4 portrait paper—70
A5 landscape paper—35
A5 portrait paper—50

letter starts 'Dear Mr . . .', 'Dear Miss . . .', etc, the complimentary close should be 'Yours sincerely'. Never type the company's name after 'Yours sincerely', unless there are special instructions to do so. Whether you type the name and designation of the writer will depend on how well the writer knows the addressee. Follow the style in previous correspondence or ask the writer.

4.11 **Name of signatory**   In business letters a male person does not append the word 'Mr', before his name. However, it is common practice for ladies to put 'Miss', 'Mrs' or 'Ms' before their name or in brackets after.

4.12 **Enclosures**   After the last line of typing, turn up a minimum of two spaces, and type Enc at left margin. If there is more than one enclosure, then type Encs. Some organizations list the enclosures. A few employers, and some examining bodies, prefer the abbreviation Att when the word 'attached' is used in the body of the letter, eg 'We attach a copy of our price-list.' If there is more than one attachment, a note must be made of the number, eg Att 3. Another method of indicating an enclosure, or enclosures, is to type three unspaced dots in the left margin opposite the line(s) in which the enclosure(s) is mentioned. This may not be possible with a word processor.

4.13 **Postscripts**   Sometimes a postscript has to be typed at the foot of a letter, either because the writer has omitted something he wished to say in the body of the letter, or because he wishes to draw special attention to a certain point. The postscript should be started two single spaces below the last line of the complete letter and should be in single spacing. Leave two character spaces after the abbreviation. PS has no punctuation with open punctuation, but a full stop after the S with full punctuation.

4.14 **Carbon copies**   It is necessary to keep in the office for filing purposes at least one carbon copy of each letter or document typed. To produce a carbon copy, take the following steps:

4.14.1   Place face downwards on a flat surface the sheet on which the typing is to be done.

4.14.2   On top of this place a sheet of carbon paper with the coated surface upwards.

4.14.3   On top of these place the sheet of paper on which the carbon copy is to be made. Pick up all sheets together and insert in machine with coated surface of carbon paper facing the cylinder.

4.14.4   All carbon copies must be a **true copy** of the original, ie any handwritten

alterations made on an original must also be made on the carbon copies.

4.14.5   Many organizations do not take carbon copies; instead the originals are photocopied. When **photocopies** have to be made, it is usual to type on the original: pc or p/c followed by the number of copies required, eg pc 6.

4.15 **Additional copies**   A copy may be required for filing and, in addition, copies of a document may have to be sent to individuals who have an interest in the subject matter. If a copy of a letter is sent to someone other than the addressee, the letters **cc** (carbon copy) or **pc** (photocopy) or simply **copy to** are typed at the bottom left margin followed by the name of the recipient. Where a copy is being sent to more than one person, the names are typed one underneath the other (usually in alphabetical order, but not necessarily) and the name of the person for whom the copy is intended is either ticked at the side or underlined on individual copies, eg:

(First copy)   (Second copy)
cc Mr Jones   cc Mr Jones
  Mrs Stone   Mrs Stone
  Mr French   Mr French
  File   File

(Third copy)   (Fourth copy)
cc Mr Jones   cc Mr Jones
  Mrs Stone   Mrs Stone
  Mr French   Mr French
  File   File

When using a word processor, additional hard copies may be printed. The term filing means that a copy of a document is placed in a drawer or filing cabinet in a particular order (alphabetical, numerical, etc). If you use a **word processor**, you record and store the text on a disk or put it into the computer memory. If the document is properly referenced, it can be retrieved easily.

4.16 **Blind copies**   It sometimes happens that the writer does not want the addressee to know that copies have been distributed, in which case the machine operator types bcc (blind carbon copy) or bpc (blind photocopy). When the letter is finished, the carbon copies or photocopies are reinserted into the machine. At the foot of these copies the operator then inserts the bcc/bpc note at the left margin, as follows:

bcc Mr H L Jones   OR bpc Mr H Jones
    Miss G Petersen   Miss G Petersen
    Mrs R Stone   Mrs R Stone

Follow **prepare to type** on page 6 and instructions given at top of page 8.

Set left margin stop at 20 (or pre-stored margin setting) use single spacing, and turn up two single spaces between exercises.

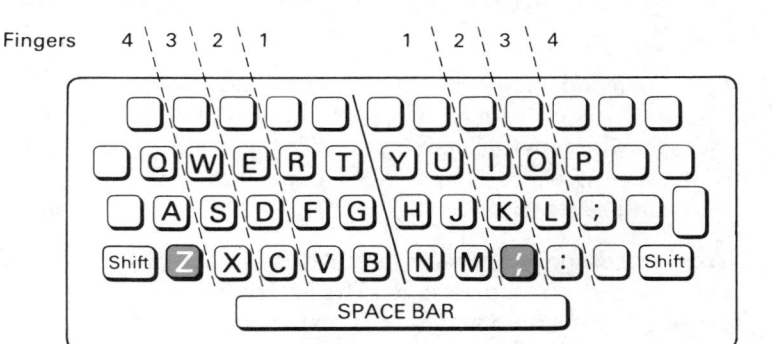

Fingers 4 \ 3 \ 2 \ 1   1 \ 2 \ 3 \ 4

Wrists and arms straight   ONE space after a comma

Keyboarding review

1 axs aqa fxf fcf axs saj sex vex tax quit aqua quad

2 *Just have one box of new grey mats packed quickly.*

3 With extra help Clive found many quite black jugs.

New key **Z**
Use A finger

4 aaa zzz aza aza zoo aza zinc aza zeal aza azure za

5 aza zip aza zero aza size aza gaze aza jazz aza za

New key **'**
(comma)
Use K finger

6 kkk ,,, k,k k,k l,k a,k s,k j,k d,k f,k hj,k g,f,k

ONE space after a comma

7 at, it, is, or, if, one, can, yes, may, for, cross

Word families

8 daze haze gaze laze maze, lazy hazy crazy, puzzle.

9 zeal zero zest zone, size prize, buzz fuzz, azure.

Homophones

Use your dictionary to check the meaning

10 affect effect; style stile; deference difference;

11 born borne; complement compliment; miners minors;

Apply the keys you know

12 Goal—9 words in half a minute   18 words in 1 minute

We do hope the right size is in stock; yes, it is;   10

we have just a few boxes, but the colour, although   20

quite pretty, is not the same. **(SI 1.15)**   26

1 | 2 | 3 | 4 | 5 | 6 | 7 | 8 | 9 | 10 |

3   Printed heading

If you are using paper with a printed heading, turn up at least two single spaces after the last line of the printed heading before starting to type. If you are using plain A5 portrait paper, or A4 paper, turn up seven single spaces.

Word processors   Some organizations provide plain paper for business documents. The letterhead, ruled forms, etc, are stored and copied on to a sheet of paper as and when required.

4   Parts of a business letter

4.1   **Reference**   If the words 'Our Ref' are already printed on the letterhead, type the reference in alignment with the print and leave at least **one** clear character space before typing the reference. If 'Our Ref' is not printed, turn up two single spaces after the printed letter heading and type at left margin. Turn up two single spaces and type 'Your Ref' if it is needed.

4.2   **Special marks applying to letters**   The words PRIVATE, CONFIDENTIAL, PERSONAL, URGENT, RECORDED DELIVERY, REGISTERED, SPECIAL DELIVERY, BY HAND or AIRMAIL are typed at the left margin at least two single spaces after the last line of the reference, or the date, if the date is typed at the left margin. FREEPOST is typed after the name of the addressee. POSTE RESTANTE means **to be called for**. The words are typed after the name of the addressee who will collect from the post office named in the address.

4.3   **Date**   Typed at least two single spaces after the reference, blocked at left margin, or typed on the same line as the reference and blocked at right margin.

4.4   **For the attention of**   It is the custom with some firms to have all correspondence addressed to the firm and not to individuals. If, therefore, the writer of a letter wishes it to reach a particular person or department, the words, 'FOR THE ATTENTION OF . . .', are typed at the left margin on the second single space after the reference, date or any special instructions. The wording is also typed on the envelope two single spaces above the name and address. (**NOTE:**   The salutation will, of course, be in the plural, ie Dear Sirs.)

4.5   **Name and address of addressee and alternate placement**   Typed in single spacing usually on the second/third single space below the reference, date, any special instructions, or 'For the attention of'.

   4.5.1   May be typed in single spacing at the foot of the page at the left margin.

   4.5.2   If the letter finishes with the complimentary close, turn up nine single spaces before typing the name and address of the addressee.

   4.5.3   If the letter finishes with the name and designation of signatory, turn up two single spaces before typing the name and address of the addressee.

   4.5.4   If you are using a continuation sheet and the name and address of addressee has not been typed before the salutation, then it may be typed at the bottom of the **first** page, two single spaces after the last-typed line and ending 25 mm (1 inch) from the bottom of the page.

   4.5.5   If you type the name and address of the addressee at the bottom of the page and the letter is marked for the attention of a particular person, the attention line is typed before the salutation. Similarly, any special instructions must be typed in the usual place and not at the bottom of the page.

   4.5.6   In a one-page letter with the name and address of the addressee at the bottom, the enclosure notation should be placed two spaces after the last line of the address.

4.6   **Salutation**   Typed on the second single space below the last line of the address and blocked at the left margin. If the correspondent wishes to write the salutation in ink, leave plenty of space. It is suggested that you turn up nine single spaces after the last line of the address before starting the body of the letter.

4.7   **Subject heading**   In fully-blocked letters, the subject heading is typed at the left margin, preferably in capitals without underscore. If lower case letters are used, the heading should be underscored. The heading must be centred if the indented style of display is being used.

4.8   **Body of letter**   Start on the second single space after the salutation or the subject heading.

4.9   **Displayed matter**   When matter is to be displayed in a fully-blocked letter, all the lines usually start at the left margin, one clear space left above and below the matter. If the display is in columns, it is usual to leave three spaces between each column. If definite instructions are given for the matter to be inset, then it must be inset, even in a fully-blocked letter. The matter is usually centred in a semi-blocked letter.

4.10   **Complimentary close**   Typed on second single space below the last line of the body of the letter. A letter with the salutation 'Dear Sir(s), Madam', should end 'Yours faithfully' which may be followed by the company's name. Sometimes the name of the company is typed after the signatory/designation. When a

Open punctuation

Many businesses and most examining bodies prefer this style for business documents. It means that the full stop is omitted from an abbreviated word (except at the end of a sentence) and is replaced by a space. Example: Mr (space) J (space) Smith, of W M Smith & Co Ltd, will discuss the terms of payment, etc, with Mrs U E St John-Browne.

Where an abbreviation consists of two or more letters with a full stop after each letter, the full stops are omitted and no space is left between the letters, but one space (or comma) after each group of letters. Example: Mrs G L Hunt, 21 South Road, will call at 7 pm today. She requires past examination papers from several bodies, eg LCCI, RSA and PEI.

Grammatical punctuation must still be used.

The major part of this book is written in open punctuation, ie no full stops are given in or after abbreviations.

Improve your typing technique

If a technique is faulty, check with the following list and carry out the remedial drill.

Faulty technique   **Remedy**

Manual machines

Faulty technique		Remedy
Raised capitals caused by releasing shift key too soon.	I may go.	Drills 4–9 page 14; drills 4–9, page 15.
Uneven left margin, caused by faulty carriage return.	I may go.	Return carriage without looking up. Any **apply the keys you know**.
Heavy strokes, caused by not releasing keys quickly.	I mmay go.	Practise finger movement drills. Any **apply the keys you know**.
Light strokes, caused by not striking the keys hard enough.	I ay go.	Practise finger movement drills. Any **apply the keys you know**.

Manual, electric and electronic machines

Faulty technique		Remedy
Omitting or inserting words (looked up from the copy).	may I go	Eyes on copy always. Page 21—lines 1–3.
Extra spaces, caused by your leaning on the space bar.	I may go.	Right thumb slightly above space bar. Drills 10–14, page 8.
Omitting spaces, caused by poor wrist position.	I maygo.	Say 'space' to yourself each time you tap space bar. Drills 10–14, page 8.
Fingers out of position.	I ,au go.	Return fingers to home keys. Any **apply the keys you know**.
Turning letters around—eyes get ahead of fingers.	I may og.	Eyes on copy always. Say each letter and space to yourself as you type. Any preceding drills.
Extra or wrong characters caused by accidentally depressing keys.	KKK may go.	Keep all fingers slightly above home keys—especially with electronic machines.

Skill measurement

*Practice routine for all **skill measurement** exercises:*
1 Type a copy of the exercise.
2 Check and circle all errors.
3 Compare your errors with those shown above.
4 Practise the remedial drills.
5 Type as much of the exercise as you can in the time suggested.
6 Check and circle any errors.

7 On your **skill measurement table** record actual number of words typed in a minute and number of errors, if any.
8 If you made more than the stipulated number of errors, continue with the timed practice and aim for accuracy.
9 If your errors were below the tolerance given, type the exercise again (timed) and endeavour to type a little faster.

Set left margin at 20 or use pre-stored margin
Skill measurement   19 wpm   1 minute   Not more than 1 error

SM1   As those shoes are too small, you should take them   10

back and have them changed for the right size. **(SI 1.00)**   19

     1 | 2 | 3 | 4 | 5 | 6 | 7 | 8 | 9 | 10 |

Borders (ornamental)

Display work, such as programmes, menus, etc, can be made more artistic by the use of a suitable ornamental border or corners, such as the following. You should be able to make up other artistic borders, but in doing so, take care not to make the border too heavy, as this will detract from the general appearance.

```
* * * * *     0: 0: 0: 0: 0: 0    * * *     * * *
*         *   :              :    *           *
* * * * *     :              :    *           *
              0: 0: 0: 0: 0: 0    *           *
                                  *           *
                                  * * *     * * *
```

Brace (brackets)

See page 67.

Brackets (handwritten or printer's bracket)

See page 68.

Brief notes

see page 107

Bring forward reminders

Very often it is important for a person to ascertain by a particular date that a certain action has been taken. The action may be the result of outgoing correspondence, incoming correspondence, a telephone call, etc. A special file, which has a variety of names such as bring-forward file, bring-up file, tickler file, follow-up file, etc, is kept for this purpose.

As a typist it may be one of your duties to keep a bring-forward file, and for that purpose you may have a concertina file with a space for each month of the year and, at the front, pockets for each day of the current month. In the various sections you will keep papers, documents and notes, that require attention on a particular date. At the end of each month, you should transfer the contents of the next month's pocket into the daily pockets. You must train yourself to look in the bring-up file each morning and take out that day's reminders so that action may be taken.

Bullet mark

This is a heavy dot, used mainly in printing and desktop publishing, to draw the reader's attention to a particular line, section or paragraph. When this facility is not available on your machine, type two small oo's, or use the asterisk.

Business letters

1   Layout

Letters can be displayed in various ways, the styles most commonly used being illustrated below.

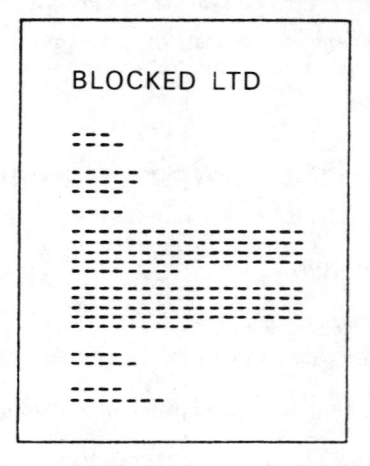

Fully-blocked (sometimes called 'blocked').

Begin every line at the left margin.

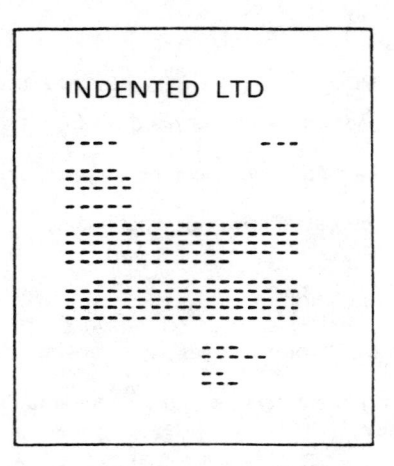

Semi-blocked (sometimes called 'indented').

Date and complimentary close as shown, with first line of each paragraph indented.

2   Punctuation

2.1   **Full punctuation**   When typing a letter with full punctuation, punctuation marks are inserted in the appropriate places in the reference, date, name and address of addressee, salutation, complimentary close and after all abbreviations.

2.2   **Open punctuation**   When typing a letter with open punctuation, no punctuation marks are inserted in the reference, date, name and address of addressee, salutation, complimentary close or abbreviations. The grammatical punctuation in the body of the letter must be inserted. If a name and address appear in continuous matter, the items are separated by a comma, or two character spaces.

Each line or sentence should be typed three times and, if time permits, type each complete exercise once. Use single spacing with double between exercises. For **skill measurement** follow instructions on page 22, and for **record your progress** follow instructions on page 24. Set left margin at 20 or use pre-stored margin.

Keyboarding review– alphabet keys

1 Five excellent school prizes were awarded and Jamy qualified for the best work in his group.

Placement of certain characters

The location of the hyphen, question mark, underscore, etc may vary with the make of machine. This also applies to a few of the signs, symbols and marks keys such as the oblique and quotation marks. When practising these keys, make sure you know whether or not you have to use the shift key, decide on the correct finger, and then practise the reach from the home key; then type the drills given.

New key hyphen

NO space before or after hyphen

2 blue-grey, one-fifth, part-time, left-hand, in-out
3 Over one-third are part-time day-release students.
4 Her father-in-law asked for all-wool yellow socks.

New key question mark

TWO spaces after ? at end of sentence

5 How? When? Where? May she? Must we? Will you?
6 Who said so? What is the time? Is it late? Why?

New key (colon) Use ; finger

7 ;;; ::: ;;; a:; l:; s:; k:; d:; j:; f:; h:; gf:;a;

Leave ONE space after colon

8 Delivery Period: one month. Prices: net ex works.

Shift-lock key

When you need to type several capital letters one after the other, the shift lock must be used. When it is depressed, the shift key remains engaged until the lock is released, and you will be able to type capitals without using the shift key. The following steps should be practised:

1 Depress shift lock, using 'A' finger of left hand.
2 Type capital letters.
3 Depress left-hand shift key to release shift lock.

New key Shift Lock Use A finger

9 BEFORE lunch please ring me in LUDLOW next MONDAY.
10 MEETINGS held in LONDON, LIVERPOOL and MANCHESTER.
11 Both LAURA and KATHLEEN were present at the party.

Skill measurement 20 wpm 1 minute Not more than 1 error

SM2 If you are good at figures, and are keen to have a   10
job in our firm, we should like you to call on us.   20
(SI 1.05)

SM3 I wish that you could have been with us on Tuesday   10
to see the new office machines which were on view.   20
(SI 1.15)

1 | 2 | 3 | 4 | 5 | 6 | 7 | 8 | 9 | 10 |

4.3 Used with figures only

am (a.m.)	= *ante meridiem* =	before noon
HP (H.P.)	= hire purchase	
No, Nos (No., Nos.)	= number, numbers	
pm (p.m.)	= *post meridiem* =	after noon
% (%)	= per centum	
v, vol (v., vol.)	= volume	
*in (in.)	= inch or inches	
ft (ft.)	= foot or feet	
*oz (oz.)	= ounce or ounces	
*lb (lb.)	= pound or pounds (weight)	
*cwt (cwt.)	= hundredweight or hundredweights	
*m	= metre, metres	
*mm	= millimetre, millimetres	
*cm	= centimetre, centimetres	
*g	= gram, grams	
*kg	= kilogram, kilograms	

* These do not require an s in the plural.

NOTE: It would seem preferable to add an s for the plural of yd and qr (yds/yds. qrs/qrs.). This style is recommended by the *Oxford Dictionary for Writers and Editors*; however, the British Standards Institution gives both examples without the s. Follow the author's copy and/or house style.

4.4 Used in cases indicated

& (&)	= ampersand = and. Used in names of firms and numbers [Nos 25 & 26 (Nos. 25 & 26)] never in ordinary matter.
BA (B.A.)	= Bachelor of Arts. Degree after a person's name.
Bros (Bros.)	= Brothers. In names of firms or companies only.
bf (b.f.)	= brought forward (accounting) *or* boldface (word processing)
c/o (c/o)	= care of. Used only in addresses. (Sometimes the word 'at' is used instead of c/o.)
Co (Co.)	= Company. Used in names of companies.
cod (c.o.d.) COD (C.O.D.)	= Cash on delivery. Used on invoices.
DSc (D.Sc.)	= Doctor of Science. Degree after person's name.
E & OE (E. & O.E.)	= Errors and omissions excepted. Used in invoices.
Junr (Junr.)	= Junior. Used in addresses after a man's name to distinguish from senior [Snr (Snr.)].
Ltd (Ltd.)	= Limited. Used in the name of a private limited company.
PS (PS.)	= Postscript. Abbreviated form

	used at end of letter and memo only.
PLC (P.L.C.)	= Public Limited Company.
plc (p.l.c.)	Used after the name of public limited company.
pro tem	= *pro tempore* (for the time being). Used after a designation, eg Secretary pro tem.
Ref (Ref.)	= Reference. Used in letters and memos.
SERPS	= State Earnings Related Pension Scheme. (May be in full or abbreviated.)

Accents

See page 67.

Agenda

See page 100.

Aligned right margin

Programmes, display, financial statements, etc, sometimes have a right column and the last character of each line of this column may have to end at the same scale point. To do this:

Decide on the exact scale point at which you wish the last character to be typed and set a tab stop one space to the right of that point. From the tab stop, backspace once for each character and space in the line to be aligned; from the point reached, type the word(s)/figure(s). This is sometimes referred to as justifying, but justifying really means inserting extra spaces between words so that the lines of the text all end at the same scale point. Electronic machines may have a 'flush right' facility to allow the information to be typed so that it will end automatically at the right margin.

Allocating space

See page 96.

Bank/bond paper

See Paper, page 189

Blocked paragraphs, double spacing

See page 31.

Boilerplating

see Document assembly, page 184

Bold print

Word processors have a facility that enables the operator to print characters with a much darker type than the normal printing. This emboldening is a very useful device for emphasizing text.

Record your progress exercises

In this edition of *Typing Two in One*, EACH **record your progress** exercise will contain ALL the letters of the alphabet.

Instructions for all **record your progress** exercises:
1 Type the exercise **once** as practice.
2 Check and circle any error.
3 With the assistance of your teacher, analyse your errors and carry out remedial work where necessary.
4 Return to your **record your progress** exercise and type as much of the passage as you can in the time allotted.
5 Check and circle any errors.
6 Record the number of words typed and the number of errors in the second typing.

Record your progress   1 minute

```
R1   I know you will be pleased to hear that Zola Coles  10

     joined this firm on a part-time basis.  Chris said  20

     I must give her a quick test next week.             28
        1  |  2  |  3  |  4  |  5  |  6  |  7  |  8  |  9  |  10  |
```

Typewriting theory and conventions

Over the years certain conventions with regard to display and layout of typewritten documents have become accepted practice. While some examining bodies and employers do not worry unduly about layout as long as the document is clean, attractive and correct (no typing, spelling or grammatical errors), we do suggest that you use the 'theory'/conventions given in this textbook as a guide. In exercise 4 on page 31, it is necessary to leave at least two clear spaces between blocked paragraphs typed in double spacing; however, it would not be 'wrong' if you left three clear, but it would be ridiculous if you left six. When you are familiar and conventions and standards suggested in this textbook, then you can adjust the layout of a document to suit the contents, your employer or the examiner.

Pre-stored margins

We do not always suggest what left and right margins should be used, and you must decide what margins will suit the particular exercise you are typing. If you wish to use the pre-stored margins on your electronic machine, you may do so provided they are appropriate.

Hard copy printout

When we refer to the insertion of paper, the instructions will also apply to typists using a computer and a printer.

DATA STORE

In addition to suggestions for the layout of documents given in the text, this **data store** (in alphabetic order) gives further information about typewriting conventions and display.

Abbreviations

In typewritten work, abbreviations should not, as a rule, be used. There are, however, a few which are **never** typed in full, and others which may be used in certain circumstances.

1 Open and full punctuation

When using **open** punctuation, no full stops are inserted after initials or in abbreviations, eg Mrs Y W T St George-Stevens is Managing Director of Y W T Stevens & Co Ltd. With **full** punctuation, full stops are inserted after initials and in abbreviations, eg Mrs. Y. W. T. St. George-Stevens is Managing Director of Y. W. T. Stevens & Co. Ltd.

Notice the spacing in the following:

Open punctuation   Mrs S J Hudson MA BSc— where an abbreviation consists of two or more letters, there is no space between the letters but one space between each group of letters. **Full** punctuation   Mrs. S. J. Hudson, M. A., B.Sc.— space between the groups is replaced by a comma, followed by a clear space.

1.1 However, with **full** punctuation, full stops need not be inserted in the following cases:
   1.1.1 **Acronyms** (words formed from initials): VAT, PAYE, UNESCO, NATO, BUPA, OPEC, NUPE, ACAS, etc.
   1.1.2 **Names** of **well-known** companies, states, countries, radio and television broadcasting stations, unions and many government departments: ICI, GKN, USA, UK, RSA, EEC, BBC, IBS, DES, etc.
   1.1.3 In metric measurements: 12 mm, 4 m, 6 kg, 30 km, etc.

2 Imperial measurements

No punctuation is inserted with open punctuation, but with full punctuation the full stops are inserted, eg 2 lb., 2 ft. 4 in.

3 Longhand abbreviations

These are used in handwriting, but the words must be typed in full. Examples: dept = department; st = street; shd = should; sh = shall; w = will; wh = which; th = that; etc. Great care must be taken to verify the correct spelling when typing

abbreviations in full, eg accom = accommodation; gntee(s) = guarantee(s); recd = received; def = definitely; sep = separate; rec(s) = receipt(s); temp = temporary; etc. Days of the week and months of the year, eg Wed, Fri, Jan, Sept, etc, **must** be typed in full. Where the names of persons, towns, countries, associations, etc, are repeated in any group of tasks, the author may write only the initial(s) or use the initial(s) followed by a long dash to represent the word(s). For example: in a letter addressed to Mrs R Green, the handwritten salutation may read, Dear Mrs G———, and the typist would be expected to type Dear Mrs Green.

4 Standard abbreviations

Lists of standard abbreviations, with their uses, are given below. Study the lists so that you will know when and when not to use the abbreviations. Full punctuation is given in brackets, although the tendency today is to use open punctuation.

4.1 **Common abbreviations**   Usually abbreviated, but may be typed in full. It is wise to follow the style used by the author and/or house style. **Be consistent.**

DSO (D.S.O.)	= Distinguished Service Order
EU	= European Union
Hon Sec (Hon. Sec.)	= Honorary Secretary. Typed in full.
IQPS (I.Q.P.S.)	= Institute of Qualified Private Secretaries
MEP (M.E.P.)	= Member of the European Parliament
MoD (M.o.D.)	= Ministry of Defence
mph (m.p.h.)	= miles per hour
RMO (R.M.O.)	= Resident Medical Officer
RNLI (R.N.L.I.)	= Royal National Lifeboat Institution
SCF (S.C.F.)	= Save the Children Fund
WCT (W.C.T.)	= World Championship Tennis

4.2 **Always used**

ad lib (ad lib.)	= *ad libitum*	= at pleasure
eg (e.g.)	= exempli gratia	= for example
Esq (Esq.)	= Esquire	= courtesy title
etc (etc.)	= et cetera	= and others
et seq (et seq.)	= *et sequentes*	= and the following
ie (i.e.)	= *id est*	= that is
Messrs (Messrs.)	= Messieurs	= courtesy title
Mr (Mr.)	= Mister	= courtesy title
Mrs (Mrs.)		= courtesy title
Ms	= courtesy title used instead of Mrs or Miss	
NB (N.B.)	= *Nota bene*	= note well

Keyboarding review— alphabet keys

1 *The taxi ranks were busy because of a sizeable jam which caused very long queues of cars up the hill.*

New key  *dash*

The hyphen key is used for the dash with ONE space **before** and ONE space **after**. There is no space before or after the hyphen.

```
2 ; - ; ; - ; Call today - no, tomorrow - after tea.
3 The book - it was his first - was a great success.
4 It is their choice - we are sure it will be yours.
```

Upper and lower case letters

Characters requiring use of shift key are called UPPER CASE characters. Characters not requiring use of the shift key are called LOWER CASE characters.

New key 1
Use A finger

```
5 We require ll pairs size ll; also ll pairs size l.
6 Add up ll plus ll plus ll plus ll plus ll plus ll.
7 On ll August ll girls and ll boys hope to join us.
8 After ll years, ll of them will leave on ll March.
```

New key 2
Use S finger

```
9  sw2s sw2s s2ws s2ws s2s2s s2s2s s2sws s2sws 2s2ws.
10 22 sips 22 seas 22 skis 22 sons 22 spas 22 sets 2.
11 We need 2 grey, 2 blue, 2 red, and 22 orange ties.
12 The 12 girls and 12 boys won 122 games out of 212.
```

New key 3
Use D finger

```
13 de3d de3d d3ed d3ed d3d3d d3d3d d3ded d3ded 3d3ed.
14 33 dots 33 dips 33 dogs 33 dads 33 dyes 33 duds 3.
15 Send 313 only to 33 Green Road and to 3 West Road.
16 Type the numbers: 3, 2, 1, 11, 12, 13, 32, 31, 23.
```

Skill measurement   21 wpm   1 minute   Not more than 1 error

```
SM4  We trust that the hints we gave for the removal of   10
     stains will be found to be of great help to all of   20
     you. (SI 1.09)                                        21
```

```
   1  |  2  |  3  |  4  |  5  |  6  |  7  |  8  |  9  |  10  |
```

Record your progress   1 minute

```
R2   At what time does the Zurich bus arrive?  You must   10
     equip yourself with: extra shoes, raincoats, brown   20
     socks, a warm jumper, a large torch, and the maps.   30
                                             (SI 1.23)
```

```
   1  |  2  |  3  |  4  |  5  |  6  |  7  |  8  |  9  |  10  |
```

PHONE

IV³ Full Call Barring

This makes sure that no calls can be made from your number to information and entertainment lines.

PROD

The figures should read: 33.1   34.0   29.7

PROP

Price – £85 999 (freehold)

RENT

Mr Laxby's address is:
16 Western Avenue
ANNAN
Dumfriesshire
DG12 6LD

SHED

Mr & Mrs L P McLennon
10 Forge Lane
Folkestone
Kent   CT17 3MT

The credit note (No 3079) is to go to:
Ms Fiona Simmons, 8 Trent Road, Folkestone,
Kent   CT15 9SY.
The invoice (No 38027) was sent 12 days ago (insert date) but one terracotta pot was chipped – £35.00, plus VAT at $17\frac{1}{2}$% = £6.13.
Calculate and insert total.

SUBS

The subscription rates are correct, except for the Under 25s which should read £12.50.

TRAV

106" and 20 kg per person
Mr & Mrs D J Fearn
3 Grove Lane
Clifton
BATH
Avon
BS3 2DO

WALK

(October to March)	9.00 am to 4.00 pm
(April to September)	8.30 am to 8.00 pm)

Keyboarding review— alphabet keys

1 The jam that he bought tasted of exotic fruit like quince, guava and pomegranate, and May ate it with zeal.

New key **4**
Use F finger

2 fr4f fr4f f4rf f4rf f4f4f f4f4f f4frf f4frf 4f4rf.
3 44 furs 44 fish 44 firs 44 feet 44 figs 44 fans 4.
4 The 4 men, 4 women, 24 boys and 4 girls go by car.
5 We ordered 434 sets and received 124 on 14 August.

New key **7**
Use J finger

6 ju7j ju7j j7uj j7uj j7j7j j7j7j j7juj j7juj 7j7uj.
7 77 jugs 77 jars 77 jigs 77 jets 77 jags 77 jaws 7.
8 The 7 boys and 77 girls sent 77 gifts to the fund.
9 Take 4 from 47, then add 27 plus 7 and you get 77.

New key **8**
Use K finger

10 ki8k ki8k k8ik k8ik k8k8k k8k8k k8kik kik8k 8k8ik.
11 88 keys 88 kits 88 kids 88 kinds 88 kilts 88 kings
12 Type 38, 83, 28, 848 and 482 with alternate hands.
13 The 8 men, 28 women, 8 boys and 78 girls are here.

New key **9**
Use L finger

14 lo9l lo9l l9ol l9ol 19191 99 laws 99 logs 99 lids.
15 Type 29, 39, 49, 927 and 939 with alternate hands.
16 Joe is 99, Bob is 89, Jim is 79, and George is 49.

New key **0**
Use right little finger

17 101 201 301 401 701 801 901 10 left 10 look 10 lie
18 The 40 men, 70 women, 80 boys and 90 girls remain.
19 See the dates: 10 March, 20 July, 30 June, 10 May.

Skill measurement   22 wpm   1 minute   Not more than 1 error

SM5 We want a first-class employee: one who has a good   10
knowledge of accounts. She must be able to manage   20
a section. **(SI 1.32)**   22

1 | 2 | 3 | 4 | 5 | 6 | 7 | 8 | 9 | 10 |

Record your progress   1 minute

R3 No charge will be made for any extra copies of the   10
GAZETTE: but their account must be paid at the end   20
of the quarter. Will this suit Kate? James would   30
like to have your reply. **(SI 1.20)**   35

1 | 2 | 3 | 4 | 5 | 6 | 7 | 8 | 9 | 10 |

DATA FILES

The following office files contain information that you will need when typing certain documents.

ACCO

Miss Dunbar's account is 185 FA 257198H. She lives at 16 Holt Lane, Folkestone, Kent CT18 5XB.

Table showing dates when interest is paid out:

Date when interest is paid out or added to an account	Date when statement will be received
30 June and 1 January	January
31 March	April
30 April	May
31 August	September
31 October	November

CAR

2   allow anyone over the age of 25 years to drive your car in an emergency, provided you are in the car; or

3   if the person needs to drive your car to your home following a medical or motoring emergency

CARD

The card is likely to be renewed every 10 years.

CON

Heating and Ventilation	47–49
Automatic Transmission	50–54
Roof Rack, Caravan and Trailer Towing	71–75

CV

The second referee is:
Mr Lional Pardoe
Personnel Officer
Pentagon Industries Ltd
Langdon Estate
Station Road
CAMBRIDGE CB12 1FY

E-MAIL

Smilies
Happy:–), sad:–(or winking;–).

EXPEN

The 1995 figures are as follows:

Grant £10 500	Interest £4
Halls £9 456	Groups £723
Publications £6	Events £255
Films £24	

Excess expenditure over income £1 555
(Please insert total figure)

FAIL

Offence	Number of points
Failing to observe pedestrian crossing regulations	3
Failing to give details of an accident	8–10

FINAN

The financial section figures should read as follows:
£877k   £978k   £340k   £221k

FOOD

Delete the word carbohydrate from the list.

HEAT

4   It is also very clean and can save on redecorating costs.

ITIN

The dates should read as follows:

Tuesday 19 November   Wednesday 20 November Thursday 21 November

Secure Building Society, 7 Temple Street

LEYS

An 8-digit LCD solar calculator, complete with wallet.

NEWS

There are now over 100 members in our region.

Keyboarding review — alphabet keys

1 The brightly coloured liquid was mixed in the jug and given to the lazy patients for sickness.

New key 5
Use F finger

```
2  fr5f fr5f f5rf f5rf 55 fill 55 flit 55 fled 55 fit
3  5 firs, 15 furs, 25 fish, 35 figs, 45 fewer, 515 5
4  25 January 1525; 15 August 1535; 15 December 1545.
```

New key 6
Use J finger

```
5  jy6j jy6j j6yj j6yj 66 jump 66 jerk 66 jest 66 jam
6  6 jars, 16 jets, 26 jabs, 36 jots, 46 jolts, 616 6
7  We need 656 green and 566 red by 16 February 1986.
```

NO space after initial " NO space before closing "

New key "
quotation marks

```
8   "Go for 30 days."   "Call at 12 noon."   "Ring now."
9   "I am going," he said.   "It is already very late."
10  Mary said, "Mr Bell is here."   "Ring me tomorrow."
```

(ONE space before NO space after
) NO space before ONE space after

New keys ( )
brackets

```
11  (1 (2 (3 (4 (5 (6 (7 (8 (9) 10) 11) 12) 13) 14) 8)
12  (22) (23) (24) (25) (26) (27) (28) (29) (30) (31).
13  Mail: (a) 2 pens; (b) 3 pins; (c) 1 tie; (d) 1 hat
```

NO space before or after the apostrophe in the MIDDLE of a word

New key '
apostrophe

```
14  It's Joe's job to clean Mary's car.   Joe's unwell.
15  Don't do that; it's bad for Mary's dog; he's nice.
16  Bill's 2 vans are with John's 8 trucks at Reading.
```

Skill measurement   23 wpm   1 minute   Not more than 1 error

```
SM6  If you feel some day that you would like a trip in  10
     the country, perhaps you could drive out to a farm  20
     to pick fruit. (SI 1.09)                            23

SM7  Do you wish to take a holiday?  Now is the time to   10
     take one of our out-of-season vacations.  Send for  20
     our brochure. (SI 1.26)                             23
```

      1 | 2 | 3 | 4 | 5 | 6 | 7 | 8 | 9 | 10 |

Record your progress   1 minute

```
R4  The gavels which Liz Max saw last July are now out   10
    of stock, and we would not be able to replace them   20
    for some weeks - perhaps a month - when we hope to   30
    receive a further quota. (SI 1.23)                   35
```

      1 | 2 | 3 | 4 | 5 | 6 | 7 | 8 | 9 | 10 |

Recall the document stored under filename WASTE.

Page one – delete the year '1996' after the words 'Waste Management' and insert 'January to December 1996' on the line underneath.

Page three – insert the following as a new item between the details for 'Quarry Pit' and 'Health Fields' – Jolly Lane

Mondays to Sundays   8.30 am to 3.30 pm

Proofread soft copy and, if necessary, correct. Print out an original in 12 point.

Recall the document stored under filename CAR. Delete item 3 in the last group of numbered items, which starts 'if the person needs …' Alter all the items numbered 1, 2, 3 etc to (a), (b), (c), etc. Embolden all the underscored words, but do not underscore

Proofread soft copy and, if necessary, correct. Print out an original and three copies in 10 point .

Recall the document stored under filename EMAIL. Perform a global search and change E-mail/e-mail back to E/electronic mail. Delete item 3 on page 2 and close up the space. Prepare an extra copy for Phil Anderson and add his name to the distribution list. Proofread soft copy and, if necessary, correct. Print out an original and three copies in 12 point

Recall the document stored under filename SHEET. Alter the figure for 'General reserve' to '238 989'; and the figure for 'Other assets' to '2134'. The totals will also need to be changed.

Proofread soft copy and, if necessary, correct. Print out original in 12 point.

Recall the document stored under filename EXPEN. Transpose the '1995' and '1996' columns.

Proofread soft copy and, if necessary, correct. Print out original in 10 point.

Recall the document stored under filename ITIN. Insert the following for 'Wednesday 20th November' in the correct time order.

'1400 hours British Air Corporation, Filton House

            Tel 01272 314769—correspondence in file No 3'

Mr Bromley's train will not now be arriving at New Street Station, Birmingham until 1245 hours on Thursday 21 November.

Proofread soft copy and, if necessary, correct. Print out original in 9 point.

Recall the document stored under filename BOND. Embolden the subject heading and the shoulder headings. Transpose items i and ii. Add the following sentence to the end of the second paragraph.

'Your Bond will come into force as soon as we have given full consideration to the information supplied or requested regarding health, occupation etc'

Proofread soft copy and, if necessary, correct. Print out original and two copies in 9 point.

Recall the document stored under filename FINAN. Delete the line about 'Education' and add the following in correct alphabetical order:

Computer Bureaux   £623   £987   £333   £420

Proofread soft copy and, if necessary, correct. Print out original in 12 point.

Please follow instructions at top of page 23.

Keyboarding review— alphabet keys

1 *A small quiet boy who lives next door to Jack came out of the gate and went down the zigzag path.*

Backspace key

Locate the backspace key on your machine. This is usually on either the top left or top right of the keyboard. When the backspace key is depressed, the carriage/carrier/cursor will move back one space at a time. On most electric and electronic machines the carriage/carrier/cursor will continue to move for as long as the backspace key is depressed.

Underscore key—underline function

Before underscoring a short word, backspace once for each letter and space in the word to be underscored. For longer words, or several words, use carriage release lever. After you finish underscoring, always tap space bar. Use shift lock when underscoring more than one character. A final punctuation mark may or may not be underscored. If you are using an electronic typewriter, follow instructions given for underscoring (underlining) in user's handbook. If you need to rule a horizontal line on a word processor, depress the underscore key in the usual way. In offices today, there is a tendency to use the word **underline** instead of the word **underscore**.

New key underscore

2 Please send them 29 only - not 9 - by air-freight.
3 John Brown, Mary Adams and Janet Kelly are coming.

ONE space before £ but NO space after. Some word processors and computers do not have a £ sign. Where this occurs, the hash sign may be used. However, it is preferable to write in the £ sign.

New key pound sign

4 Buy 5 at £15, 8 at £68, 17 at £415 and 30 at £270.
5 £1, £2, £3, £4, £5, £6, £7, £8, £9, £10, £20, £30.

ONE space before and after &

New key ampersand

6 Jones & Cutler Ltd, 67 & 68 North Street, Falkirk.
7 Mr & Mrs Weston, 18 & 19 Main Street, Cirencester.

NO space before or after oblique

New key oblique or slash

8 I can/cannot be present. I do/do not require tea.
9 Jim Minett will take an aural and/or written test.

Skill measurement   24 wpm   1 minute   Not more than 1 error

SM8 The account for May should now be paid, and I must 10
     ask you to let me have your cheque for the sum due 20
     as soon as you can. **(SI 1.04)**   24

SM9 When you leave the office at night you should make 10
     sure that your machine is covered up and that your 20
     desk is quite clear. **(SI 1.12)**   24

     1 | 2 | 3 | 4 | 5 | 6 | 7 | 8 | 9 | 10 |

Record your progress   1 minute

R5   Our parents are fond of telling us that, when they 10
     were quite young they were expected to work harder 20
     than we do today; however, we will, no doubt, tell 30
     our lazy children the same joyful tale. **(SI 1.29)**   38

     1 | 2 | 3 | 4 | 5 | 6 | 7 | 8 | 9 | 10 |

Page 41
Recall the document stored under filename ANSER. To save retyping this letter for exercise 5, alter Muriel Fletcher's name and address to that of Jack Phillips. Close up the extra linespace and change the salutation to 'Dear Sir'. Proofread soft copy and, if necessary, correct. Print out original only in 10 point.

Page 43
Recall the document stored under filename MOVE. Add the following sentence to the end of the second paragraph.
'It has been designed to the highest standard offering greatly improved facilities.'
Proofread soft copy and, if necessary, correct. Print out original in 10 point.

Page 71
Recall the document stored under filename SALE. Add the extra items shown in the letter in exercise 3 to Mrs Jacquie Freeman.
Proofread soft copy and, if necessary, correct. Print out an original and one copy in 10 point.

Page 72
Recall the document stored under filename HEAT. Add the following as item number two (change the numbers of the following items accordingly).
'The solar heating system is simple to install and causes the minimum of disruption. It can be completed within 48 hours.'
Proofread soft copy and, if necessary, correct. Print out an original in 12 point and take one copy.

Page 80
Recall the document stored under filename CAN. Underline the first three words in each of the numbered paragraphs. Add the following, in brackets, to item II.
(In 1993, in response to concerns about the environment, British Steel developed a push-button Ecotop can which is opened by pressing a raised button the size of a 20p coin, to release the pressure in the can.)
Proofread soft copy and, if necessary, correct. Print out an original in 12 point and take one copy.

Page 86
Recall the document stored under filename NEWS. The number of members is now 132. Delete the word 'over' and insert the new figure. Insert the word **important** before information at the end of the second paragraph. Embolden the main heading and the words **DO NOT** in the third paragraph.
Proofread soft copy and, if necessary, correct. Print out an original and one copy in 10 point.

Page 88
Recall the document stored under filename DATE. Transpose the section under the heading 'Died' before the section 'Born'. Embolden these two headings.
Proofread soft copy and, if necessary, correct. Print out an original in 12 point.

Page 91
Recall the document stored under filename SALE. The telephone answering machine was £102.50. The sale price is correct. The personal word processor is to be reduced again in price in the sale to £350.99. Please alter the figures accordingly. Delete the leader dots. Change the introductory paragraph to double spacing.
Proofread soft copy and, if necessary, correct. Print out an original in 10 point.

Page 97
Recall the document stored under filename ARAB. Highlight 'Lawrence of Arabia' where it appears in the second paragraph. Add the following sentence to the beginning of the last paragraph.
'To avoid the fame his exploits had attracted, Lawrence joined the Royal Air Force in 1922 under an assumed name – first J H Ross and later T E Shaw.'
Proofread soft copy and, if necessary, correct. Print out an original in 10 point.

Page 99
Recall the document stored under filename SAFE. Perform a global search and change the word 'typist(s)' back to 'operator(s)'. Justify the right margin.
Proofread soft copy and. if necessary, correct. Print an original in single spacing and 12 point.

Please follow instructions at top of page 23.

Keyboarding review— alphabet keys

1 *In spite of the likely hazard, a decision was made to grant their request and give him the extra job.*

ONE space before and after, in continuous text

New key
at

2 f@f f@f d@d j@j 9 @ 10p; 8 @ 11p; 7 @ 12p; 3 @ 8p.
3 Please send 44 @ £5; 6 @ £7; 13 @ £8; and 28 @ £9.
4 Order 420 @ £12, 50 @ £5, 40 @ £6 and 5 @ £8 each.

Numeric keypad

Some machines with electronic keyboards have a numeric keypad, usually placed to the right of, and separate from, the alphabet keyboard. This keypad may be used in addition to, or instead of, the figure keys on the top row of the keyboard. When using the 10-key pad, employ the **456** as the home keys on which you place the **J K L** fingers. The fingers and thumb will then operate the keypad as follows:

J = 1 4 7   **K** = 2 5 8   **L** = decimal point 3 6 9
Thumb = 0   **Little finger** = enter, comma, minus

The layout of the keypad will differ from one machine to another. Study your keyboard and, if you have a keypad, note any differences from the layout above and the characters to which the suggested fingering applies.

Practise on numeric keypad

5 456 654 147 258 369 041 520 306 470 508 906 159 02
6 417 528 639 159 350 256 107 369 164 059 378 904 38
7 4.5 6.9 4.1 4.7 5.2 5.8 4,655 3,987 2,541 8,465 79

Skill measurement   25 wpm   1 minute   Not more than 1 error

SM10 I have just moved to my new house and, when I have   10
      put it straight, I would be glad if you could then   20
      spend a few days with me. **(SI 1.00)**   25

SM11 I am delighted to tell you that we have now joined   10
      the team. We had hoped to do so last year, but we   20
      were then not old enough. **(SI 1.12)**   25

      1 | 2 | 3 | 4 | 5 | 6 | 7 | 8 | 9 | 10 |

Record your progress   1 minute

R6   I was sorry to find that my cheque - sent to Suzie   10
      on Monday - had not been received. I think it has   20
      just gone astray in the post. Shall I ask my bank   30
      to stop it now? Please excuse the delay. **(SI 1.18)**   38

      1 | 2 | 3 | 4 | 5 | 6 | 7 | 8 | 9 | 10 |

Keys to proofreading exercises

Page 148—exercise 1
Line 1—program; line 2—visual; 3—100; line 4—a daisy-wheel printer; line 5—stock; line 6—Spreadsheet.

Page 148—exercise 2
Line 1—your; line 2—top and bottom; line 3—interrupt; line 4—dictation.; line 5—omit the word 'the';
line 6—omit comma after 'pencil'.

Page 148—exercise 3
Line 1—GARDENING; line 2—month; line 3—or; line 4—lettuces; line 5—spring-flowering; line 6—line not at left margin;
line 7—omit the word 'ANY'.

Page 149—exercise 4
Line 1—definite; line 2—two spaces after full stop; line 3—handling; line 4—index cards; line 5—loose-leaf; line 6—omit
'they may'.

Page 149—exercise 5
Line 1—retrieval; line 2—accessed; line 3—insert 'an' before annual; line 4—varied,; line 5—retrieve; line 6—a telephone
line; line 7—adapted; line 8—insert full stop after 'use'.

Page 150—exercise 6
FIELD WALK; 10 April; Shân; Mow'; A4057; Route; reference; SU637856).; hear; binoculars; 3¾ miles. (two spaces before)
Suitable.

Page 150—exercise 7
GCSE; General Certificate of Secondary Education; Visual Display Unit (without the semicolon); RSA; Cultural;
Organization; Beginners'; Telegraphy; Errors and Omissions Excepted.

Page 151—exercise 8
Brook-Little; PB-L/TSEV; SEPTEMBER 1996 TO DECEMBER 1996; enrolment; run,; follows–; underline column headings:
type the whole line 'Audio Typing' before 'Beginners' Typing'; B207; I shall be glad; dates and times.

Page 152—exercise 9
Address; Installed; Treatments; Tel: (01603) 623091; postcode on the same line as Norwich; Computer; (01272); BS16 1RP;
10A; Felton; Peterborough (without full stop); April (without comma).

Page 153—exercise 10
countryside; town. (2 spaces after full stop, s omitted); obedient; dog-training; know; told,; which is hard to break; line space
between each numbered item; dog's lead; when there are farm; and (not the ampersand).

Page 153—exercise 11
manufacturers; Their furniture; companies; e.g.,; executive's; approximately; £981.50; The colours; yellows, (2 errors—
delete apostrophe, add comma); inset 5 spaces for second paragraph; year's; breaking; 27.7%.

Page 154—exercise 12
Prestel; and (in full, not the ampersand); British; world's; service. (2 spaces); computers; you are given; modem; device; do
not indent the third paragraph; stories; advertisements; information,; etc.; goods,.

Page 154—exercise 13
all day; headaches,; miscarriages; worries; stress comes highest; that not 'than'; breaks; possible; detachable; swivel; screen;
(one space); adjust; processor; typewriter.

Language arts—apostrophe

Page 155—	Lines 1 and 3	Singular (one only) noun not ending in **s**, add an apostrophe **s**.
	Lines 2 and 4	Plural noun ending in **s**, add an apostrophe.
	Lines 5 and 6	If the singular noun ends in **s**, or an **s** sound, and the addition of an apostrophe **s** makes the word **difficult to pronounce**, add the apostrophe only. What one considers difficult to pronounce is debatable.
	Lines 7 and 8	Plural nouns (children, men) **not** ending in **s**, add an apostrophe **s**.
	Line 9	The contractions **don't** and **it's** require the apostrophe to show the omission of **o** and **i**. The pronoun **its** (The dog chased its tail.) does not require an apostrophe.
	Line 10	The apostrophe is sometimes used in place of quotation marks to indicate the exact words of a speaker or writer.
	Line 11	Used as the sign for feet. Is also the sign for minutes: 1' equals 60".
	Line 12	To avoid confusing the reader, the apostrophe is used around the word 'embarrass' and between the single letter and the **s** that follows. Electronic typewriters usually have an emboldening facility and one would then embolden the word(s)/letter(s) instead of using the apostrophe.

Language arts—agreement of subject and verb

Page 155—	Line 1	**daisywheel** (singular noun) requires singular verb **is**.
	Line 2	**disks** (plural noun) requires plural verb **are**.
	Line 3	A plural verb is always necessary after **you**.
	Line 4	Although **s** or **es** added to a noun indicates the plural, **s** or **es** added to a verb indicates the third person **singular**.
	Line 5	When singular subjects are joined by **nor**, the verb must be singular.
	Line 6	Singular subjects joined by **and** require a plural verb.

KEYBOARDING SKILLS

Before proceeding to the exercises below, you should type the following skill building exercises:

improve your spelling Nos 1 and 2, page 155.   **alphabetic sentence** No 1, page 156.
skill measurement No 12, page 158.   **record your progress** No 7, page 164.

PRODUCTION DEVELOPMENT

Types of display headings

Main headings

The main heading, the title of a passage, is blocked at the left margin when using blocked display. Unless otherwise instructed, turn up seven single spaces, 25 mm (1 inch), from the top edge of the paper before starting the main heading. It may be typed in:

1   closed capitals—leave one space between each word;
2   spaced letters—leave one space between each letter and three spaces between each word;

3   lower case with initial capitals;
4   bold print.

Any of these headings may be underlined. Generally it is wise to follow the display indicated in the exercise to be copied. Lower case headings, particularly, can be given greater emphasis by the use of underlining. The underline must not extend beyond the typing.

1   Type the following on A5 landscape paper. (a) Single spacing. (b) Suggested margins: 12 pitch 22–82, 10 pitch 12–72, or pre-stored margins where appropriate.

> Turn up 7 single spaces

```
WORD PROCESSOR OPERATORS
```
> Turn up 2 single spaces

```
If you are using a word processor it is wise to study the
manufacturer's manual that accompanies the machine, and make
yourself familiar with its various techniques and functions.
```
> Turn up 2 single spaces

```
Initially, make sure you understand how to create a new
document and open an existing one; save your work for future
use and print it.  You will also need to be able to close
documents and switch off your machine.
```

Subheadings

The main heading may be followed by a subheading which further clarifies the contents of the passage. Turn up two single spaces after typing the main heading and then type the subheading.

2   Type the following on A5 landscape paper. (a) Single spacing. (b) Suggested margins: 12 pitch 22–82, 10 pitch 12–72, or pre-stored margins where appropriate.

> Turn up 7 single spaces

```
WORD PROCESSOR OPERATORS
```
> Turn up 2 single spaces

```
Further tips
```
> Turn up 2 single spaces

```
If you are using a computer with a word processing package,
do not use the spacebar to move the cursor or to indent or
align text.  Instead, use the arrow keys or click the mouse.
```
> Turn up 2 single spaces

Press the spacebar only to insert a space between words.

R32 For the better-paid typist's job you should have appropriate   12
qualifications: a Stage III in Typing, Stage II/III in Audio   24
Transcription, and a good knowledge of English. This job   35
usually demands common sense, initiative, and tact. However   47
rushed you may be, you will have to be pleasant to the bore   58
who will often deviate from the topic and perhaps waste your   70
time. If you have a question, ask for advice - there may be   82
a maze of regulations that you will not understand.   92

You may be required to deal with internal and external tele-   104
phone calls and to make certain decisions. The typist often   116
has to operate a filing system. Typing is also a means of   127
providing input for word processors and computers and it may   139
be that you will have extra pay for using these machines.   150
Employment prospects for typists are excellent. Thousands   161
of typists are added to the work-force each year, and the   172
typist who is familiar with processing equipment has an even   184
better chance. **(SI 1.45)**   187

1 | 2 | 3 | 4 | 5 | 6 | 7 | 8 | 9 | 10 | 11 | 12 |

R33 A FAX or facsimile machine is a copier which will transmit   11
a document by electronic means usually over telephone lines   22
from one location to another. At the distant end it appears   34
as a printed copy, or facsimile, of the original.   44

Almost anything that can be put on paper can be transmitted   55
by facsimile - text, graphs, charts, etc, can be sent and   66
also received. Quotations, orders, price-lists, delivery   77
schedules, specifications, etc, are just a few examples.   88
As originally planned it was slow and only small sizes of   99
paper could be used. The equipment used today takes advan-   110
tage of today's technology which means that it is much   121
faster.   122

One of the great advantages of facsimile is the reduction of   134
keyboarding errors because if the original copy is correctly   146
prepared, no further typing or checking is necessary, and no   158
carbon copies, envelopes, postage, etc, are required. Also,   170
you will know that the document cannot get lost in the post.   182
These machines have answering devices and other automatic   193
mechanism which means they can receive documents without an   204
individual being present, and documents may be sent when   215
phone prices are at a lower rate, such as in the evening.   226
(SI 1.54)

1 | 2 | 3 | 4 | 5 | 6 | 7 | 8 | 9 | 10 | 11 | 12 |

Paragraph headings

Apart from the main heading and the subheading at the beginning of a passage, paragraph headings are used to give emphasis to the first few words of a paragraph. In blocked style the paragraph heading starts at the left margin as in exercise 3 below. They may be typed:

1 in upper case, with or without underlining;
2 in lower case with underlining;
3 with a full stop and two spaces, or just the two spaces without the full stop;
4 running straight on into the following words of the paragraph, but may be emphasized by using capitals, underlining and/or bold print.

3 Type the following on A5 portrait paper. (a) Single spacing. (b) Suggested margins: 12 pitch 13–63, 10 pitch 6–56, or pre-stored margins where appropriate.
NB The coloured figures after the paragraph headings indicate the number of character spaces to be left and should not be typed.

DATA PROCESSING   *Turn up 7 single spaces*

      Turn up 2 single spaces

Database and Spreadsheet   *Turn up 2 single spaces*

DATABASE[2] This is a means of entering and saving information on computer in a card index system, eg, price lists, customer details, stock records, personnel records, etc.

SPREADSHEET[2] The screen appears as a grid of columns and rows and the data is entered into the cells. The operator can then perform calculations such as addition, subtraction, multiplication and division quickly and easily on screen.

Blocked exercises typed in double spacing

If the text is typed in double spacing it is wise and easier for the reader, if an extra space, or spaces, is left after the headings. It may by simpler for you to return twice on double, but three single spaces are equally acceptable.

4 Type the following on A5 portrait paper. (a) Double spacing. (b) Suggested margins: 12 pitch 13–63, 10 pitch 6–56, or pre-stored margins where appropriate.

DATA PROTECTION ACT   *Turn up 7 single spaces*

      Turn up 2 single spaces

REGISTRATION OF INFORMATION

      Turn up 3 single spaces

The Data Protection Act of 1984 stated that any

organization holding information on computer, that

could identify individuals, must register with the

data protection registrar.

      Turn up 3 single spaces

Registration forms can be obtained from main post

offices.

R28 A typed document which is not 'mailable' is not acceptable.   11
By mailable copy we mean: the contents must make sense; no   22
omissions; no uncorrected errors (misspellings, incorrect   33
punctuation, typing errors, etc); no careless corrections   44
(if part of the wrong letter(s) is showing, the correction   55
is not acceptable); no smudges; no creases.   63

When using the VDU screen, it is fairly easy to text edit a   74
document that has been amended by the author. The data is   85
retrieved from the file and displayed on the screen. The   96
backspace-strikeover method is normally used to correct typ- 108
ing errors and, with the use of the function keys, text- 119
editing techniques are used to change information in the 130
text. If the text on the VDU looks hazy, you should clean 141
the screen or adjust the luminous intensity. 149

Whilst corrections and amendments are easily made on the 160
VDU screen, these changes may take up a lot of time which 171
could better be spent on other work. Try to produce a 182
correct copy on the first printout. **(SI 1.43)** 189

1 | 2 | 3 | 4 | 5 | 6 | 7 | 8 | 9 | 10 | 11 | 12 |

R29 All of you will be glad to hear that I now have a scheme for   12
refunding to staff the part of their expenses for travelling   24
long distances to work. Just details of local conditions,   35
the grades of staff, and travel zones, will help settle your   47
queries. **(SI 1.31)**   48

1 | 2 | 3 | 4 | 5 | 6 | 7 | 8 | 9 | 10 | 11 | 12 |

R30 Electronic mail will justify its use because of the speed   11
with which it is known to deliver large amounts of infor-   22
mation: it offers immediate delivery if this is required.   33
There are one or 2 points you should remember about this   44
means of communication. We were amazed to find that dif-   55
ferent kinds of equipment can communicate with each other -   66
telephone lines, telegraph lines, satellites are good   77
examples. The message is communicated in the form of elec-   89
tronic signals, not a copy on paper. **(SI 1.35)**   96

1 | 2 | 3 | 4 | 5 | 6 | 7 | 8 | 9 | 10 | 11 | 12 |

R31 Zodiac Travel, our branch in High Street, can help you in a   11
number of ways to solve your travel and transport queries.   22
In these days, when time seems to be the most important com-   33
modity of all, you can depend on Zodiac Travel to deal with   44
all your problems. Just telephone Karen Gallagher and she   55
will use both her own and her staff's time in dealing with   66
the hundred and one irritating little things that crop up,   77
but which are so easily overcome by the expert who has made   88
the whole subject her own intimate profession. Should you   99
wish to do business with a country with which you are not 110
in touch, our agents will be pleased to help you. **(SI 1.31)** 119

1 | 2 | 3 | 4 | 5 | 6 | 7 | 8 | 9 | 10 | 11 | 12 |

When this form of heading is used, it is typed at the left margin and may be in closed capitals or in lower case with initial capitals, with or without the underscore, and/or in bold print. It is preceded and followed by one blank line when using single spacing. When using double spacing, it is preceded by two or three blank lines and followed by one.

5   Type the following on A5 landscape paper. (a) Single spacing. (b) Suggested margins: 12 pitch 22–82, 10 pitch 12–72, or pre-stored margins where appropriate.

INFORMATION TECHNOLOGY

Terms used

If you use a computer it is wise to learn some of the terms involved.

TOUCH SENSITIVE SCREEN

A computer screen that responds to pressure from a finger or pointer. The user is usually offered a choice from a menu, and by touching the appropriate part of the screen a selection can be made.

MOUSE

This is the name given to a pointing device used with a Computer.

Turn up 2 single spaces (after INFORMATION TECHNOLOGY)
Turn up 2 single spaces (after Terms used)
Turn up 2 single spaces (after involved.)
Turn up 2 single spaces (after TOUCH SENSITIVE SCREEN)
Turn up 2 single spaces
Turn up 2 single spaces

6   Type the following on A5 portrait paper. (a) Double spacing. (b) Suggested margins: 12 pitch 13–63, 10 pitch 6–56, or pre-stored margins where appropriate.

NETWORKS

COMPUTER LINKING

Local Area Network

Computers can be linked together so that data can

be passed from one to another. This link-up is

called a network. The local area network refers

to an office, or a building.

Wide Area Network

This network links offices in different parts of

the country, or even in different parts of the

world.

Turn up 2 single spaces (after NETWORKS)
Turn up 3 single spaces (after COMPUTER LINKING)
Turn up 2 single spaces (after Local Area Network)
Turn up 3 single spaces (after to an office, or a building.)
Turn up 2 single spaces (after Wide Area Network)

R25 The number of guide cards used and their arrangement depend   12
on the filing system; however, the purpose of the guide card   24
is the same in all systems: to guide the eye when filing and   36
finding papers, and to support the folders. Guide cards can   48
be bought in all standard sizes, as well as for special sys-   60
tems such as fingerprint, medical, and insurance classifica-   72
tions. Most guide cards have a tab along the top edge, and   83
the space contains a plain and clear reference to the folder   95
behind. It is important that this reference should be easy   106
to read, and the marker show the exact order of the folders.   117
These cards, quite rightly, justify their existence. (SI 1.36)   127

  1 | 2 | 3 | 4 | 5 | 6 | 7 | 8 | 9 | 10 | 11 | 12 |

R26 We were very glad to learn from your letter of 16 April that   12
the prospects we discussed when you visited us some 3 months   24
ago are now materializing. You inform us that you have pur-   36
chased a new truck for business purposes and that you intend   48
saving storage charges by housing it in your factory; doubt-   60
less you have calculated well and the truck will cut down on   72
your expenses.   75

Have your insurance brokers reviewed your policies since you   87
bought the truck? We do venture to suggest that you go over   99
your insurance cover with your brokers to make sure that you   111
have comprehensive protection. The fact that you have this   122
truck in your works may change the rates and may invalidate   133
the policies. (SI 1.39)   135

  1 | 2 | 3 | 4 | 5 | 6 | 7 | 8 | 9 | 10 | 11 | 12 |

R27 Visitors to the border county of Hereford may be impressed   12
by the deep-red colour of its fertile soil. Then perhaps we   24
will notice the striking appearance of many of its houses   35
built in the half-timbered style, with dark wooden beams   46
which form the framework and contrast with the white plaster   58
in between. But a very short stay will make us realize that   70
the great charm of this county is its air of peace. It has   82
industries, but they are unobtrusive, using local products.   94
and employing local labour; its many beauty spots have never   105
been unduly publicized. It is a county of cattle pasture   117
and cornland, of apple and orchard, of homely village and a   129
small but flourishing county town.   136

The boundaries of the county are marked out partly by hill   148
crests and partly by rivers. To the west they traverse the   159
foothills of the Radnor Forest. (SI 1.37)   167

  1 | 2 | 3 | 4 | 5 | 6 | 7 | 8 | 9 | 10 | 11 | 12 |

KEYBOARDING SKILLS

Before proceeding to the exercises below, you should type the following skill building exercises:

proofreading No 1, page 148.   **techniques and reviews** No 1, page 157.

skill measurement No 13, page 158.   **record your progress** No 8, page 164.

PRODUCTION DEVELOPMENT

- *Standard sizes of paper*—See, pages 10–13.
- *Vertical linespacing*—See, page 20.
- *Horizontal linespacing*—See, pages 9–13.

Display

Some types of matter such as notices, menus and advertisements are much more attractive if items are displayed on separate lines and good use is made of capital letters, small letters, the underscore and bold print. In its simplest form, and to save time, decide on a *suitable* left and top margin depending on the length of the longest line and the actual number of lines to be typed. Then type each line at the left margin, leaving extra lines between items, as required, for emphasis.

Spaced letters

Important lines may be given prominence by using spaced capitals, ie leave one space between each letter and three spaces between each word.

NB   When using closed capitals, it is usual to leave one space between each word.

Notice the use of spaced capitals, closed capitals, and lower case and a variation in linespacing to place emphasis and stress on individual lines, in the exercises that follow. Examining bodies use the word 'emphasize' or 'highlight' when they wish the typist to give prominence to a particular word, words or lines of text.

Automatic emboldening

If you are using an electronic machine, you may be able to make use of the bold function key. See note on page 34: Automatic display functions.

1   Display the following on A5 portrait paper. (a) Leave 51 mm (2 inches) at the top of the page, ie turn up 13 single spaces. (b) Suggested left margin: 12 pitch 13, 10 pitch 11, or pre-stored margins where appropriate. (c) Copy the exercise line for line.

1	Line 1	THE WORD PROCESSOR	Turn up 13 single spaces
2	Space		Turn up 2 single spaces
3	Line 2	I N P U T	Turn up 2 single spaces
4	Space		
5	Line 3	Alternative methods	Turn up 2 single spaces
6	Space		
7	Line 4	Mouse	Type the last 4 lines in
8	Line 5	Touch screen	single spacing
9	Line 6	Voice recognition	
10	Line 7	Optical character recognition	

2   Display the following on A5 landscape paper. (a) Leave 51 mm (2 inches) at the top of the page. (b) Suggested left margin: 12 pitch 25, 10 pitch 21, or pre-stored margins where appropriate. (c) Copy the exercise line for line.

1	Line 1	A R E C E P T I O N I S T	Turn up 13 single spaces
2	Space		Turn up 2 single spaces
3	Line 2	PERSONAL QUALITIES REQUIRED	Turn up 3 single spaces
4	Space		
5	Space		
6	Line 3	A good receptionist will be:	Turn up 2 single spaces
7	Space		
8	Line 4	Neat and well groomed	Type the last 3 lines in
9	Line 5	Polite, friendly and helpful	single spacing
10	Line 6	Well informed	

R19 Many people who pay rent are entitled to a rent allowance or   12
rebate - an allowance if a private tenant or a rebate if you   24
are a council tenant.   28

You should write to your local council. Then they will need   40
to know your income, and the larger your family the more you   52
are justified in seizing the chance of getting help, and the   64
more quickly you may expect help. **(SI 1.36)**   70

  1 | 2 | 3 | 4 | 5 | 6 | 7 | 8 | 9 | 10 | 11 | 12 |

R20 If you are asked to compile a business letter, you must: (a)   12
use short words if they express clearly what you want to say   24
and (b) also keep your sentences short. Tackle the job with   36
zeal, acquire a good style, and avoid vague statements. **(SI 1.25)**   47

  1 | 2 | 3 | 4 | 5 | 6 | 7 | 8 | 9 | 10 | 11 | 12 |

R21 Dear Ms Knight, Since July 1987 we have had your name on our   12
mailing lists, and although we have, from time to time, sent   24
you details of many exclusive properties, you have not tele-   36
phoned as you said you would. We are now anxious to know if   48
you have any queries and still wish to buy a desirable resi-   60
dence at an amazingly low price. **(SI 1.33)**   66

  1 | 2 | 3 | 4 | 5 | 6 | 7 | 8 | 9 | 10 | 11 | 12 |

R22 In September 1985, 9,000 people were killed in an earthquake   12
in Mexico City. Also, in June 1986 slight damage was caused   24
by a weak tremor which recorded as 5.4 on the Richter scale.   36
In March 1986, an earthquake struck southern Turkey and some   48
14 people were injured in 4 villages as houses fell. We are   60
lucky in Great Britain as there are only one or 2 zones that   72
have slight earth tremors. **(SI 1.32)**   77

  1 | 2 | 3 | 4 | 5 | 6 | 7 | 8 | 9 | 10 | 11 | 12 |

R23 When you arrive, you should follow the clearly marked black-   12
on-yellow 'arrivals' signs to immigration. If you are going   24
to take an onward flight, follow the signs to the 'Transfer   36
Desk'. After clearing immigration, wait in the lounge until   48
your flight number appears on the TV screen indicating which   60
carousel in the Baggage Hall to go to. Just place your bag-   72
gage on one of the unique, free-of-charge trolleys and go on   84
through customs to the exit zone on the terminal concourse.   96
(SI 1.35)

  1 | 2 | 3 | 4 | 5 | 6 | 7 | 8 | 9 | 10 | 11 | 12 |

R24 A wide range of tax-free goods is available on the aircraft,   12
and a list of the products, with prices and comparative UK   24
retail prices, will be found in the seat pocket. Your cabin   36
staff will let you know in good time as to when the tax-free   48
products will be on sale. For your guidance a list of items   60
you can hear on the audio channels is in the pocket - adjust   72
the sound to suit your needs, but keep the volume low. Some   84
flights have a film and you should select a suitable channel   96
to listen to the sound-track and channel 2 for quality jazz.   108
Your headset should be placed in the seat pocket before you   120
leave the aircraft. **(SI 1.27)**   124

  1 | 2 | 3 | 4 | 5 | 6 | 7 | 8 | 9 | 10 | 11 | 12 |

Effective display

Displayed work looks more effective when it is centred on the page. The underscore, closed capitals or bold type may be used to emphasize or highlight important lines.

Backspace key

Refer to page 28 and locate the backspace key on your machine.

Horizontal centring—blocked style

When centring a piece of display in the full width of the paper, take the following steps:

1 See that the left edge of the paper is at 0 on the paper guide scale.
2 Move margin stops to extreme left and right.
3 Divide by two the total number of spaces between 0 and the scale point reached by the right edge of the page; this gives the centre point of the paper.
4 Bring carriage, carrier or cursor to the centre point.
5 Locate the backspace key and backspace once for every two characters and spaces in the longest line. Ignore any odd letter left over.
6 Set the left margin at the point reached.
7 All lines in the exercise start at the left margin.

Automatic display functions

On electronic keyboards there are usually:

1 An automatic centring function which centres the typed line.
2 An automatic underline function and
3 Automatic emboldening where the chosen text appears in a heavier print.

---

3 Display the following on A5 landscape paper. (a) Leave 25 mm (1 inch) at the top of the page. (b) Centre the longest line horizontally. (c) Set the left margin and start all lines at this point.

	Turn up
	7 single spaces
TRAVEL ARRANGEMENTS	2 single spaces
REFERENCE MANUALS	3 single spaces
ABC Railway Guide	Use single
ABC World Airways Guide	spacing for the
ABC Shipping Guide	last five items
ABC Hotel Guide	
ABC Travel Guide	

NOTE: The left margin will be set at
12 pitch 39
10 pitch 30

4 Display the following on A5 portrait paper. (a) Leave 25 mm (1 inch) at the top of the page. (b) Centre the longest line horizontally. (c) Set the left margin and start all lines at this point.

	Turn up
	7 single spaces
B R E A K F A S T M E N U	2 single spaces
Sunday, 4 February 1996	3 single spaces
Grapefruit, cereal	2 single spaces
Bacon and eggs	1 space
Scrambled egg on toast	1 space
Smoked haddock	2 spaces
Toast and marmalade	1 space
Tea or coffee	

R13 A thick haze covered the headland, and the wind, now at gale 12
force, was sharp and biting. I walked on and in a long time 24
I judged I had done only 3 miles. Anxious and quite worried 36
I sat down for a short time. **(SI 1.12)** 41

1 | 2 | 3 | 4 | 5 | 6 | 7 | 8 | 9 | 10 | 11 | 12 |

R14 Have you ever been to a large airport just to watch the end- 12
less movement of people and planes? You can see hundreds of 24
folk getting on and off these exciting jets, and it makes me 36
wonder how such unique planes zoom so gently into the air or 48
land without skidding. **(SI 1.27)** 52

1 | 2 | 3 | 4 | 5 | 6 | 7 | 8 | 9 | 10 | 11 | 12 |

R15 She exhaled deeply as they crossed the frozen lake and moved 12
swiftly past the hole lined with jagged ice. The sleds were 24
light and the 6 dogs well rested; consequently, there was no 36
need to think about a stop until we were in the next hamlet. 48
Then a sudden squall brought more snow and the track's mark- 60
ings were lost. **(SI 1.22)** 63

1 | 2 | 3 | 4 | 5 | 6 | 7 | 8 | 9 | 10 | 11 | 12 |

R16 From our magazine you will see that we have spent many years 12
fitting all kinds of carpets - all our staff are specialists 24
and quietly complete their jobs. In truth, they are experts 36
who have spent their lives in this trade. **(SI 1.25)** 44

1 | 2 | 3 | 4 | 5 | 6 | 7 | 8 | 9 | 10 | 11 | 12 |

R17 Different kinds of wild plants do not grow in the same place 12
because they need the soil and conditions to suit them, just 24
as you have your likes and dislikes. If you acquire a plant 36
which excels in a warm, dry place, it is prone to die if you 48
move it to a zone which is cold and damp. It is possible to 60
alter its habits over a period of time. **(SI 1.20)** 68

1 | 2 | 3 | 4 | 5 | 6 | 7 | 8 | 9 | 10 | 11 | 12 |

R18 It may be next June before I can be certain of the number of 12
folk who may be present at the Market Square for this year's 24
Fair.. Four years ago our efforts added up to zero, but I am 36
sure we have already sold more tickets than in 1987. **(SI 1.22)** 46

1 | 2 | 3 | 4 | 5 | 6 | 7 | 8 | 9 | 10 | 11 | 12 |

5 Display the following on A5 landscape paper. (a) Leave 25 mm (1 inch) at the top of the page. (b) Centre the longest line horizontally.

		Turn up
	FOSTER AND ELLIOTT	1 single space
	Solicitors	3 single spaces
The left margin will be set at: 12 pitch 33 10 pitch 24	Personal and professional attention on all types of property matters	1 single space 2 single spaces
	Appointments by arrangement	2 single spaces
	0121-456 5433	

Spaced capitals

To centre words that are to be typed in spaced capitals:

1 Say the letters and spaces in pairs.
2 Backspace once for each complete pair, including the two extra spaces between the words, eg S space P space A space C space E space D space space space C space A space, etc.

3 Do NOT backspace for the last letter in the final word and remember to leave three spaces between each word. Practise centring the following two words.

S P A C E D C A P I T A L S

6 Display the following on A5 portrait paper. (a) Leave 25 mm (1 inch) at the top of the page. (b) Centre the longest line horizontally.

		Turn up
	C O M P U T E R S U P P L I E S	3 single spaces
	One-year guarantee	2 single spaces
The left margin will be set at:	DELIVERY WITHIN 24 HOURS	4 single spaces
12 pitch 19 10 pitch 13	Security cable lock Mouse mat and jacket Bar code reader Adjustable footrest	Type the last 4 lines in single spacing

7 Display the following exercise on paper of a suitable size.

THE SINGLE MARKET
How does it affect you?
KEEP UP TO DATE
The United Kingdom and
The Irish Republic
are members of —
THE EUROPEAN UNION

1½ minutes

R7 Many thanks for your notes about the dozen desks we ordered.   12
They are not required right away, but if we may have them by   24
Thursday you may expect our remittance quite soon.   We will   36
adjust our records when we receive your invoice and the bill   48
is paid. **(SI 1.29)**   49

    1 | 2 | 3 | 4 | 5 | 6 | 7 | 8 | 9 | 10 | 11 | 12 |

2 minutes

R8 There seems to be quite an amazing lack of simple, and easy-   12
to-follow guides to operate the more complicated machine; in   24
fact, I looked at 2 or 3 of the books and felt they made the   36
operations seem a little hard - indeed, they were not.   Just   48
one foreign text gave a lucid account of what the typist had   60
to do. **(SI 1.30)**   61

    1 | 2 | 3 | 4 | 5 | 6 | 7 | 8 | 9 | 10 | 11 | 12 |

3 minutes

R9 Have you ever followed modern machine manuals in any detail?   12
They seem to be written in a complex language which contains   24
a great deal of jargon - quantity rather than quality with a   36
lack of easy-to-follow wording.   I did read 3 books in which   48
the message was plain, and one told me how to produce clear,   60
dazzling graphics in a simple way.   Students using this book   72
would find it easy to follow because there are many diagrams   84
and notes that are very clear. **(SI 1.37)**   90

    1 | 2 | 3 | 4 | 5 | 6 | 7 | 8 | 9 | 10 | 11 | 12 |

1 minute

R10 Enclosed please find our price-lists.   When you have studied   12
the range of goods, you will be amazed at the quality of the   24
vast majority of the articles.   Our agent will keep in touch   36
and you may expect a visit. **(SI 1.31)**   41

    1 | 2 | 3 | 4 | 5 | 6 | 7 | 8 | 9 | 10 | 11 | 12 |

1½ minutes

R11 Dear Hazel, It is exactly 6 months since you moved from this   12
Sales Office to join our Accounts Section; therefore, as you   24
now qualify for a transfer and your work is highly regarded,   36
we would be happy to discuss the future with you.   May I see   48
you one day soon? **(SI 1.31)**   51

    1 | 2 | 3 | 4 | 5 | 6 | 7 | 8 | 9 | 10 | 11 | 12 |

2 minutes

R12 As requested, I give below the pay scales objected to at our   12
last 2 meetings.   May I say that I am still quite puzzled by   24
the large increases suggested, and I feel that the new rates   36
should not be made effective at the present time.   May I ask   48
you not to inform your staff before we next meet. **(SI 1.26)**   58

    1 | 2 | 3 | 4 | 5 | 6 | 7 | 8 | 9 | 10 | 11 | 12 |

Fractions

8 Find the ½ key and the % key on your keyboard and make certain you know whether or not you have to use the shift key. Type each of the following lines three times. Margins: 12 pitch 22–82, 10 pitch 12–72, or pre-stored margins where appropriate.

```
; ; ;   ½½½   ; ; ;   ½½½   ; ½;   ; ½;   1½;   2½;   3½;   4½;   5½;   6½;   7½;   8½;   90½;
; ; ;   %%%   ; ; ;   %%%   ; %;   ; %;   ½%;   2%;   3%;   4%;   5%;   6%;   7%;   9%;   19%;
```

NOTE: In addition to the ½, most typewriters have keys with other fractions. Examine your machine to find what fractions it has. These are all typed with the ; finger. Some will require the use of the shift key. Practise the reaching movement from the home key to the fraction key you wish to type. Remember ALWAYS return your finger quickly to the home key.

Sloping fractions

When fractions are not provided on the typewriter, these should be typed by using ordinary figures with the oblique, eg 2 fifteenths = 2/15; 3 sixteenths = 3/16. Where a whole number comes before a 'made-up' fraction, leave a clear space (NOT a full stop) between the whole number and the fraction. Fractions already on the keyboard and sloping fractions may both be used in the same exercise.

9 Type the following on A5 landscape paper. (a) Double spacing. (b) Margins: 12 pitch 22–82, 10 pitch 12–72.

```
2½, 3¼, 6 2/5, 2 5/16, 3 7/8, 4 8/9, 8 2/9, 17 3/7, 16 3/10.
The following widths are in inches: 7½, 5 3/8, 16¾, 17 1/10.
```

Decimals

1 Use full stop for decimal point. This is usually typed in the normal position of the full stop.
2 Leave NO space before or after decimal point.
3 No punctuation required at the end of figures except at the end of a sentence.
4 Always insert the number of decimal places required by using zero.
   Examples: Two decimal places: type 86.40 not 86.4.
   Three decimal places: type 95.010 not 95.01.

10 Type the following sentences three times.

```
Add up 12.54, 13.02, 24.60, 6.75 and 0.20 and you get 57.11.
The sheet measures 1.200 × 5.810 × 2.540 m; the gross weight
is approximately 50.802 kg and the net weight is 38.102 kg.
```

Sums of money in context

1 If the sum comprises only pounds, type as follows: £5, £10 or £5.00, £10.00.
2 If only pence, type: 10p, 97p.
   NOTE: No space between figures and letter p and no full stop after p (unless, of course, it ends a sentence).
3 With mixed amounts, ie sums comprising pounds and pence, the decimal point and the £ symbol should always be used, but NOT the abbreviation p.
   Example: £7.05.
4 If the sum contains a decimal point but no whole pounds, a nought should be typed after the £ symbol and before the point.
   Example: £0.97.

11 Type the following exercise in double spacing.

```
We have purchased goods to the value of £200.50, and we must

send our cheque for this amount; however, we still await a

credit note for £61.49 which means the cheque should be for

£139.01.   The latest discount we were offered was 2½% and

not 3½% as stated in their letter.
```

SM40

Have you ever 'met' a person for the very first time over 11
the telephone? How did you know what kind of person she/he 23
was? By the voice, of course! Was it gruff or pleasant, 35
calm or excited? How do you sound over the telephone? You 46
cannot be seen, only heard, and your voice will convey your 58
personality. 61

You should speak clearly and distinctly, and be very tactful 73
and logical in expressing your thoughts. The good telephon- 85
ist will handle all telephone calls courteously and intelli- 97
gently by speaking in a well-modulated voice, enunciating 108
distinctly, choosing words that convey her thoughts clearly, 120
and expressing through her tone sincere interest in the per- 132
son calling. How well you represent your employer on the 143
telephone will depend on your telephone technique. 153

Answer all calls promptly. Make a habit of having pen and 165
paper ready so that you can record any messages. **(SI 1.46)** 175

1 | 2 | 3 | 4 | 5 | 6 | 7 | 8 | 9 | 10 | 11 | 12 |

SM41

Input is the information prepared by the author and entered 12
into the system by means of the keyboard. The input may be 24
in the form of typed or handwritten drafts, or shorthand/ 36
audio dictation. Whatever kind of input you work from, 47
typing letters and reports will always predominate. You 58
must use: the correct paper for the printout - letterhead, 70
memo, plain bond, and, of course, bank paper for the carbon 81
copies; the preferred house style; accurate spelling, gram- 93
mar, and punctuation. You must proofread thoroughly, mak- 105
ing correction on the soft copy before printout. 115

Converting the input to usable form requires processing. 126
You should follow instructions precisely, use your time 137
wisely, apply common sense and initiative, and type mail- 149
able copy, within a given time, ready for approval, sign- 160
ing and/or comment. Processed input in its final form is 171
known as 'output'.   **(SI 1.51)** 175

1 | 2 | 3 | 4 | 5 | 6 | 7 | 8 | 9 | 10 | 11 | 12 |

KEYBOARDING SKILLS

Before proceeding to the exercises below, you should type the following skill building exercises:

improve your spelling Nos 3 and 4, page 155
skill measurement No 14, page 158.

alphabetic sentence No 2, page 156.
record your progress No 9, page 164.

PRODUCTION DEVELOPMENT

- *Personal letters*—See **data store**, page 189.

1   Type the following formal personal letter on plain A5 portrait paper. (a) Suggested margins: 12 pitch 13–63, 10 pitch 6–56. (b) Follow the layout and capitalization exactly. NB Leave one clear character space between the two parts of the postcode.

Turn up
4 single spaces

Sender's home
address

2 single spaces

2 single spaces

2 single spaces

2 single spaces

2 single spaces

5 single spaces

```
        6 Watson Lane
        MILLOM
        Cumbria
        LA18 4DG

        7 February 1996

        Dear Dr Rivers

        As secretary of our local history society I am
        writing to ask if you would be willing to come and
        talk to our members on Friday 19 April at 7.30 pm
        on the history of our town during the early part
        of this century.

        The talks take place in the Memorial Hall and
        usually last about an hour.  I do hope the date is
        suitable for you.

        Yours sincerely




        Angela Harriman
```

2   Type the following letter on a sheet of plain A5 portrait paper. (a) Suggested margins: 12 pitch 13–63, 10 pitch 6–56. (b) The letter is from Angela Harriman to Dr Rivers; therefore, apart from the date, which is 12 February 1996, follow layout and wording in the letter above, as far as the salutation, then type the following.

I was delighted to learn from your recent letter that you will be able to talk to the members of the history society on 19 April. We shall have a slide projector and screen available for your use.

I will call and collect you in my car at 7.00 pm.

Type the complimentary close and Miss Harriman's name as in the letter displayed in exercise 1.

SM34 If the new shop is to be ready in June, there are a few jobs   12
that must be done at once. First, we must find a person who   24
will make some effort to put the business on its feet. **(SI 1.14)** 35

SM35 My brothers and I were terrors when we were boys, but I do   12
not believe we were really bad. In those days there were no   24
movies or radio, and television was a thing of the future,   35
(SI 1.31)

1 | 2 | 3 | 4 | 5 | 6 | 7 | 8 | 9 | 10 | 11 | 12 |

SM36 A dozen climbers, roped together, had struggled for hours   12
up one of the Swiss heights, and the summit lay only half a   23
mile ahead. Behind them a snow slope fell steeply away for   35
more than a third of a mile. The group was nearly across   46
the slope when they heard a deep tearing noise, and a crack   59
appeared in the snow and ice just five yards above them.   70
(SI 1.23)

SM37 There has always been a great deal of good advice available   12
for the person seeking a job. Much of this excellent advice   24
lays stress on making a good first impression, and I do feel   36
that the first few minutes are critical to your chances of   47
being selected for a job. This means that you should carry   59
out some careful planning before you attend an interview.   70
(SI 1.31)

1 | 2 | 3 | 4 | 5 | 6 | 7 | 8 | 9 | 10 | 11 | 12 |

SM38 We understand that you will be leaving this country shortly   12
to take a job overseas, and we thought that your friends and   24
family might like an up-to-date photograph of you before you   36
leave. We can supply large prints, and we should be pleased   48
to arrange a sitting at short notice when convenient to you.   60
May we also mention that we offer a service for business men   72
which is both efficient and complete in every way. We will   84
be pleased to show you numerous pictures which show clearly   96
the eye-catching style presented by our cameraman. **(SI 1.35)** 106

1 | 2 | 3 | 4 | 5 | 6 | 7 | 8 | 9 | 10 | 11 | 12 |

SM39 Yes, they should call here to see the goods which I spoke to   12
you about last Monday. I do not send stock out on approval.   24
I shall be very pleased to do business with you and to allow   36
you monthly credit of £10,000. In the late autumn I hope to   48
offer some first-class quality goods, and in the meantime I   60
can let you have the best value in woollens, with a special   72
line in sweaters. I am sorry that I am unable to suggest a   84
reliable house for socks: this is part of the trade in which   96
I have not done business, and it would not be fair of me to   108
pass an opinion on the firms whose names you mention in your 120
letter. I have always kept my prices low, and will write to 132
you when next I have some special offers. **(SI 1.23)** 140

1 | 2 | 3 | 4 | 5 | 6 | 7 | 8 | 9 | 10 | 11 | 12 |

● *Personal business letters*—See **data store**, page 189.

3   Type the following personal business letter on plain A5 portrait paper. (a) Suggested margins: 12 pitch
13–63, 10 pitch 6–56. (b) Type the letter in fully-blocked style with open punctuation. (c) Follow the layout
and capitalization precisely.

Turn up
4 single spaces

Sender's home
address

11 Martin Lane
BOSCOMBE
Dorset
BH7 4AQ

2 single spaces

12 November 1996

2 single spaces

Name and address
of addressee

Mr P F Osborne
Osborne Business Machines
26 High Street
BOSCOMBE
Dorset
BH3 8MM

2 single spaces

Dear Mr Osborne

2 single spaces

The laser printer I purchased from you in January
of this year is not working as efficiently as it
should.

2 single spaces

As the machine is under contract with you I should
be very glad if a maintainence engineer would
call at the above address as soon as possible.

2 single spaces

If you will let me know a date and time for this
call I will make sure that I am at home at that
time.

2 single spaces

Yours sincerely

5 single spaces

Martyn C Fowler

4   Type the following letter on a sheet of plain A5 portrait paper. (a) Use margins of 12 pitch 13–63, 10 pitch
6–56. (b) The letter is from Martyn C Fowler to Mr Osbourne; therefore, apart from the date, which is
19 November 1996, follow layout and wording in the letter above, as far as the salutation, then type the
following:

Thank you for your letter dated 15 November 1996.

The contract number for my laser printer is MB216.
I shall be here on Monday 2 December at 2.30 pm when
your engineer will call to service the printer.

(c) Type the complimentary close and Mr Fowler's name as in the letter displayed in exercise 3.

SM31 Please note that as from 2 October there will be an increase   12
of 9% in air fares because of higher landing charges, a drop   24
in the value of sterling, and a surge in the price of fuel.   36

May we again remind you that you must comply with police and   48
immigration regulations at the points of arrival and depar-   60
ture and at any place along the route. Your journey may be   72
broken at most stops (except on package tours) with no extra   84
charge, provided you complete your journey within the dates   96
stated. As there are a number of formalities, the check-in 107
time quoted is the time you must register at the check-in 118
desk. **(SI 1.37)** 119

  1 | 2 | 3 | 4 | 5 | 6 | 7 | 8 | 9 | 10 | 11 | 12 |

SM32 Before your employer leaves on a business trip, obtain from   12
her/him instructions as to what business or private letters   24
may be opened and what correspondence should be forwarded by   36
mail. If you decide to send on the actual letters, make a   47
copy of each as a safeguard against loss or damage in the   58
post. When posting, make sure that the envelope used is of   70
a suitable size and that it is addressed to the town your   81
employer will have reached by the time the letter arrives.   92

Mark the letter/package clearly TO AWAIT ARRIVAL, and state 104
your business address to which the letter should be returned 116
if not claimed within a certain time. You must also record 127
the date of posting mail. **(SI 1.35)** 132

  1 | 2 | 3 | 4 | 5 | 6 | 7 | 8 | 9 | 10 | 11 | 12 |

SM33 When you apply for your first post, how should you look? Is   12
the prospective employer going to say to himself, "This per-   24
son is smart looking and I will be pleased to introduce her   36
to the office staff." Or will he feel that your clothes are   48
'way out', your hair is too startling and unkempt, and your   60
finger nails look dirty. Make certain that your appearance   72
is suitable for the job you are seeking, and forget about it   84
until after the interview.   89

At an interview you will be required to answer and ask ques- 101
tions. The interviewer will have your application form and 113
will perhaps ask you questions that you have answered on 124
paper; however, he wishes to have the information repeated 135
orally. When answering questions, speak clearly and do not 147
bite your words. **(SI 1.37)** 150

  1 | 2 | 3 | 4 | 5 | 6 | 7 | 8 | 9 | 10 | 11 | 12 |

KEYBOARDING SKILLS

Before proceeding to the exercises below, you should type the following skill building exercises:

proofreading No 2, page 148. **techniques and reviews** No 2, page 157.
skill measurement No 15, page 158. **record your progress** No 10, page 164.

PRODUCTION DEVELOPMENT

*Business letters—open punctuation—fully-blocked—see also data store,
page 177.*

Letters are ambassadors and advertisements for the organization that sends them; therefore, you must ensure that your letters are well displayed and faultlessly typed. Businesses have a variety of forms of display, and the examples that follow are in fully-blocked style with open punctuation, which you used in the letters in unit 26.

A business organization will always have paper with a printed letterhead and you should turn up a minimum of two single-line spaces after the last line of the printed heading before starting to type. The originator (writer or author) of a business letter will also have a reference at the top and this, in its simplest form, consists of the initials of the dictator followed by an oblique and the typist's initials. Many organizations today use the dictator's initials, followed by the disk number, the document number and the typist's initials, eg PD/15/22/AH. It is also accepted practice, but by no means essential, to type the dictator's name five single spaces after the complimentary close with her/his designation (official position) typed underneath.

1 Type the following letter on A4 letterhead paper (available from the publishers). (a) Suggested margins: 12 pitch 22–82, 10 pitch 12–72. (b) Follow the layout and capitalization given.

Printed
heading

LEYS ENTERPRISES

Registered No 241199 (England)
Freefone 01270 700014
Telex 76335   Fax 01270 709822

Registered Office 6-9 Druce Road
Cox Bank
CREWE CW3 2AF
Telephone 01270 701387

Turn up
3 single spaces

```
Ref  FW/JP
```

2 single spaces

```
12 January 1996
```

2 single spaces

```
Miss G Patel
19 Haywoods Street
Bearwood
SMETHWICK
West Midlands
B65 0WQ
```

2 single spaces

```
Dear Miss Patel
```

2 single spaces

```
Thank you for the interest you have shown in our products
and for requesting our latest catalogue.
```

2 single spaces

```
Unfortunately, the catalogue is being reprinted to show our
new spring range.  We expect to receive it from the printers
sometime next week.  I will send you 2 copies as soon as
possible.
```

2 single spaces

```
Yours sincerely
```

5 single spaces

```
Frank Warrender
SALES MANAGER
```

SM26 You will be pleased to learn that we have made more machines 12
this year than we did last year, and that we are also making 24
all vital spare parts. Over the next 2 months we shall take 36
orders only for the new models we are producing. **(SI 1.22)** 45

1 | 2 | 3 | 4 | 5 | 6 | 7 | 8 | 9 | 10 | 11 | 12

SM27 Some large offices have a pool of typists who share the work 12
to be done, but we do not know whether or not this is a good 24
plan. It is a matter upon which each firm should make a de- 36
cision based on the pressure of work and the number of staff 48
employed as typists. You may prefer a job in a typing pool. 60
(SI 1.22)

1 | 2 | 3 | 4 | 5 | 6 | 7 | 8 | 9 | 10 | 11 | 12 |

SM28 The Chairman of the Board tells me that Tom Younger has been 12
badly hurt in an accident on the M5, and points out that Tom 24
will not be at work for at least 18 months. You are aware, 36
no doubt, of the fact that he has a large number of speaking 48
engagements in many different cities, and these will have to 60
be cancelled at once unless we are able to engage someone to 72
take over from him. **(SI 1.25)** 76

1 | 2 | 3 | 4 | 5 | 6 | 7 | 8 | 9 | 10 | 11 | 12 |

Speed building

Speed is built up more easily on short, simple exercises and, as we have now reached 2½ minutes at 30 wpm, and will continue at 30 wpm with increased lengths of timing, we suggest that you use the earlier **skill measurement** exercises as practice material for speed building. For example, to increase your speed from 30 wpm to 35 wpm, use SM12 on page 158. As a guide, we suggest that if have more than one error for each minute typed, then should strive for greater accuracy. With less than one for each minute typed, you may wish to build your spee using short exercises of low syllabic intensity.

SM29 When travelling in an aeroplane, make sure that none of your 12
hand luggage obstructs the aisle or seat areas. It should 24
be stored in the overhead lockers or under the seat in front 36
of you. Enjoy your flight! Sit back, relax, and make your- 48
self comfortable - the cabin staff will be pleased to attend 60
to your needs. Hot or cold meals will be served during the 72
flight, depending on the time of day and length of flight. 83
Radio and tape players may be used. **(SI 1.27)** 90

1 | 2 | 3 | 4 | 5 | 6 | 7 | 8 | 9 | 10 | 11 | 12 |

SM30 You get basic tax relief on most mortgages by paying less to 12
the society who lent you the money, so no allowance is made 24
in your code. If you pay higher rate tax, your code will be 36
adjusted to give the extra relief due. If you pay interest 48
in full on mortgages or other loans for such things as home 60
improvements, an estimate of the amount of interest payable 72
will be given in your code. If you have a mortgage on prop- 84
erty that you let for a commercial rent (during 6 months of 95
each year) interest will be allowed as a deduction. **(SI 1.33)** 105

1 | 2 | 3 | 4 | 5 | 6 | 7 | 8 | 9 | 10 | 11 | 12 |

Keyboarding skills—skill measurement SM26–SM30   **160**
1½, 2, 2½, 3 and 3½ minutes at 30 wpm
Speed building

2 Type the following fully-blocked letter in open punctuation, from Leys Enterprises, on A4 letterhead paper (available from the publishers). (a) Suggested margins: 12 pitch 22–82, 10 pitch 12–72. (b) Keep to the spacing and layout indicated at this elementary stage of your learning process.

● For an explanation of the different parts of the letter, see **data store**, page 178.

Reference	Our ref JM/FG	Turn up 2 single spaces
Date	22 January 1996	2 single spaces
Name and address of addressee	Dr T P Townsend 6 Florence Drive Harborne BIRMINGHAM B32 2JZ	2 single spaces
Salutation	Dear Dr Townsend	2 single spaces
Body of letter	Further to your telephone call received this morning, I am writing to let you know that I have now looked into the fact that you have not received your order made early in December.	
	Because of the popularity of this particular item it has had to be reordered. I will let you know immediately the item is received by us and when you may expect delivery.	2 single spaces
	In the meantime, I am enclosing a copy of our latest catalogue. Should you wish to order any item from it before the end of March, we can offer you a 10% discount.	
	Please accept our sincere apologies for the delay.	
Complimentary close	Yours sincerely	5 single spaces
Signatory Designation	JONATHAN MATKINS Customer Services Department	1 single space
Enclosure	Enc	Minimum of 2 single spaces

3 Type the following fully-blocked letter in open punctuation, from Leys Enterprises, on A4 letterhead paper. (a) Suggested margins 12 pitch 22–82, 10 pitch 12–72. (b) The details as far as the salutation are exactly as those given in the letter above, except for the date which is 12 February 1996. (c) After typing the salutation, turn up two single spaces and type the following paragraphs.

I am delighted to inform you that your Order No 329076 was received this morning and will be despatched to you today.
Please accept our very sincere apologies for the delay.

(d) The complimentary close etc, is the same as in the letter above. Omit 'Enc'.

SM19 At the moment, there is no guide to help us to judge how far   12
we are from the roadside or from the car in front of us. We   24
know that a device is being made that will help us gauge how   36
far away we may be. **(SI 1.22)**   40

1 | 2 | 3 | 4 | 5 | 6 | 7 | 8 | 9 | 10 | 11 | 12 |

SM20 He said that if you want a garden then you will have to do a   12
great deal of work, but in these days you can buy many tools   24
which will be helpful for the heavy work, and thus save time   36
and effort. You would not need to employ hired help, and so   48
you could then save some money. **(SI 1.13)**   54

1 | 2 | 3 | 4 | 5 | 6 | 7 | 8 | 9 | 10 | 11 | 12 |

SM21 A computer is now being made that will store voice patterns.   12
It will know your voice when you speak to it, and it will be   24
able to reply to you. **(SI 1.21)**   28

1 | 2 | 3 | 4 | 5 | 6 | 7 | 8 | 9 | 10 | 11 | 12 |

SM22 When you eat your Brazil nuts at Christmas do you ever think   12
of the men who pick them and of the risks they run to do so?   24
One of the risks is the falling of nuts from the trees which   36
grow to a very great height. What we usually call nuts are,   48
in fact, really the seeds from the tree. **(SI 1.20)**   56

1 | 2 | 3 | 4 | 5 | 6 | 7 | 8 | 9 | 10 | 11 | 12 |

SM23 Against the clear blue morning sky, the white sails of their   12
graceful yachts made an ever-changing pattern as they danced   24
and swayed in the breeze. **(SI 1.21)**   29

1 | 2 | 3 | 4 | 5 | 6 | 7 | 8 | 9 | 10 | 11 | 12 |

SM24 One of the great problems of today is the pressure of noise: 12
noise in the streets, in the home, by day, and sometimes far   24
into the night. Are buses and lorries the chief cause? No.   36
As we hear these all day, we get used to them. So it is the   48
infrequent sounds, such as those made by jet planes. **(SI 1.16)**   58

1 | 2 | 3 | 4 | 5 | 6 | 7 | 8 | 9 | 10 | 11 | 12 |

SM25 The weather is likely to remain mild in the south, with some   12
light rain, but in the north there may be ground frost which   24
could cause ice on some roads. **(SI 1.10)**   30

1 | 2 | 3 | 4 | 5 | 6 | 7 | 8 | 9 | 10 | 11 | 12 |

Keyboarding skills—skill measurement   SM19–SM25   **159**
1½ and 2 minutes at 27 wpm   1 and 2 minutes at 28 wpm   1 and 2 minutes at 29 wpm
1 minute at 30 wpm

NOTE TO WORD PROCESSOR AND VDU OPERATORS From this point in the textbook you will find various exercises with specific instructions for word processor and VDU operators. It is understood that the basic procedures of word processing will have been achieved at this stage and that you are able to start up the equipment, create a new file, use the pre-stored margins, key in text, proofread and correct the document on screen, print the document, store it on disk and close down (log off) the equipment.

4   Type the following fully-blocked letter in open punctuation from Leys Enterprises, on A5 letterhead paper. (a) Suggested margins: 12 pitch 13–63, 10 pitch 6–56. (b) Insert today's date.

●   For an explanation of **subject heading** see **data store**, page 178.

```
Ref KM/42/53/RO

Miss Muriel Fletcher OBE
Everest & Gould
Solicitors
16 New Street
BIRMINGHAM
B1 2SP
```
                                                                         Turn up
                                                                         2 single spaces
```
Dear Madam
```
                                                                         2 single spaces

Subject heading   `TELEPHONE ANSWERING MACHINE`
                                                                         2 single spaces
```
Thank you for your letter asking for details of
our telephone answering machines.

I am enclosing leaflets of our various machines,
but I feel that AUM580 would be suitable for you.
This machine has many facilities including full
remote operation with high quality recording.

The price of this machine is £191.25, but if you
order before the end of next month we will allow
15% discount.

Yours faithfully



Kim Charrington (Ms)
Sales Department

Encs
```

 Key in document 4 (filename ANSER) for 10-point printout. Use the word wraparound function and embolden the subject heading. When you have completed this task, save under filename ANSER and print out one original. Recall the document and follow the instructions for text editing on page 171.

5   Type an identical letter to the one given in exercise 4, but address it to: Mr Jack Phillips, 32 Martin's Way, Henley-on-Thames, Oxon, RG9 1UG. Except for the name and address of the addressee and the salutation, the wording will be exactly as that given above.

Skill measurement

Follow instructions on page 23.

Margins: 12 pitch 22–82, 10 pitch 12–72

25 wpm   1½ minutes   Not more than 2 errors

SM12   Just a year ago I said that you should be given a trial as a   12
clerk in our sales section, and, as one of the staff will be   24
leaving a week today, I would like you to take her job.   Let   36
me know. **(SI 1.16)**   38

1 | 2 | 3 | 4 | 5 | 6 | 7 | 8 | 9 | 10 | 11 | 12 |

25 wpm   2 minutes   Not more than 2 errors

SM13   There must be little imps who sleep until we start to do our   12
work, and then they visit our office and begin to harass us.   24
We must all try to keep our minds on the work that has to be   36
done, and avoid letting our line of thought be broken by any   48
visitors. **(SI 1.24)**   50

1 | 2 | 3 | 4 | 5 | 6 | 7 | 8 | 9 | 10 | 11 | 12 |

25 wpm   3 minutes   Not more than 3 errors

SM14   We have not yet been able to send the goods you ordered last   12
week as they are not stock lines, but we shall do all we can   24
to let you have some of the goods, if not all, by Tuesday of   36
next week.   We trust that you will excuse the delay in send-   48
ing your requirements, and that we may look forward to meet-   60
ing your requests more promptly in the future.   We enclose a   72
new price list. **(SI 1.21)**   75

1 | 2 | 3 | 4 | 5 | 6 | 7 | 8 | 9 | 10 | 11 | 12 |

26 wpm   1 minute   Not more than 1 error

SM15   In spite of the rain all of us thought it had been an excel-   12
lent evening; but the guests could not travel till the storm   24
had passed. **(SI 1.15)**   26

1 | 2 | 3 | 4 | 5 | 6 | 7 | 8 | 9 | 10 | 11 | 12 |

26 wpm   1½ minutes   Not more than 2 errors

SM16   As a good typist you must be fast, accurate, and able to set   12
out all kinds of documents.   In your first post there may be   24
some forms of layout that are not clear.   If that is so, you   36
may need help. **(SI 1.18)**   39

1 | 2 | 3 | 4 | 5 | 6 | 7 | 8 | 9 | 10 | 11 | 12 |

26 wpm   2 minutes   Not more than 2 errors

SM17   Last May we had a chance to buy a large stock of fine cotton   12
sheets, and we are now selling these at a reduced price.   If   24
your own stock of sheets is low, now is the chance to obtain   36
some of these goods at half price or less.   Send an order by   48
July at the latest. **(SI 1.13)**   52

1 | 2 | 3 | 4 | 5 | 6 | 7 | 8 | 9 | 10 | 11 | 12 |

27 wpm   1 minute   Not more than 1 error

SM18   The day was sunny but cool.   After we had rested and had our   12
snack, we packed our bags and set out for the distant cliffs   24
some 2 miles off. **(SI 1.15)**   27

1 | 2 | 3 | 4 | 5 | 6 | 7 | 8 | 9 | 10 | 11 | 12 |

- *Forms of address*—See **data store**, page 180.
- *Envelopes and labels*—See **data store**, page 185.
- For an explanation of **special marks**—See **data store** page 178.

Addressing envelopes and labels

Approximately one-third from left-hand edge.

First line half way down ————————→ Mrs Margot Lawden BSc JP
Moorend
177 Barry Avenue
Sedgebrook

Each item on a separate line

Post town in capitals ————————→ GRANTHAM
Lincs

One space between the two halves of ————→ NG32 2EL
postcode

DL envelope—110 × 220 mm (4¼″ × 8⅝″)

```
FOR THE ATTENTION OF MR DAVID MRAMBA

Grosvenor Studios
Grosvenor House
Watlington Trading Estate
Bletchley
MILTON KEYNES
Bucks
MK2 3EY
```

6 Display the above addresses, given as examples, on DL envelopes or labels. Type the following addresses on envelopes or labels. Mark the first one URGENT and the second one PERSONAL. Start a new line where two blank spaces have been left between items. The letter to Dan Corrigan should be marked AIRMAIL.

```
Sir Joseph Bliss JP  Oak Lodge  Four Oaks  SUTTON COLDFIELD  West Midlands  B74 4EH
Dr Jeremy Brooker  1 St Julian's Avenue  St Peter Port  GUERNSEY  Channel Islands
Mr & Mrs Harold Hunter  Orchard Cottage  Webb Way  GREAT DUNMOW  Essex  CM6 2BR
Miss Gwyneth Jones  26 Ely Road  Bryn Mawr  PWLLHELI  Gwynedd  LL53 2AR
Joan McKenzie  41 Dalkeith Road  EDINBURGH  EH16 5BU
The Global Manufacturing Co  FREEPOST  Clifden Buildings  CIRENCESTER  Glos  GL7 1CU
Youngs Motors Ltd  High Street  TAUNTON  Somerset  TA1 3SX
Dan Corrigan  2 Ennis Road  RATHKEALE  Co Limerick
Messrs J Cranleigh & Co  PO Box No 21  Surrey Road  NORWICH  Norfolk  NR1 3NG
Mr Yeoh Chee Yam  104 West Street  BRADFORD  West Yorkshire  BD1 1NL
```

7 Type envelopes or labels for exercises 1–5 in this unit.

Freepost

An organization wishing to receive a reply (or response to an advertisement) from customers, without them having to pay postage, may (by obtaining a licence from the Post Office) tell the customers to use the word FREEPOST on the envelope. The word is usually typed in capitals on a line by itself after the name of the organization.

Techniques and reviews

Knowledge of display, of word division and of tabulation are useless if you cannot operate the machine efficiently. Therefore, the basic need of all typing courses is the development and consolidation of good techniques. Technique and review drills may be used as 'warming-up' exercises or for remedial work. Type each line or sentence three times, and then type the complete exercise.   Left margin 15

1   *Improve control of space bar*

as is so or be in am if an me go my do he by us ask may you.
It is so.   Ask me to go.   You must be in time.   I may do so.
Who is she?   He can go home on 6 May.   It is a 65-page book.

2   *Improve control of down reaches*

Ac lack back rack hack jack track crack brace vacant accents
Ab cabs dabs tabs jabs able table gable sable labels enables
Ask Jack to bring back the labels for that one vacant table.

3   *Build speed on fluency drills*

Did for the key all dog why see you put car ask new her site
She did not see the new bus.   Ask her for all the old shoes.
I will talk to him as soon as he is ready to go to the play.

4   *Improve control of up reaches*

Ki kick kirk kite kind king skim skips taking asking napkin.
Aw awed laws saws paws yawn Shaw shawl crawls brawls straws.
He is taking the skips of straw to Crawley on Monday 3 June.

5   *Review hyphen key*

full-time, up-to-date, blue-grey, 48-page, re-cover, co-opt.
Full-time students wore pin-striped blue-grey ties.   He considered that the up-to-date 248-page document was now ready.

6   *Build accuracy on punctuation review*

"Is John - John Mann, not John Green - here, please?"   "No."
Send me the documents immediately; I cannot wait any longer.
Call on me today.   I require: 2 books, 3 ribbons, 4 pencils.

7   *Improve control of out reaches*

Ga game gape gave gates gales garlic galley baggage Algarve.
Up upon sups cups upset soups couple duplex couplet superior
The superior baggage belongs to the couple going to Reigate.

8   *Improve control of shift keys*

Dear Sir, Yours faithfully, Mr J Brown, New York, Hong Kong.
Dear Mr Brown, Dear Mrs Green, Miss R Grey, Miss Jean R Dua.
The book Advanced Word Processing is by J and D Stananought.

9   *Improve control of figures*

ewe 323 woe 293 our 974 rye 463 you 697 tour 5974 writ 2486.
Drill: 10, 29, 38, 47, 56, 123, 456, 789, 010, 343, 678, 86.
Accounts: 00-11-2345, 00-12-6789, 00-13-5858, 00-14-2679-80.

10   *Improve control of jump reaches*

Ve five live jive dive even vain pave have rave valve events
On loan zone cone tone hone bone fond only once bonus lesson
Five of these events have a once only bonus for the winners.

11   *Improve control of in reaches*

Ar are art ark lark dark park arch larch tartar barter March
Ou out our sour dour pour tour ounce pounce bounced trounced
It was dark in the park and the rain poured on the tourists.

12   *Improve control of adjacent keys*

Oi toil boil soil foil join voice noise coins choice adjoins
Rt tart part dart cart sort forts sport mirth berths sported
The many voices joined in cheering the sporting darts teams.

8 Type the following fully-blocked letter in open punctuation, from Leys Enterprises, on A4 letterhead paper.
(a) Suggested margins: 12 pitch 22–82, 10 pitch 12–74. (b) Type an envelope.

Turn up

```
Our ref   GP/AV407914R/FJ                           2 single spaces

Your ref   DK/INV                                   2 single spaces

27 March 1996                                       2 single spaces
```

Special   `FOR THE ATTENTION OF DEREK KINGSWAY`   2 single spaces
mark

```
Kingsway, Boulter and Meade
27 The Broadway
WALSALL
West Midlands
WS1 6EF

Dear Sirs

RELOCATION OF PREMISES

I am pleased to inform you that our Birmingham branch will
be moving to new premises as from 6 May 1996. It will close
at 1700 hours on Friday 3 May and all business will be
transferred to the new office which will be open from
0900 hours on Monday 6 May.

I am enclosing a leaflet giving full details of address,
telephone number and the various services we shall be offer-
ing at our new branch.

You can be assured of the same friendly and helpful service
at our new offices that you have received in the past.

Yours faithfully
```
Name of   `LEYS ENTERPRISES`
organization

```
Glyn Payne
Area Director
```

NOTE: This exercise contains all the
parts of a business letter.
Keep your copy and refer to it
when necessary.

```
Enc
```

 Key in document 8 (filename MOVE) for 10-point printout. Embolden all words in block capitals and use the
word wraparound function. When you have completed this task, save under filename MOVE and print out one
copy. Recall the document and follow the instructions for text editing on page 171.

KEYBOARDING SKILLS

Alphabetic sentences

It is very important that you start each typing period with a 'warm-up' drill, and the alphabetic sentence is excellent material because it gives intensive practice on the alphabet keys and, therefore, improves accuracy. Type each sentence three times.   Left margin 15

1 The pretty girl gave a cry of terror as those ravens quickly seized the jewels from the box.

2 The fox came quietly into the open, and enjoyed walking over the field which was bathed in hazy sunshine.

3 The bold pilot was unable to land the jet owing to extremely thick fog which quite covered the whole zone.

4 The thick haze over the lake meant that Jacques would not be expected to visit his good friends living nearby.

5 I saw the grey squirrel relax by the very old trees and then jump with zest from one piece of bark to another.

6 The breakfast Jackson requested was excellent even though it was cooked for him in a frying pan over a brazier.

7 The male patient lay back quietly in the oxygen tent dozing, just after his operation for a broken hip was over.

8 Flexible working is generally favoured and requested by most employees as they can just avoid the crazy traffic.

9 When we walked among the foxgloves and bluebells on that hot day in June, the crazy paving looked quite attractive.

10 The exquisite butterflies flew past, and Kathy could see the amazing colours of jade, blue, and mauve on their wings.

11 Mike was so full of zeal for the project but exaggerated his abilities very much, and they were not quite up to the task.

12 An extract from the magazine on the technique of painting in oils was requested by the majority of folk who were revising art.

13 The dozens of climbers were frequently exhausted when trying to complete the fantastic job of climbing the very high rock mountain.

14 With maximum efficiency vivacious Eliza completed the formal tests, was judged to be the best candidate, and acquired the highest marks.

15 Then we saw the five models at the waxworks, which were just amazing, as the exact resemblances to folks in the past were quite remarkable.

16 The executive was next in line for the position of editor on the Gazette as the skills required for the job were just the ones possessed by him.

17 The examination was very difficult for the lazy boy who just managed to complete the first question; but unfortunately he did not gain many marks.

18 The azure blue sky was quite a breathtaking event for Trixie to see, but it lasted just a few moments as the storm clouds blew up and covered the sun.

KEYBOARDING SKILLS
Before proceeding to the exercises below, you should type the following skill building exercises:

improve your spelling Nos 5 and 6, page 155.   **alphabetic sentence** No 3, page 156.
skill measurement No 16, page 158.   **record your progress** No 11, page 164.

PRODUCTION DEVELOPMENT

- *Correction of errors*—See **data store**, page 182.

- *Proofreading*—See **data store**, page 190.

1   In the exercise below, the sentences in COLUMN ONE have been repeated in COLUMN TWO. Those in column one are correct, but in each sentence in column two there is a typing error. Compare the sentences and see how quickly you can spot the errors. Then type the sentences correctly.

COLUMN ONE

1   Allan Osborn has a sister, Jayne.
2   Word processing saves a lot of time.
3   The operator's work was praised.
4   Anna, the receptionist, was efficient.
5   The word processor cost £3,980.00.
6   Did Marion print a copy of the letter?
7   The engineer repaired the machine.
8   I shall take the post to Mr Fearn.
9   The disk from Purchasing is faulty.
10 Please have your work ready by 5.00 pm.

COLUMN TWO

1   Allan Osborne has a sister, Jayne.
2   Word processing save a lot of time.
3   The operators work was praised.
4   Anna, the receptionist was efficient.
5   The word processor cost £3,890.00.
6   Did Marion print a copy of the letter.
7   The Engineer repaired the machine.
8   I will take the post to Mr Fearn.
9   The disk form Purchasing is faulty.
10 Please have you work ready by 5.00 pm.

Further exercises on **proofreading** are on pages 148–154.

Typing from manuscript copy

You will have to type letters or documents from handwritten drafts. Take particular care to produce a correct copy. Before typing, read the manuscript through to see that you understand it. Check the completed document and correct any errors *before* removing the paper from the typewriter or *before* printing out the document, if you are using a computer.

2   Type the following on A5 landscape paper. (a) Read the whole passage through before you start to type and locate and correct the three circled errors. (b) From the top edge of the paper turn up seven single spaces. (c) Suggested margins: 12 pitch 22–82, 10 pitch 12–72. (d) Single spacing. (e) Keep to the line-endings in the copy and follow the abbreviations used.

SAVE ENERGY AT HOME

There are (sevaral) ways you could save energy in your home. Some won't cost you any money; they simply mean thinking more about the way you use energy — but they will all save money and help protect the environment.

These include such things as (swiching) off (unecessary) lights, not leaving the TV on when you are not watching it, boiling only the amount of water you actually need in the kettle, and turning down the thermostat by a degree or so.

Improve your spelling skill

Type each line of an exercise three times, then type the complete exercise once. Set the left margin at 15 or use pre-stored margins.

```
 1  view until merge awful chaos quiet forty really absorb centre
 2  lose occur gauge audio among video weird choice losing prefer

 3  paid guard media input recur queue depot canvas govern pursue
 4  quay basic alter diary truly lying reign height eighty ascend

 5  cheque usable cursor buffet unique wholly mislaid acknowledge
 6  debtor tariff fulfil coming friend humour leisure undoubtedly

 7  hungry murmur choose format argues misuse omitted immediately
 8  modern cancel except access genius serial console transferred

 9  mislaid relying dismiss useless forceful privilege stationery
10  editing college twelfth benefit February principal admissible

11  liaison minutes cursory woollen harassed Wednesday difference
12  usually grammar centred certain achieved dependent receivable

13  movable pastime synonym justify withhold perceived compliment
14  arguing marriage valuable omission function parallel envelope

15  develop exercise physical planning expenses guardian pleasant
16  believe courtesy received decision occasion familiar definite

17  pitiful forcible sentence transfer separate reducing feasible
18  proceed exercise physical hardware expenses guardian pleasant

19  knowledge agreeable competent underrate absorption colleagues
20  vaccinate committee benefited possesses accessible accidental

21  technical recognize inoculate recommend courageous wraparound
22  recipient erroneous transient emphasize especially repetition
23  courteous aggravate aggregate competent enthusiasm pagination
```

Language arts—apostrophe   See explanation on page 170

```
 1  My clerk's new word processor has many useful function keys.
 2  All our clerks' income tax records were in the Staff Office.
 3  The company's new laser printers were very swift and silent.
 4  The directors' cars were parked just in front of the office.

 5  Mr & Mrs Bob Cross's house was put up for sale on Wednesday.
 6  Kenneth Andrews' farm was put up for auction on 21 November.
 7  My children's playground was unusable because of the floods.
 8  The men's cricket bat will be found near the pavilion gates.

 9  We don't know at what time it's possible to visit her today.
10  James said, 'Do write and let me know your time of arrival.'
11  The desks measured 5' 11" x 2' 10" x 2' 6" and 6' x 3' x 3'.
12  I am certain that the word 'embarrass' has 2 r's and 2 s's.
```

Language arts—agreement of subject and verb   See explanation on page 170

```
 1  A daisywheel is a fast spinning disk that prints characters.
 2  Floppy disks are used for recording and storing information.
 3  You were our first customer when we opened our shop in town.
 4  He agrees with me, I agree with you, and they agree with us.
 5  Neither William nor Brian was at the meeting on Monday last.
 6  A new diary and a phone index are necessary for your office.
```

Tabulation

Arrangement of items in columns

You may be required to arrange items in column form in such a way that they are horizontally centred on the page, with equal spaces between the columns and with equal margins. This can be done easily by means of the backspacing method you have already used in display work, or by using the arithmetical method.

Word processing programs have facilities to allow you to create tables quickly and simply.

Tabulator key

All typewriters have three tabulator controls which you should locate on your machine as their positions vary on the different makes.

1 A tab set key to fix the tab stops.
2 A tab clear key to clear the tab stops.
3 A tab bar or key to move the carriage/carrier/cursor to wherever a tab stop is set.

Refer to the user's handbook for information on how to set tab stops on your computer.

Preliminary steps for arranging items in columns

1 Move margin stops to extreme left and right.
2 Clear all previous tab stops that may be already set.
3 Set the left margin and tab stops at the points given.
4 Test you tab stops by returning the carriage, carrier or cursor and then depressing the tab bar or key.

Typing the table

1 Type the main heading at the left margin.
2 Turn up two single (one double) spaces.
3 At left margin type first item in first column.
4 Tabulate to the second column and type first item; then tabulate to each of the remaining columns and type the first item.
5 Continue in the same way with the rest of the table.

3 Carrying out the instructions given above, type the following table on A5 landscape paper. (a) Leave 51 mm (2 inches) at the top of the page, ie turn up 13 single-line spaces from the top edge of the paper. (b) Set the left margin at the point given; the figures in brackets are for 10 pitch. (c) Set the tab stops as shown. (d) Double spacing.

Left margin:
33(24)

WORD FORMATION

1st tab: 43(34)
2nd tab: 58(49)

control	controllable	controlled
use	usable	useful
like	likeable	liking
benefit	benefited	beneficial

Exercise 12

Keys on page 170
Proofreading target: 7 minutes
Typing target: 4 minutes

The following exercise contains 15 errors. A correct version is not provided, so you will have to identify the errors by using your knowledge of typing layout, spelling, punctuation and correct grammatical expression. When you have noted all the errors, type a corrected version, proofreading your typed copy very carefully.

P R E S T E L

Prestal is a collection of specialist, educational and general databases which provide a wide range of information & services for a variety of users. It is part of british Telecom and was the worlds first viewdata service. At the end of 1987 there were about 300,000 pages of information and interactive services held on Prestel's own computors, from more than 1,000 organizations.

When you subscribe to Prestel you is given an identity number and password and a telephone number to dial to connect you to the Prestel network. The information is held on mainframe computers situated in different parts of the country and linked together to form a network. The services are made available to your microcomputer via the telephone and modem at local call telephone rates. The moden is a devise which allows a computer to be connected to a telephone line.

        The information includes news articles, storys, advertisments, reference information statistics, ect. A Prestel user can book holidays, send messages to other subscribers, order goods; etc.

The following exercise contains 14 errors. A correct version is not provided, so you will have to identify the errors by using your knowledge of typing layout, spelling, punctuation and correct grammatical expression. When you have noted all the errors, type a corrected version, proofreading your typed copy very carefully.

HEALTHY VDU SCREENS?

Is it safe to sit in front of a visual display unit allday? Or does it cause eye strain, backache, headaches frozen shoulders, or even misscarriages?

If there are any health worrys, it may be that stress come highest on the list caused by sitting with a fixed posture in front of a screen for more than four hours a day on work than is repetitive and requires a high degree of accuracy. It is wise to take plenty of brakes, get up and walk around a little, or do a different type of work for a short time, if poss. Make sure the lighting and ventilation in your office are adequate, and that your chair is adjustable so that you are sitting in a comfortable position; a detatchable keyboard is useful, as is a tilt and swivle screen; ajust the brightness of the print on the screen to suit your eyes. Remind yourself how lucky you are to have all the advantages of typing on a word processer! Or would you prefer to use an old manual type writer?

4 Following the instructions given on the previous page, type this table on A5 landscape paper. (a) Leave 51 mm (2 inches) at the top of the page. (b) Set the margins and tab stops at the points given; the figures in brackets are for 10 pitch. (c) Double spacing.

Left margin:
26(17)

H O M O P H O N E S

Same sound - different spelling and meaning

1st tab: 44(35)
2nd tab: 61(52)

berth - birth	sell - cell	chute - shoot
some - sum	creak - creek	draw - drawer
draft - draught	flour - flower	hair - hare
hear - here	main - mane	plane - plain

● **Horizontal centring (*steps to determine starting point for each column*)—*backspacing method*—**See **data store,** page 187.

Horizontal centring (steps to determine starting point for each column)—arithmetical method

1 Move margin stops to extreme left and right.
2 Clear all previous tab stops that may be already set.
3 Insert paper seeing that the left edge is at 0.
4 Calculate the number of characters and spaces in the longest item in each column and write these figures clearly in a rough diagram on a separate sheet of paper.
5 Allow three spaces between each column. Write these figures in the diagram.
6 Subtract the total calculated in point 5 from the total number of spaces across the page.

7 Divide the sum arrived at in point 6 by two, which will give you the point at which to set your left margin.
8 From the left margin, space along for each character and space required for the longest item in the first column, plus the three spaces allowed between the first and second columns. Set a tab stop and make a written note on your diagram of the point on the scale at which the tab stop is set.
9 Repeat for the remaining columns.
10 Type the table as described on the previous page.

5 Carrying out the instructions given above, type the following table on A5 landscape paper. (a) Leave 51 mm (2 inches) at the top of the page. (b) Leave three spaces between columns. (c) Double spacing.

Rough calculations for exercise 5.

$$\boxed{14} + 3 + \boxed{7} + 3 + \boxed{7} + 3 + \boxed{11} = 48$$

	12 pitch	10 pitch
A5 landscape paper		
Number of characters across	100	82
Less	48	48
Number of spaces remaining	52	34
Divide by two	26	17
Set left margin at	26	17

Left margin:
26(17)

THE EUROPEAN UNION

Members of the Single Market

1st tab: 43(34)
2nd tab: 53(44)
3rd tab: 63(54)

United Kingdom	Germany	France	Italy
Spain	Belgium	Greece	Netherlands
Portugal	Denmark	Ireland	Luxembourg

Exercise 10

Keys on page 170
Proofreading target: 5 minutes
Typing target: 3 minutes

The following exercise contains 12 errors. A correct version is not provided, so you will have to identify the errors by using your knowledge of typing layout, spelling, punctuation and correct grammatical expression. When you have noted all the errors, type a corrected version, proofreading your typed copy very carefully.

WALKING DOGS IN THE COUNTRYSIDE

It is just as important to keep your dog under control in the country-side as it is when walking him in a towns. Your dog should be trained to be obediant. There are dog — training classes in most areas. Take your dog — both you and he will enjoy it, and it will give you confidence to now that you can control your dog. He should stay when he is told come when called, sit and walk to heel on command.

Remember the following points when in the country —

1 Never allow your dog to chase anything — it is a bad habit which are hard
   to break.
2 The dogs lead should always be on when their are farm animals about, and do
   not allow him to run on to cultivated fields.
3 Make sure you know the country code yourself, & then you can train your dog
   in countryside awareness.

The following exercise contains 14 errors. A correct version is not provided, so you will have to identify the errors by using your knowledge of typing layout, spelling, punctuation and correct grammatical expression. When you have noted all the errors, type a corrected version, proofreading your typed copy very carefully.

      Staverton International Ltd., office furniture and equipment manufactures, have reported losses for a number of years, but have now staged a strong recovery. They were in good form last year, breaking the £1 million pre-tax profit barrier for the first time. There furniture is modern and functional and within the price bracket of the smaller companys, eg, an executives desk in mahogany will sell for approximatly £981.50p. the colours are bright and imaginative with yellow's blues and greens being used for the upholstery.

Last years record braking results reflect a 27.7 % return on shareholders' funds. This year has started strongly and there is a good order book.

Vertical centring

At this early stage in your training it is not necessary to centre the tables vertically with equal top and bottom margins. Follow the instructions given or leave a top margin of 25–51 mm (1–2 inches).

Typing column headings—blocked style

1 Remember that the column heading may be the longest item in the column, so you must take this into account when making your calculations for horizontal centring.
2 Column headings and column items start at the left margin and at the tab stops set for the longest item of each column.
3 Turn up two single (one double) after the main headings.
4 Turn up two single (one double) after the column headings, which may be typed in capital letters or small letters with initial capitals. The column headings are usually underlined if they are typed in small letters.
5 In an examination use the style shown in the copy.

6 Type the following table on A5 landscape paper. (a) Leave 51 mm (2 inches) at the top of the page. (b) Centre the table horizontally. (c) Leave three spaces between columns. (d) Double spacing.

DIFFICULT SPELLINGS

Abbreviation	Word in full	Abbreviation	Word in full
sep	separate	recom	recommend
Feb	February	cos	companies
Wed	Wednesday	sinc	sincerely
secs	secretaries	gntee	guarantee

7 Type the following on A5 portrait paper. (a) Leave 51 mm (2 inches) at the top of the page. (b) Centre the table horizontally. (c) Leave three spaces between columns. (d) Double spacing. (e) Before you type this exercise, find the missing dialling codes from your telephone directory and enter them correctly in your finished copy.

INTERNATIONAL DIALLING CODES

Country	Code	Country	Code
Ireland	00 353	Italy	00 39
France	00 33	Germany	00 49
Denmark	00 45	Greece	00 30
Netherlands		Portugal	

8 Centre the following horizontally on A5 portrait paper in double spacing according to the instructions given for the previous exercises.

APPOINTMENTS

Fullerton Enterprises Ltd

Designation	Salary
European Sales Manager	£50 000
Head of Information Technology	£40 000
Business Development Manager	£35 500

Exercise 9

Keys on page 170
Proofreading target: 5 minutes
Typing target: 7 minutes

The details given in the handwritten exercise 9(b) are correct. There are a number of errors in the typewritten version in exercise 9(a). When you have noted the errors, type a corrected version, making sure that you proofread your own typed copy very thoroughly.

Exercise 9(a)

ADDRESSES OF PREMISES WHERE OUR EQUIPMENT IS INSTALLED

Name	Addresses	Date Instaled	Inspection due on
P M Coker & Sons Tel: (01373) 62445	Watermore House 21 Castle Street Frome Somerset BA11 3AS	September 1992	January 1996
Acoustic Treatment PLC Tel: (0603) 624091	Castle House Norwich NR2 1PJ	January 1993	September 1996
Batley Computor Services Ltd Tel: 01272 548967	2 Old Gloucester Road Hambrook Bristol BS16 1RP	March 1993	November 1996
Dandy Agency plc Tel: (01733) 653312	10a High Street Old Felton Peterborough PE2 9DY	April, 1993	December 1996

Exercise 9(b)

ADDRESSES OF PREMISES WHERE OUR EQUIPMENT IS INSTALLED

Name	Address	Date Installed	Inspection due on
P M Coker & Sons Tel: (01373) 62445	Watermore House 21 Castle Street Frome Somerset BA11 3AS	Sept. 1992	Jan 1996
Acoustic Treatments PLC Tel: (01603) 623091	Castle House Norwich NR2 1PJ	Jan 1993	Sept 1996
Batley Computer Services Ltd Tel: (01272) 548967	2 Old Gloucester Road Hambrook Bristol BS16 1RP	March 1993	Nov. 1996 *(months in full, please)*
Dandy Agency p lc Tel: (01733) 653312	10a High Street Old Felton Peterborough PE2 9DY	April 1993	Dec 1996 *(Do NOT type postcodes on a separate line)*

CONSOLIDATION PRACTICE

We have reserved this unit for consolidation so that you have an opportunity to apply the practices and procedures introduced in the previous units thus enabling you to revise where necessary, or practise keyboard techniques and drills in order to type more accurately or more quickly.

The examiner, and your employer, will be interested in how many documents you type in a given time; therefore, in addition to accuracy and acceptable layout, we have set a **production target time** for each exercise. It may be that at first you will only reach this target after concentrated practice.

If you make an error, stop and correct it. Of course, the more errors you make the more time you waste (!) in making corrections. When you have typed the complete exercise, check the whole document carefully and correct any errors you may find *before* removing the paper from the machine or *before* printing out the document if you are using a computer.

At the top of each page, type the date and the **production target**.

Production target—6 minutes

1   Type the following on A5 portrait paper. (a) Leave 25 mm (1 inch) clear at the top of the page. (b) Double spacing. (c) Suggested margins: 12 pitch 13–63, 10 pitch 6–56.

```
TOMORROW'S MOTORING

Electronic palm readers


As a means of preventing theft, electronic palm

readers are used in banks, and it is felt there is

a case for them being used in cars.


The technology already exists for a vehicle to

recognise its owner's palm print as a means of

preventing a thief from literally 'getting his

hands on it'.


Voice-operated door locks and ignition switches

could also be used.  This means that a car would

be able to recognise its owner's voice as well as

members of the family.
```

Exercise 8

Keys on page 170
Proofreading target: 4 minutes
Typing target: 5 minutes

The details given in the handwritten exercise 8(b) are correct. There are a number of errors in the typewritten version in exercise 8(a). When you have noted the errors, type a corrected version, making sure that you proofread your own typed copy very thoroughly.

Exercise 8(a)

MEMORANDUM

FROM Paula Brooke-Little   DATE   11 September 1996

TO Giles Ladell   REF   PB-L/TS/Eve

TIMETABLE FOR THE WINTER SESSION - SEPTEMBER 1996-DECEMBER 1996

Following enrolement, I am pleased to tell you that we have sufficient students for your two evening classes to run as folows:

Subject	Day	Time	Starting Date	Room No
Beginners' Typing	Monday	6.30-8.30 pm	23.9.96	B204
Audio Typing	Wednesday	6.15-8.15 pm	25.9.96	H207

I should be glad if you will confirm with your senior lecturer that you are still willing to take these extra classes, and that the times and dates are suitable for you.

Exercise 8(b)

MEMORANDUM

FROM *Paula Brooke-Little*   DATE *11 September 1996*

TO *Giles Ladell*   REF *BB-L/TSEV 1996*

TIMETABLE FOR THE WINTER SESSION — SEPTEMBER/TO DECEMBER 1996

Following enrolment, I am pleased to tell you that we have sufficient students for your two evening classes to run, as follows —

Subject	Day	Time	Starting Date	Room No
Beginners' Typing	Monday	6.30 – 8.30 pm	23.9.96	B 204
Audio Typing	Wednesday	6.15 – 8.15 pm	25.9.96	B 207

I shall be glad if you will confirm with your senior lecturer that you are still willing to take these extra classes, and that the dates and times are suitable for you.

2   Type the following on A4 letterhead paper (Leys Enterprises). (a) Suggested margins: 12 pitch 22–82, 10 pitch 12–72. (b) Create an envelope to Sir Joseph Bliss.

Our ref   KC/AT

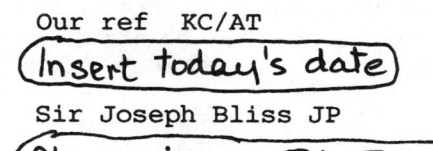
(Insert today's date)

Sir Joseph Bliss JP

(Please insert Sir Joseph's address here.
You will find it on page 42.)

Dear Sir Joseph

HANDMADE DISPLAY CABINETS

Thank you for your letter enquiring about our mahogany,
handmade display cabinets.

As you can see from the enclosed illustrated leaflet, one
of our cabinets would be very suitable to display the small,
Victorian items you mentioned in your letter. If you wish
we can offer you the option of having your cabinet made from
other woods, such as yew, pine, rosewood or walnut.

The quotation on the leaflet is for a mahogany cabinet.
Delivery will be approximately 30 days from the date of your
order.

Yours sincerely

Kate Corrigan

Enc

3   Display the following on A5 landscape paper. (a) Leave a top margin of 51 mm (2 inches). (b) Centre the table horizontally. (c) Leave three spaces between columns. (d) Double spacing.

F O O D   S E N S E

Healthy eating

Breakfasts	Lunches	Evening meals
Wholemeal toast	Salads	Grilled fish
Bran flakes	Baked beans	Pasta dishes
Kippers	Wholemeal rolls	Wholemeal pizzas
Fruit juices	Baked potatoes	Chicken

Exercise 6

Keys on page 170
Proofreading target: 3 minutes
Typing target: 2 minutes

The information given in exercise 6(a) has been typed from exercise 6(b) given below. Exercise 6(b) is accurate, but there are 12 typing errors in exercise 6(a). When you have noted the errors, type the exercise. Proofread your own typed version very thoroughly and compare with exercise 6(b).

Exercise 6(a)

```
FIELD WALK

Sunday, 9 April                                    Leader: Shan Porter

Meet at car park opposite the 'Barley Mow; turn off A4047 Wallingford—Reading
road at Black Root Farm.  (Map ref SU637856)  8.30—10.30 am.  A walk to see
marsh marigolds and here snipe drumming.  Wellies advised, binoculers useful.
No dogs.  Length of walk approximately 3½ miles. Suitable for all ages.
```

Exercise 6(b)

```
F I E L D   W A L K

Sunday, 10 April                                   Leader: Shân Porter

Meet at car park opposite the 'Barley Mow'; turn off A4057 Wallingford—Reading
road at Black Route Farm.  (Map reference SU637856).  8.30—10.30 am.  A walk
to see marsh marigolds and hear snipe drumming.  Wellies advised, binoculars
useful.  No dogs.  Length of walk approximately 3¾ miles.  Suitable for all
ages.
```

The details given in exercise 7(b) are correct. There are 11 errors in exercise 7(a). When you have noted the errors, type a corrected version, in alphabetical order, making sure you proofread your own typed copy very thoroughly.

Exercise 7(a)

```
PAYE   — Pay As You Earn
GSCE   — General Certificate in Secondary
         Education
VDU    — Visual Display Unit;
R.S.A. — Royal Society of Arts
UNESCO — United Nations Educational,
         Scientific and Culture
         Organisation
BASIC  — Beginners All-Purpose
         Symbolic Instruction Code
FAX    — Facsimile telegraphy
EFTA   — European Free Trade Association
PTO    — Please Turn Over
E & OE — Errors & ommissions accepted
```

Exercise 7(b)

```
BASIC  — Beginners' All-Purpose Symbolic
         Instruction Code
E & OE — Errors and Omissions Excepted
EFTA   — European Free Trade Association
FAX    — Facsimile Telegraphy
GCSE   — General Certificate of Secondary
         Education
PAYE   — Pay As You Earn
PTO    — Please Turn Over
RSA    — Royal Society of Arts
UNESCO — United Nations Educational,
         Scientific and Cultural
         Organization
VDU    — Visual Display Unit
```

4   Type the following on A5 landscape paper. (a) Read the passage through before starting to type. (b) Turn up 25 mm (1 inch) from the top of the page. (c) Suggested margins: 12 pitch 22–82, 10 pitch 12–72. (d) Double spacing. (e) Keep to the line-endings shown in the copy.

SAFETY IN THE HOME

SMOKE ALARMS

What is a smoke alarm?

These are small devices about the size of a man's hand which are fitted to the ceiling and are able to detect fires in their earliest stages. They sound a loud warning signal.

Looking after your smoke alarm

About once every month you should check the battery by pressing the test button; also test the sensor by holding a recently extinguished candle under the alarm. About once a year change the battery, and vacuum the inside to make sure that dust is not blocking the sensor chamber.

Production target—8 minutes

5   Type the following on A5 portrait paper. (a) Read through the passage before starting to type. (b) Turn up 25 mm (1 inch) from the top of the page. (c) Suggested margins: 12 pitch 13–63, 10 pitch 6–56. (d) Single spacing. (e) Keep to the line-endings shown in the copy.

UNDERSTANDING FOOD LABELS

The facts behind claims.   If a label makes a claim like 'made from fresh egg yolk', it also has to back it up by showing the amount of egg yolk used.

Facts about healthy eating.   More and more foods label the amount of calories, fat, sugar, fibre, carbohydrates and salt in them, as well as additives. This means we can avoid ingredients we do not want.

Check from the Data Files (filename FOOD) on page 173, that this list is correct. If not, please alter accordingly.

Keys on page 170
Proofreading target: 4 minutes ⎱ for each
Typing target: 5 minutes ⎰ exercise

Read each passage carefully and compare with the correct copy typed below. Each line in the incorrect copy contains an error that may be spelling, spacing, hyphenation, omission of apostrophe, etc. When you have found and noted the errors, type the corrected passage using margins of 12 pitch 22–82, 10 pitch 12–72. Use blocked paragraphs. Do not type the figures down the left side.

Exercise 4

Exercise to be corrected

1 Visible indexing systems have the definate advantages of easy access

2 and clear labelling or indexing. The information can be seen at once

3 with very little or no handeling. Also cards can be inserted or removed

4 without disturbing others in the container. Visible card indexes may

5 be held flat in trays, in loose leaf binders, or they may hang from

6 walls, or they may be free-standing on table tops or desks.

Correct copy

1 Visible indexing systems have the definite advantages of easy access

2 and clear labelling or indexing. The information can be seen at once

3 with very little or no handling. Also cards can be inserted or removed

4 without disturbing others in the container. Visible index cards may

5 be held flat in trays, in loose-leaf binders, or they may hang from

6 walls, or be free-standing on table tops or desks.

Exercise 5

Exercise to be corrected

1 Prestel is a public database Retrieval service operated by British
2 Telecom. The data is stored on computers and accesed via telephone
3 lines. Various agencies subscribe to input information for annual
4 fee. The information is very varied: eg, household hints, sports
5 results. In order to retreive information a Prestel user can call
6 the computer centre on telephone lines, using a keypad. The informa-
7 tion will be shown on his television screen, which can be adopted for
8 Prestel use

Correct copy

1 Prestel is a public database retrieval service operated by British
2 Telecom. The data is stored on computers and accessed via telephone
3 lines. Various agencies subscribe to input information for an annual
4 fee. The information is very varied, eg, household hints, sports
5 results. In order to retrieve information a Prestel user can call
6 the computer centre on a telephone line, using a keypad. The informa-
7 tion will be shown on his television screen, which can be adapted for
8 Prestel use.

KEYBOARDING SKILLS

Before proceeding to the exercises below, you should type the following skill building exercises:

proofreading No 3, page 148   **techniques and reviews** No 3, page 157.
skill measurement No 17, page 158.   **record your progress** No 12, page 164.

PRODUCTION DEVELOPMENT

Securing an acceptable right margin

Up to this stage in the book, you have always returned at the same point as the line-ends in the exercise from which you have been copying. This is not usually possible, of course, and in a great many exercises you will have to decide on your own line-endings and also see that you do not have an untidy right margin. If you are using a manual or electric typewriter, a bell will ring to warn you that you are nearing the right margin.

Before you can practise making your own line-endings, it is necessary for you to become accustomed to listening for an audible signal (margin bell, etc) that warns you that you are nearing the end of the typing line. On your own typewriter, find out how many spaces there are after you hear the margin bell or warning device before you reach the set right margin. If you are using an electronic typewriter, we suggest that you do not utilize the automatic return for the time being. Find out how the manual return works and what audible signal, if any, there is.

Word wraparound

Most electronic typewriters have normal carrier return, justified right margin and automatic return. This automatic return is referred to as automatic word wraparound. Some have devices that indicate that you are approaching the right margin and some do not. Consult the handbook that accompanies your machine. Word processing packages have automatic word wraparound and the choice of justified or unjustified right margin.

1   Type the following on A5 landscape paper and note the instructions in the text. (a) Use single spacing. (b) Suggested margins: 12 pitch 22–82, 10 pitch 12–72. (c) Listen for the audible signal, but follow the copy line for line.

> RIGHT MARGIN AUDIBLE-WARNING DEVICE
>
> Five to 10 spaces from the right margin a bell or other sig-
> nal on your machine will warn you that you are almost at the
> end of the writing line. It is necessary to train yourself
> to listen for this signal, and to react as follows:
>
> If the bell/device signals at the beginning of a new word of
> more than 5-10 letters, divide the word at the first avail-
> able point.
>
> If the bell/device signals at the end of a word, do not type
> a further word on that line unless it has less than 5-10
> characters (or 2 words such as 'for it' or 'I am', etc) or
> unless the new word can be divided at an appropriate point.

Margin-release key

If you cannot complete a word at the right margin, press the margin-release key (usually found at the top right or left of the keyboard). The word can then be completed. The margin-release key will release the left margin as well as the right one.

2   Type each of the following sentences exactly as it appears, using the margin-release key when necessary. (a) Use A5 landscape paper. (b) Double spacing. (c) Suggested margins: 12 pitch 22–82, 10 pitch 12–72.

> Text which is unjustified provides an uneven or ragged right margin.
> Reformatting text on a VDU will result in a change in line-endings.
> A system/program which is simple to use is known as 'user friendly'.

Proofreading

Keys on page 170
Proofreading target for each exercise: 2 minutes
Typing target for each exercise: 3 minutes

In the exercises below, the sentences in COLUMN ONE have been repeated in COLUMN TWO. Those in column one are correct, but in each sentence in column two there is a typing error. Compare the sentences and see how quickly you can spot the errors. Then type the sentences correctly.

Exercise 1

Column one	Column two
1 A program for a computer is recorded on a disk.	1 A programme for a computer is recorded on a disk.
2 The visual display unit looks like a TV screen.	2 The vizual display unit looks like a TV screen.
3 A disk can hold 100 kilobytes or more.	3 A disk can hold 10l kilobytes or more.
4 A matrix printer is faster than a daisy-wheel printer.	4 A matrix printer is faster than daisy-wheel printer.
5 Bar codes may be used in stock control.	5 Bar codes may be used in Stock control.
6 Spreadsheet programs may be used for management accounting.	6 Spread sheet programs may be used for management accounting.

Exercise 2

Column one	Column two
1 Keep your shorthand notebook handy.	1 Keep you shorthand notebook handy.
2 Date each page at top and bottom.	2 Date each page at bottom and top.
3 Do not interrupt the dictator.	3 Do not interupt the dictator.
4 Raise any queries at the end of dictation.	4 Raise any queries at the end of dictation
5 Rule a left margin for reminders.	5 Rule a left margin for the reminders.
6 Keep a pen or pencil by your notebook.	6 Keep a pen or pencil, by your notebook.

Exercise 3

Column one	Column two
G A R D E N I N G - October	G A R D N I N G - October
Tasks for the month	Tasks for the Month
Plant fruit trees or soft fruit canes	Plant fruit trees of soft fruit canes
Transplant cabbages, and lettuces	Transplant cabbages, and lettuce
Plant hardy, spring-flowering plants	Plant hardy, spring flowering plants
Mark out boundaries of new borders	Mark out boundaries of new borders
SWEEP UP DEAD LEAVES	SWEEP UP ANY DEAD LEAVES

3 Copy each of the following lines once for practice and then once for accuracy. (a) Use A5 landscape paper. (b) Suggested margins: 12 pitch 22–82, 10 pitch 12–72. (c) Single spacing. (d) Note that the hyphen indicates where the word would be divided at the end of a line. Observe where the word is divided and if no hyphen is given, where division is not possible.

```
tele-phones, trans-mitted, play-ing, atten-tion, ship-ments,
fisher-man, pre-eminent, self-confidence, prod-uct, kin-dred
satel-lites, excel-lent, pos-sible, bag-gage, magis-trates,
desig-nation, radi-ator, manu-script, per-fect, under-stand,
book, books, looked, shakes, paved, cleaned, ended, sailed,
entry, amazed, invent, sadly, £30.89, Coventry, Miss Reading
```

4 Type the following making your own right margin. If you feel it necessary, in order to avoid a ragged right margin, divide words at the end of the lines. (a) Suggested margins: 12 pitch 22–82, 10 pitch 12–72. (b) Double spacing.

```
T Y P E W R I T I N G

Homework Assignments


Once you have completed the keyboard, under the super-

vision of your tutor, it may be beneficial for you to

practise on your own typewriter, at home.


If you do not have a typewriter, you can still undertake

a certain amount of work.  You can prepare exercises by

reading them through; there are points of theory that

you must know and be able to apply without hesitation;

exercises that you type in class can be checked and read

through at home.
```

If you spend some extra time working on your own, you will become a fast and accurate typist.

(6)

(20 mins)

URGENT
MEMORANDUM

(Inset heading —
EXOTIC HOLIDAY BROCHURE 1996/97)

To Phil Stewart-Leigh
From (My name & designation)
DATE

I hv noticed from the final draft copies th there is an omission on page 87 of our Exotic Holidays Brochure for 1996/97. The climate + part of the travel info are missing from the details of the holidays to Singapore.

CLIMATE   (Highlight both headings)

Hot, sunny and humid all the year, with the temperature hovering around 82° F. The wet season is from November to February, but the rain tends to be in short bursts, quickly followed by sunshine. You will need a jumper or cardigan for the cool of the air-conditioning.

TRAVEL INFORMATION

Flying Time: 12-14 hours
Distance: 6 743 miles
Local Time: GMT + 8 hours

As we are hoping to ho the brochure in circulation by the end of next month it is most important that the printers receive the above asap. Please see to this for me urgently.
Thank you.

TW / (Yr initials)

(// The following is taken from our 1995/96 brochure + needs to be inserted in the appropriate place.)

PRODUCTION DEVELOPMENT

Typing measurements

When typing measurements note the following:

1 The letter 'x' (lower case) is used for the word 'by', eg 210 mm × 297 mm (space before and after the 'x').
2 ONE space is left after the numbers and before the unit of measurement, eg 210 (space) mm; 2 (space) ft 6 (space) in.
3 Groups of figures should not be separated at line ends.
4 Most abbreviations do not take an 's' in the plural, eg 6 in; 6 lb; 2 mm; 4 kg.
5 When using open punctuation there is no full stop after any abbreviation, unless at the end of a sentence.

1 Type each of the following lines three times on A5 landscape paper. (a) Suggested margins: 12 pitch 22–82, 10 pitch 12–72. (b) Pay particular attention to the spacing in the measurements.

```
One rug measures 82 cm x 76 cm; and the other, 65 cm x 44 cm.

The carpets were all 6 ft 6 in x 5 ft 7 in or 16 ft x 15 ft.

Send me 5 lb of potatoes, 2 oz of pepper, and 500 g of sugar.
```

Use of words and figures

1 Use words instead of figures for number one on its own and for numbers at the beginning of a sentence. But if number one is part of a list of figures, it should be typed as a figure, eg 'Follow instructions 1, 2 and 3'.
2 Use figures in all other cases.

2 Display the following exercise on A5 portrait paper. (a) Suggested margins: 12 pitch 13–63, 10 pitch 6–56. (b) Leave 25 mm (1 inch) clear at the top of the page. (c) Single spacing. (d) Read the passage through before starting to type. (e) Make your own line-endings. (f) Note the use of words and figures.

TELEVISION SHOPPING

A television revolution,

Sky subscribers can tune into television shopping 24 hours a day, 7 days a week and 365 days of the year to order a vast range of goods directly via their television screens. Shoppers phone in their orders, paying by credit card, and should receive the goods within 3 to 5 days.

It is estimated that, by the year 2000, the U.K. television shopping market will be worth more than £170 million.

Americans have been able to order goods offered on television for over 9 years, and sales are rising steadily.

(4)   (20 mins)

Please prepare a letter + envelope to Mr & Mrs Fearn. They have enquired about "foreign currency", so use th as a hdg. Thank them for their enquiry abt whether to take cash or Traveller's cheques, or to pay by credit card when on their holiday to Europe. Tell them the answer is to take a combination. Cash + credit cards will be sufficient when staying in the large tourist centres, but in the more remote locations they will need Eurocheques or traveller's cheques, as well. Say that credit cards have a double use. As well as paying bills, they can withdraw foreign currency from compatable machines and/or banks.
Wish them a happy holiday.
Dont forget 'Our ref' (my initials followed by yr own), the date and Mr & Mrs Fearns name + address wh you wl find in the Data Files (Filename TRAV) p 174. The salutation wl be Dear & Mr + Mrs Fearn — and finally, of course my name + designation.

L lc

(5)

(15 mins)

Display the following information on one side of a card + address the reverse side to DAN CORRIGAN. His address is on p 42.

SUPERDEAL   TRAVEL   AGENCY
(Insert our address + tel no here)
Ref TW/(Yr initials)   (Date)
$ INSURANCE ←——— (Sp caps)
Premiums
Up to 17 days holiday   £ 34- 90
18 to 23 days holiday   42- 90
24 — 30   "   "   47- 90
Each additional/ days   5- 00

- *Longhand abbreviations*—See **data store**, page 175.

3 After studying the list of abbreviations in the **data store** on page 175, read the following passage to see that you understand it; then type a copy on A5 landscape paper. (a) All abbreviations to be typed in full. (b) Suggested margins: 12 pitch 22–82, 10 pitch 12–72. (c) Single spacing. (d) Make your own line-endings.

MOTORWAY TOLLS

The first step to bringing tolls to motorways has already bn taken. The project shd be ready for the road testing stage sometime in 1997-1998.

Toll booths, wh are a feature in some parts of Europe, hv bn ruled out in Britain. It is thought th the system here may be an electronic one, wh shd cause less traffic hold-ups.

There is a major fear th if the tolls charged are too high the traffic wl move to unsuitable rural roads wh cd cause more accidents, congestion & pollution.

4 Type the following on A5 portrait paper. (a) Suggested margins: 12 pitch 13–63, 10 pitch 6–56. (b) Single spacing. (c) Make your own line-endings.

CLEAN AIR MOTORING

The electric car

Do electric cars hv a future? You may hv seen electric milk floats used by milkmen, but wd you be willing to buy an electric car for everyday use?

If yr car is fully-charged it may be possible to drive for approx 50 miles before recharging it. Ten minutes' worth of top-up cd give you up to 10 miles of driving with a full load. It wd take up to 8 hrs to recharge yr car fully.

A pilot scheme is taking place in France & Coventry to see whether electric cars hv a realistic role to play in urban transport systems of the 21st century.

③

(15 mins)

CUSTOMER BOOKING FORM

Holiday or Cruise Code _____

Holiday start date _____ Duration _____

Resort or Tour name _____

Special requests _____

_____

_____

YOUR DETAILS

Name _____

Address _____

_____ Postcode _____

Date of birth _____ Tel no _____

Passport no _____ 10 year* ____ 1 year* ____

If non-British please state nationality _____

TRAVELLING COMPANION

(Repeat details here)

* Tick as appropriate

TW/hol. 2016/ (yr initials)

KEYBOARDING SKILLS

Before proceeding to the exercises below, you should type the following skill building exercises:

proofreading No 4, page 149.   **techniques and reviews** No 4, page 157.
skill measurement No 19, page 159.   **record your progress** No 14, page 165.

PRODUCTION DEVELOPMENT

Enumerated items

Paragraphs and items are sometimes numbered or lettered as follows. The numbers or letters may stand on their own or be enclosed in brackets. Always leave one clear linespace between enumerated items. Two character spaces follow the last figure, letter or bracket. There is always one clear linespace before and after enumerated items, eg

```
1²  Address          (1)²  Address          A²  Address          (a)²  Address
2   Telephone Number  (2)   Telephone Number  B   Telephone Number  (b)   Telephone Number
```

1   Display the following on A4 paper. (a) Use single spacing with double between each item. (b) Suggested margins: 12 pitch 22–82, 10 pitch 12–72. (c) Leave two character spaces after the item number. (d) Top margin: 51 mm (2 inches), ie turn up 13 single spaces from the top edge of the paper.

> WORD PROCESSOR OPERATIONS
>
> The different functions that can be undertaken on any particular word processor will depend not only on the equipment used, but also on the word processing program.
>
> The following basic text-editing functions can be carried out on most word processors -
>
> 1 format and edit text;
>
> 2 simple calculations;
>
> 3 communicate with other equipment;
>
> 4 process files;
>
> 5 integrate data from other programs.

2   Display the following on A5 paper. (a) Use single spacing with double between each item. (b) Suggested margins: 12 pitch 13–63, 10 pitch 6–56. (c) Leave two character spaces after the bracketed letters.

> LIGHTING FOR YOUR VDU
>
> It is important to think carefully about the lighting in the room when you are using a VDU as the images on the screen are already tiring on the eyes and the wrong lighting can make them even more so.
>
> (a) Don't have bright lighting in the room when the screen is on. Dimmer switches make it easier to adjust the lighting.
>
> (b) Check on your screen for reflections or bright spots of glaring light. The brain learns to ignore these, but that in itself can be tiring on the eyes.
>
> (c) Have adjustable blinds at the windows.
>
> (d) Remove objects th may be causing a reflection on the screen, such as mirrors + pictures.
>
> (e) Make sure neither you nor the screen is facing a window.

②

(30 mins)

Our ref TW/4657 (my initials)

(Month + year only)

(leave sufficient space here for name + address)

(Two copies please. Mark only the copies for Rudi Gossingham + File)

Dr

Holidays 1996/1997 ←— (Caps)

Thank you for the interest you hv shown in our new 1995/1996 holidays. The brochures you hv requested are enclosed together with details of our early booking special offer. If you book a hol. within the next mth we will send you a free gift — one of six specially selected (books λ travel described in the enclosed leaflet.

TRAVEL BOOKS

// As a previous client of ours
As λ you ∝ know th it is our philosophy to do all we can to ensure th we meet yr high standards. When you take a ~~holiday~~ with SUPERDEAL you find th it is more than an annual recharging of the batteries — it is an opp for widening yr horizons, mtg new people & exploring different places.

Whether you are looking for a chance to escape to the sun for the winter mth~~z~~ or wd like to set sail on an exotic cruise ~~to a~~ ~~far away place~~, we wl make ~~sure~~ th extra effort to ensure th yr hol is a success. // Please complete the slip at the fod of this letter stating wh particular holiday takes yr eye, + we wl send you further details by return of post.

Yrs sinc

(planning a British break)

(my name + designation here please)

- -

NAME (in capitals) - - - - - - - - - - - - - - - -

ADDRESS (in capitals) - - - - - - - - - - - - - - -
- Tel. No - - - - - - - - - -
I would like more information on holiday - - - - - - (state holiday code)
DATE - - - - - - - - - - - -

JFR/264

UNIT 55   **Integrated production project—No 5**   144

Insetting matter from left margin

Matter may be inset from the left margin to give a certain part of the work greater emphasis. This matter may or may not consist of numbered items. You must follow any instructions given to you as to how many spaces to inset. There is always one clear linespace before and after inset matter.

When insetting matter you may either:

1 Set a tab stop at the point where each of the lines in the inset portion will commence; or

2 re-set the left margin.

When using this method, it is most important to remember to go back to the original margin when you have finished typing the inset portion. It is wise to make a reminder mark on the copy at the point where you need to revert to the original margin again.

Most electronic typewriters and word processing packages have automatic tab indents, and you may find it easier to line up the inset portion at the tab stops rather than setting a temporary second margin. Refer to the user's handbook, or ask your tutor if you need help.

3 Display the following on A4 paper. (a) Use single spacing, with double between the paragraphs and numbered items. (b) Suggested margins: 12 pitch 22–82, 10 pitch 12–72.

S U R N A M E S

In the past families often took their names from their villages, occupations, a local landmark or even descriptions of family characteristics.

The following are a few examples.

Inset 5 spaces

1 If your surname is Devonshire, your family probably lived there in the past, and became known by that name when they moved away.

2 The origins of names such as Baker and Carpenter are obviously derived from occupations.

3 Surnames such as Long, Short or Wise were descriptions of the people.

It may be interesting to find out more about your own name.

4 Display the following on A5 portrait paper. (a) Single spacing. (b) Suggested margins: 12 pitch 13–63, 10 pitch 6–56.

PERSONAL PHONE NUMBER

In the near future ea member of yr family wl be able to hv their own personal tel no, if they wish. It wl give a distinctive tone every time it is used in yr home.

Inset 5 spaces

(a) With one of the new '0700' nos, calls cd be redirected from yr home to office, car or a friend's home, at the touch of a button.

(b) It wl even be poss for the no to travel with the user across the world.

Personal phone nos are already being used by thousands of subscribers in America.

SUPERDEAL TRAVEL AGENCY

Holiday information ← ⟨Sp caps⟩

Our reputation is built on offering the widest choice and best value at the lowest prices. In over 25 years we have carried around 4 million holidaymakers to all parts of the globe - and many of them return to us year after year.

1 Passports and Visas   ⟨Highlight all numbered hdgs⟩

You must be in posession of a valid full passport before going on one of our holidays overseas. We must emphasize that neither ourselves, nor the carrying airlines, can accept any liability should your passport and/or visa requirements not be in order.

2 Flight Information and Timings

   2.1 Getting to the airport   ⟨In full⟩

   We offer special-rate return coach and rail travel to most UK airports.
   Prices for return travel to Gatwick and London (Heathrow) are:

From	Rail		Coach
	Standard	First	
	£*	£*	£*
London	11.00	18.00	6.00
England and Wales	17.00	32.00	13.00
Scotland	38.00	53.00	17.00

   * All prices are £s per person.

   2.2 Schedules

Airline schedules are liable to change, occassionally at short notice. Your timings will be shown on your airline tickets and they should be checked carefully immediately upon receipt.

3 Baggage Allowance   ⟨Please check these figures +, if nec, alter accordingly. You wl find them in the Data Files (filename TRAVp 124)⟩

Aircraft baggage allowance consists of 2 bags, the total measurements of which (height + length + width) must not exceed 106" and 21 kg per person. In addition, one cabin bag is allowed but this must be small enough to fit under the aircraft seat.
NB On coach tours only one piece of baggage per person (plus reasonable hand luggage) is permitted.

PRODUCTION DEVELOPMENT

Variable linespacer

The variable linespacer is found on the left or right platen knob. By pressing this in, the platen roller can be moved to any position desired. Its purpose is to ensure that you have proper alignment of the details to be typed on dotted lines, ruled lines or when inserting details in a form letter or memo.

Memoranda (memorandums)

A message from one person to another in the same firm, or from the Head Office to a Branch Office, or to an agent, is often in the form of a memorandum—usually referred to as a 'memo'. Memoranda (the plural 'memorandums' is now widely accepted) may be typed on any of the usual sizes of paper. The layout of headings may vary from organization to organization.

Important points to remember when typing memos on headed forms

1   Margins: 12 pitch 13–90, 10 pitch 11–75. These margins may vary depending on the size of the form and the length of the message to be typed.
2   After the words in the printed headings leave two clear character spaces before typing the insertions and use the variable linespacer to ensure their alignment.
3   Date: correct order—day, month, year. The month is not usually typed in figures.
4   Some memos have a subject heading which gives the reader information about the contents of the memo. The heading is typed two single spaces below the last line of the printed headings, ie turn up two single spaces.
5   If there is no subject heading, start the body of the memo two single spaces after the last line of the printed headings.
6   The body of the memo is usually typed in single spacing, with double between paragraphs.
7   When using blocked headings after the last line of the body, turn up two single spaces and type the reference. This is usually the dictator's and typists initials which identify the department or person dictating the memo. The reference may also by typed at the top of the memo (see page 58) if the headings have been printed in this way.
8   If an enclosure is mentioned in the body of the memo, this must be indicated by typing Enc (or Encs if more than one enclosure) at the left margin. After the reference turn up at least two single spaces before typing Enc or Encs.

NOTE: Memos with printed headings are available from the publishers and may be copied.

Templates

With a word processing package, it is possible to store a master template containing printed headings for memos (and letters). The details can then be inserted in subsequent memos without the necessity to type the printed headings each time. See your user's handbook for details on **templates**.

1   Display the following memo on a printed A5 memo form. (a) Follow the instructions given above. (b) Suggested margins: 12 pitch 13–90, 10 pitch 11–75.

MEMORANDUM

From Franklyn Ogden   Office Services Manager

To   All word processor operators

Date 2 April 1996

DISK STORAGE

Would you please ensure that all disks not being used are kept in their pro-tective envelopes, and stored in the boxes provided, which should be locked.

FO/IP

SUPERDEAL TRAVEL AGENCY

OFFICE SERVICES—REQUEST FORM

This sheet contains instructions that must be compiled with when typing the documents. Read the information carefully before starting, and refer back to it frequently.

Typist's Log Sheet

Originator *Trudi Weston* Designation *Tours Director*   Date *Today's*   Ext No *2 1*

 Typists operating a word processor, or electronic typewriter with appropriate function keys, should apply the following automatic facilities: top margin; carrier return; line-end hyphenation; underline OR bold print (embolden); error correction, centring; any other relevant applications.

Remember to (a) complete the details required at the bottom of the form; (b) enter typing time per document in the appropriate column; and (c) before submitting this **Log Sheet** and your completed work, enter TOTAL TYPING TIME in the last column so that the typist's time may be charged to the originator.

Docu-ment No	Type of document and instructions	Copies— Original plus	Input form[1]	Typing time per document	Total typing time ¥
1	Holiday Information	1 original	AT		
2	Letter - circular	1 + 2	MS		
3	Customer booking form	1 original	MS		
4	Letter from brief notes (+ envelope)	1 original	MS		
5	Card	1 original	MS		
6	Memo	1 + 1	MS.		
	(you will need headed paper for the letter & the memo)				
				TOTAL TYPING TIME	

TYPIST—please complete:

Typist's name:

Date received: Date completed:
Time received: Time completed:

If the typed documents cannot be returned within 24 hours, the office services supervisor should inform the originator. Any item that is urgent should be marked with an asterisk(*).

¶T = Typescript   AT = Amended Typescript   MS = Manuscript   SD = Shorthand Dictation   AD = Audio Dictation
¥ to be charged to the originator's department   AP = Amended Print.

2   Display the following on a printed A5 memo form. (a) Suggested margins: 12 pitch 13–90, 10 pitch 11–75.
    (b) Mark the memo URGENT as indicated.

URGENT   **MEMORANDUM**

From Jocelyn Trueman Finance Director   Ref JT/0893/FD

To All Departmental Heads   Date 10 April 1996

DEPARTMENTAL EXPENDITURE

I require the total of your department's expenditure for the last 3 months
by the end of April at the latest. If you cannot get the figure to me by
that date would you please let me know as soon as possible.

3   Display the following on a printed A5 memo form. (a) Suggested margins: 12 pitch 13–90, 10 pitch 11–75.

                                MEMORANDUM

From Adrian Tranter Personnel   Ref AT/fg

To Mark Finstall Accounts   Date 15 April 1996

LEAVE OF ABSENCE

I understand that you are due to take your driving test 2 weeks today. As
you have used up all your holiday entitlement I should be glad if you would
complete the enclosed form so that you can apply for leave of absence.

I can see no reason why this should not be granted, and best of luck for the
test.

Enc

4   Display the following on a printed A5 memo form. (a) Suggested margins: 12 pitch 13–90, 10 pitch 11–75.

FROM Lucinda Farmer Senior Production Manager
TO Jack Abbot Maintenance Dept
        (Insert today's date)
INFORMATION TECHNOLOGY ROOM 16A

It has bn decided th the room used by our information processors
shd hv a fitted carpet, as well as acoustic tiles fitted to the
ceiling.

Wd you please see th this work is carried out satisfactorily
at the earliest poss date, + with the least disturbance to
those working in this area.

(Please insert reference here – Mrs Farmer's initials followed by yr own.)

4 Centre and rule the following table.

Building Insurance ← (Caps)

Sum Insured	Annual Premium		
	Standard Cover	Premium Cover	Economy Cover
	£	£	£
£18,000	29.80	35.50	27.20
£20,000	33.00	39.00	30.50
£25,000	48.00	41.00	35.20
£40,000	66.00	78.00	58.30
£50,000*	82.50	89.50	73.50

* For each £1,000 thereafter add £2.00

(£30,000   48·25   56·50   42·00)

5 Centre and rule the following table.

ADVERTISEMENT RATES[1]

From January 1996

Paper[2]	Classified		Per line (minimum 3 lines)
	Cars	Situations Vacant	
	£	£	£
The Herald	3.95	4.50	1.16
The Tribune	4.10	4.85	1.16
Evening News	2·30	2·75	0·65
Advertiser	1·82	1·72	0·70

1 Per single column
2 Weekly

KEYBOARDING SKILLS

Before proceeding to the exercises below, you should type the following skill building exercises:

proofreading No 5, page 149.   **techniques and reviews** No 5, page 157.
skill measurement No 21, page 159.   **record your progress** No 16, page 165.

PRODUCTION DEVELOPMENT

Forms

Information that is to be typed opposite headings should be on the same line as the base of the printed heading and, therefore, it is important to know how close your typewriter prints to its alignment scale. Type a sentence and study exactly the space between the typing and the scale so that, when you insert a form and wish to align your typing with the bottom of the printed words, you will know how much to adjust the paper with the variable linespacer.

When typing over ruled or dotted lines, no character should touch the ruled or dotted line. Therefore, with the variable linespacer adjust the typing line so that, when typed, the descending characters y, p, g, etc, are very slightly above the dotted or ruled line. Business organizations have a great variety of forms that have been printed, or duplicated, with guide headings, boxes, columns, etc, and the typist has to type in additional information.

When the insertion is typed on the same line as the printed heading, there are two clear spaces before the start of the insertion. Where the insertion comes below a printed heading, it is typed on the next line. However, if the column is deep and the information to be inserted is short, it will look better with a clear space between the printed heading and the inserted matter.

1 Insert a copy of the form below into your typewriter and then type in the handwritten words, following the layout given. (A skeleton of this form is available from the publishers; it may be photocopied.)

DIRECT DEBITING INSTRUCTION

Please complete, then return the form to Broadlands Trust, Park Avenue, GRANTHAM, Lincs, NG31 5LL

Membership No TV 2496 ....

The Manager   Somerton   Bank

Full address of your bank branch 2 White Street ....

Great Dunmow Essex .... Postcode CM6 2BR ....

Name of account holder Cliff T Ware ....

Account No | 8 | 4 | 6 | 0 | 1 | 5 | 3 | 9 |

I instruct you to pay Direct Debits from my account at the request of Broadlands Trust.

Signature .... Date 15 May 1996 ......

---

2 Complete another form, dated today, in respect of Joan MacKenzie. Her membership number is PY07298 and she banks with Lowshire Bank, 26 Queen Street, Edinburgh, EH2 3ER (Account number 65096511).

TYPIST — I am not sure whether Ms Mackenzie's name is spelt correctly. Would you check it please? You wl. find it on p.42.

3 Type and rule the following table.
  Note: K equals thousand; retain the abbreviation.

THE COMPUTER INDUSTRY *(all caps no u/score)*
Expenditure - 1995-1996

User Section	Expenditure			
	Hardware		Software	
	1995 £K	1996 £K	1995 £K	1996 £K
Engineering	460	368	121	125
Retail and Distribution	710	437	107	99
Public Utilities	941	724	260	244
Financial	877	987	360	212
Education	355	343	104	48
Public Administration	578	520	90	109
Process Industry	467	505	186	128
Other Industry	433	477	128	99
Research	324	299	102	84

(Insert Leader Dots)

(Please check these figures in the Data Files (filename FINAN page 173.)

18 Key in document 3 (filename FINAN) for 12-point printout. Embolden the main headings, use the save function for the first horizontal line and copy this where necessary. Also use the vertical line key. When you have completed this task, save under filename FINAN and print one copy. Recall the document and follow the instructions for text editing on page 172.

3 Using a copy of the printed form (available from the publishers), complete the details for Sir Joseph Bliss. You will find his address on page 42. Date the form for tomorrow.

LEYS ENTERPRISES *(Typist - Please type in the handwritten details.)*
6-9 Druce Road, Cox Bank, CREWE, Cheshire, CW3 2AF
Telephone 01270 701387   Fax 01270 709822

Item *5 boxes Facsimile rolls - Code No 3184*

I enclose crossed cheque/PO for the total amount £ _____ payable to LEYS ENTERPRISES, or I wish to pay £ *43·43*   by

(Please tick appropriate box) *(TYPIST - Insert tick in ink)*

☐ Access   ☑ Visa   ☐ Diners   ☐ American Express

Your card expiry date *August 1996*

Card No *4929 601 424 828*

Signature _____   Date _____

Name and address for delivery (BLOCK CAPITALS):

TITLE | S | I | R | | | | INITIALS | J | | | | | | | *BLISS*

SURNAME | B | L | I | S | S | | | | | | | | | | | | | | | | | | | |

NUMBER AND ROAD | | | | | | | | | | | | | | | | | | | | | | | | |

DISTRICT | | | | | | | | | | | | | | | | | | | | | | | | | |

TOWN | | | | | | | | | | | | | | | | | | | | | | | | | |

COUNTY | | | | | | | | | | | | | | | | | | | | | | | | | |

POSTCODE | | | | | | | | TEL NO | 0 | 1 | 2 | 1 | | 3 | 5 | 4 | | 5 | 3 | 8 | 3 |

Deletions

It is sometimes necessary to delete letters or words in a form, form letter or a circular letter. For instance, in the exercise below the Rev N P Carter-Bond wishes to pay Leys Enterprises by cheque. You will therefore need to delete the oblique sign and PO. To delete printed characters, use an x aligned with the characters already printed.

4 *Complete another form, dated today, for the Rev N P Carter-Bond of 12 High View, Chorlton, Crewe, Cheshire, CW4 3PF. The remaining details are in the Data Files (filename LEYS) on p. 173*

KEYBOARDING SKILLS

Before proceeding to the exercises below, you should type the following skill building exercises:

agreement of subject and verb Nos 1–6, page 155.   **alphabetic sentence** No 14, page 156.
skill measurement Nos 40 and 41, page 163.   **record your progress** No 33, page 169.

PRODUCTION DEVELOPMENT

● *Blocked style tabulation—subdivided headings*—See **data store**, page 196.

1   Type the following table and rule on completion.

S A V I N G S   P L A N

Investment of £20 per month

over 11 years

Age at outset		Cash Sum Paid	Yield
Female	Male		
		£	%
18–35	18–31	5,492	12.68
44	40	5,461	12.59
54	50	5,357	12.26
64	60	5,222	11.83

2   Type the following table and rule on completion.

lc/   Price-List

Uniform medal ribbons*   } 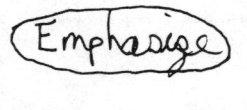 Emphasise

Retain ditto marks

Length of ribbon	Price per metre			
	16 mm	25 mm	32 mm	35 mm
	£	£	£	£
50 metres	1.15	1.30	1.50	1.55
100 "	0.70	0.85	0.95	1.05
200 "	0.52	0.56	0.71	0.82
500 "	0.44	0.50	0.62	0.68
1,000 "	0.40	0.45	0.59	0.62

Double spacing

* Corded finish

KEYBOARDING SKILLS

Before proceeding to the exercises below, you should type the following skill building exercises:

improve your spelling Nos 11 and 12, page 155.   **alphabetic sentence** No 6, page 156.
skill measurement No 22, page 159.   **record your progress** No 17, page 165.

PRODUCTION DEVELOPMENT
Typing sums of money in columns

Refer to the instructions given on page 36 with regard to the typing of decimals. Then note the following:
The £ sign is typed over the first figure in the £'s column.
Units, tens, hundreds, etc, fall under one another

Example	£
	461.76
	34.99
	1.21
	956.00

1 Type the following on A5 portrait paper, taking care to type the decimal points, units, tens and hundreds figures under one another. (a) Leave three spaces between the columns. (b) Double spacing.

£	£	£
384.89	217.80	789.45
108.00	209.12	387.45
90.07	40.87	30.76
2.00	9.77	3.66

Interliner lever

The interliner lever may be found on the right or left side of the typewriter. Locate this on your machine. The interliner lever frees the cylinder from the ratchet control, so that the cylinder may be turned freely forward or backward as required. When the lever is returned to its normal position, your machine will automatically return to the original spacing.

Double underscoring of totals

If you have to type double lines underneath the totals, use the interliner. When typing totals, proceed as follows:
1 Type the underscore for the first lines above the totals. (Do not turn up before typing the first lines). These lines extend from the first to the last figure of the longest item in each column, including the total.
2 Turn up twice and type the totals.
3 Turn up once and then type the lines below the totals.
4 Turn the cylinder up slightly by using the interliner lever and type the second lines. Then return the interliner lever to its normal position.

2 Display the following on A5 landscape paper. (a) Single spacing for the main part. (b) Leave three spaces between columns. (c) Follow the instructions for the total figures. (d) Decimal points must fall under one another.

£	£	£	£	
228.90	12.34	212.34	109.87	
404.75	566.78	33.44	654.57	
323.25	90.12	105.62	1,010.85	
1,234.56	35.45	1,212.05	354.25	
789.00	1,237.95	343.18	1,213.65	
654.32	220.16	331.26	434.12	← Do not turn up
				← Turn up 2 single spaces
3,634.78	2,162.80	2,237.89	3,777.31	
				← Turn up 1 single space
				← Use interliner

Enumerated items – roman numerals blocked to the right

See page 79 for information about enumerated items. As well as being blocked to the left, roman numerals may be blocked to the right with or without full stops. Full stops are never used with brackets. There should be two spaces after the full stop, bracket or after the numeral without a full stop. With open punctuation it is not usual to type a full stop after the enumeration. As indented paragraphs are used in the exercise below, the roman numeral with the most characters, ie, iii, starts at the indent, which means that it will be necessary to indent an extra two spaces for i and an extra space for ii and iv, eg

```
          i
         ii
        iii
         iv
```

2 Type an original and two copies of the following semi-blocked letter. **On the copies only** mark one for Jasper Worthington, Project Manager, and the other for the file. Prepare a label for Dr. Stanhope-Jones.

```
Our ref.  JGY/PB/FE216.4

Dr. L. T. Stanhope-Jones,
The Nook,
2 Upton Drive,
EDINBURGH.
EH18 4EW
```

centre heading in caps
↓

```
Dear Dr. Stanhope-Jones,

UNIT INESTMENT BOND 216.4

     Thank you for your application and your remittance for the first premium
shown below.

     Units are being reserved in respect of your premium (subject to the
payment being made under any cheque) and will continue to be reserved for a
period up to 6 weeks from the date of this letter,
```
pending yr Bond coming into force.

```
Standard Policy Provisions

     A booklet, containing the standard policy provisions is enclosed.  It
should be kept in a safe place because this booklet, and the policy schedules
which will be issued later, will form your Bond documents.

Retain for reference

     You should also retain for reference -
```

centre in double spacing →

```
     i.   the descriptive booklet;
    ii.   this letter;
   iii.   any accompanying forms
```
; and
```
    iv.
```
the Bond itself.

```
     Please do not hesitate to let us know if there is any further informa-
tion or assistance you require.
```

On copies only insert -
```
                              Yours sincerely
```
c.c. Jasper Worthington Project Manager
File

```
                              Commercial Controller
```

Key in document 2 (filename BOND) for 15-point printout. Use the word wraparound function. When you have completed this task, save under filename BOND and print one original and two copies. Retrieve the document and follow the instructions for text editing on page 172.

Form letters

Many documents that businesses use will contain similar information and wording and, in order to save time, form or skeleton letters, containing the constant (unchanging) information, are prepared and are duplicated or printed, and only the variable items (name and address, etc) are inserted by the typist in the blank spaces that have been purposely left to accommodate them.

Skeleton letters

The introduction of word processing has made production of repetitive text very much easier and time saving. The skeleton letter, containing the constant information, is keyed in and stored on a disk. When required, it can be retrieved and any insertion can be made quickly and easily (there is no difficulty with alignment when you use a word processing package, and the complete letter printed out, so that it looks like an original—as distinct from a duplicated or printed document with the variables added.

Filling in pre-printed form letters

The following steps should be taken when you fill in a pre-printed form letter:

1 Insert the form letter into the machine so that the first line of the body of the letter is just above the alignment scale.
2 By means of the paper release adjust the paper so that the base of an entire line is in alignment with the top of the alignment scale (this position may vary with different makes of machines) and so that an 'i' or 'l' lines up exactly with one of the guides on the alignment scale.

3 Set margin stops. The margins should be set to correspond to the margins already used in the duplicated letter.
4 Insert the details in the appropriate spaces. Remember to leave one clear space after the last printed character before starting to type the 'fill in'. The date, the name and address of the addressee and the salutation should be typed against the left margin.
5 Complete the insertion details.

3 Following the instructions for pre-printed form letters given above and using a copy of the printed letter (available from the publishers), type in the handwritten details.

THE CENTRAL HOSPITAL
Park Hall, OXFORD, OX2 1AL   Telephone 01865 432968

Our ref OG/261/42/Spr

23 May 1996

Mrs Olive Patterson
3 Partridge Lane
Boar's Hill
OXFORD
OX3 2BC

Dear Mrs Patterson

An appointment has been made for you to attend Mr Maynard's clinic on Monday, 10 June   at 2.00 pm for a consultation.

If you are unable to keep this appointment, please notify the hospital immediately.

Yours sincerely

O GRANTHAM
Medical Records Officer

KEYBOARDING SKILLS

Before proceeding to the exercises below, you should type the following skill building exercises:

use of apostrophe Nos 9–12, page 155. **alphabetic sentence** No 13, page 156.
skill measurement Nos 38 and 39, page 162. **record your progress** Nos 31 and 32, pages 168–69.

PRODUCTION DEVELOPMENT

Semi-blocked letters

The following points should be noted when typing semi-blocked letters.

1 **Date:** This ends flush with the right margin. To find the starting point, backspace from the right margin once for each character and space in the date.
2 **Reference:** Type at the left margin on the same line as the date.
3 **Special marks:** PERSONAL, PRIVATE, URGENT, etc, are typed in the same style and position as in fully-blocked letters.
4 **Subject heading:** Centre the heading in the typing line.
5 **Body of letter:** The first word of each paragraph is indented, usually five spaces, from the left margin. Tap in and set a tab stop for paragraph indent.

6 **Complimentary close:** Start this approximately at the centre of the typing line.
7 **Signature:** As in fully-blocked letters, turn up a minimum of five single spaces to leave room for the signature. Type the name of the person signing, starting at the same scale point as the complimentary close.
8 **Designation:** Begin to type the official designation (if any) at the same scale point as the complimentary close, ie immediately below the name of the person signing.
9 **Enclosure:** Typed in the same style and position as in fully-blocked letters.
10 **Punctuation:** Semi-blocked letters and fully-blocked letters may be typed with open or full punctuation.

1 Type the following semi-blocked letter from Leys Enterprises on headed A4 paper, with two copies, one for Stewart R. Froggatt and the other for the file. Use full punctuation and prepare an envelope to Mrs Alstone.

Our ref. KS/8904R/WB   15th November 1996

URGENT

Mrs. J. L. Alstone,
6 Kingsway,
Highbury Lane,
WORCESTER.
WR4 8BT

Dear Madam,

                    MORTGAGE ACCOUNT NO 8904R ← *Centre*

    I am pleased to enclose the official notice of a reduction in the rate of interest for your mortgage account.

    If you wish to pay more each month than the amount shown in the notice, please complete and return the enclosed form, and we will then calculate the approximate remaining amount of time your mortgage has to run.

Commence at centre point.

[If at this stage you require further info, please contact yr local branch.

Yours faithfully,

Katrina Scott (Ms)
General Manager

c.c. Stewart R. Froggatt
     File

4 On another copy of the form letter from The Central Hospital complete the following details.

The reference is OG/264/42/fpr & the date is 29.5.96. The letter is to be sent to MR GARY ARNOLD, 18 ELAND LANE, JERICHO, OXFORD, OX2 6PR, & he must attend the skin clinic on Wed 12 June at 1045 hrs for an x-ray.

Invoices

An invoice is the document sent by the seller to the purchaser and shows full details of the goods sold. The layout of invoices varies from organization to organization according to the data to be recorded. Invoices are printed with the seller's name, address and other useful information. A trader registered for VAT who supplies taxable goods to another taxable person, must issue a VAT invoice giving the VAT registration number, tax point, type of supply, etc.

5 Type the following invoice on a copy of the form below (original available from the publishers). Set the left margin and tab stops for each column at the starting point for the headings in each column and then type the information exactly as it appears.

INVOICE 1234

JAMES CORRIGAN & SONS LIMITED
Dublin Road
Thurles
Co Tipperary

Telephone (0162) 56986

12 June 1996
Mr & Mrs J O'Rourke
39 Cranston Drive
Thurles
Co Tipperary

Quantity	Description	Price	Total
		£	£
2	Crystal Vases	75.00	150.00
1	Crystal Fruit Bowl	86.00	86.00
3	Crystal Sherry Glasses	25.00	75.00
1	Crystal Decanters	120.00	120.00
			431.00
	Delivery charge		8.50
			439.50
	Prices include VAT E & OE		

Indented paragraph headings

See page 31 for paragraph headings. The paragraphs may be indented and the headings displayed in either of the forms given on page 31. A full stop may be typed after the paragraph heading, two spaces being left after the full stop.

2   Type the following in single spacing with indented paragraphs.

CHILD SAFETY

The Electronic Child Tagger

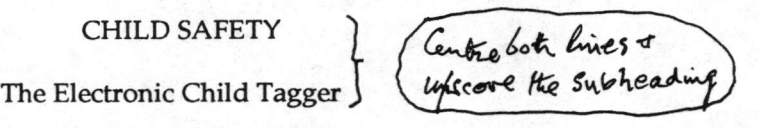

Centre both lines & underscore the subheading

A radio-controlled child alarm that warns parents if their son or daughter strays outside a certain pre-set range is now on the market.

Radio-based. The alarm is radio-based and warns the parent if a child strays by more than 20m. There are no wires or leads to be connected up and the device is quite small. *It works by emitting a frequent radio pulse from the parent's unit to the child's alarm. Beyond 20 m the child's alarm is too far to respond to the pulse & without a response the 'parent's unit automatically triggers a warning signal.* [ARMBAND]

Armband. The child's tagger, worn in the form of an armband, also sounds on the parent's unit if the child were to turn off the unit or fall over. If the parent wishes to page the child to signal to return, this can be done up to a range of 60 m.

Panic button: The child's armband also incorporates a panic button. This, together with the parent's unit, w/ emit a shrill sound if activated by the child, or someone grabbing him/her.

Shoulder headings

See page 32 for shoulder headings. The paragraphs that follow the shoulder headings may be indented, but the shoulder headings are displayed in the same form as they are when followed by blocked paragraphs.

3   Type the following in double spacing with indented paragraphs.

ON-SCREEN EYE TESTS ← *Centre*

VDU USERS

An on-screen eye test for thousands of office workers who use regularly computers and word processors with VDUs has been developed, so that within 5 minutes, and for as little as 79p per person, VDU users can test their sight at their desks.

European Directive ← *CAPS*

A European Directive, introduced in 1993, entitles employees using VDUs to an eye examination paid for by the employer.

USER-FRIENDLY SOFTWARE

The system can be run on a floppy disc, or installed on a hard disc, so employees can remain at their desk & call up the eye test programme on their computer screen.

STATISTICS

Statistics show 70% of those tested hv no sight problems.

6 Type the details that follow on to another invoice form.

Invoice No: *8390*   Supplier: *As ex 5 p 63*   Date: *19 June 1996*
Purchaser: *McCluskey Bros 10 Castle Street Thurles Co Tipperary*

6 cut glass goblets   £35.00   £210.00
2 "   " candlesticks 30.00   60.00
1 "   " bowl   75.50   75.50
The delivery charge is £6.50. Please calculate and insert
*   totals.*

7 Type the details from the invoice below on to a suitable form. (An original form is available from the publishers.)

INVOICE   NO 8301

MAGNET OFFICE EQUIPMENT PLC
33 Magnet Buildings
ENNISKILLEN   Co Fermanagh   BT74 6DX

Telephone (01365) 23480
VAT registration No 008 3765 87   Fax (01365) 25879

                                          Date 5 June 1996

T MacMannus & Co Ltd	Tax point 5 June 1996
2 Dowell Lane	Type of supply Sale
ENNISKILLEN	
Co Fermanagh BT74 7AA	

Your order No PUR 7/96   Account No P/3209   Advice note No   23456

Quantity	Description	Unit cost	Total cost
		£	£
3	Open plan acoustic screens	128.63	385.89
1	Roller blind cupboard	178.99	178.99
1	Double pedestal desk	359.95	359.95

VAT SUMMARY
Code % Goods Tax
1   17½ £924.83 £161.84

Total goods	924.83
Discount	0.00
Total VAT	161.84
TOTAL	1 086.67

Subject to our conditions of
sale. Copy on request.

E & OE

KEYBOARDING SKILLS

Before proceeding to the exercises below, you should type the following skill building exercises:

proofreading Nos 12 and 13, page 154.   **techniques and reviews** No 12, page 157.
skill measurement Nos 36 and 37, page 162.   **record your progress** No 30, page 168.

PRODUCTION DEVELOPMENT

Paragraphing

There are three different forms of paragraphing, viz, indented, hanging and blocked.

Blocked paragraphs

As you have already learnt, all lines in blocked paragraphs start at the left margin. When typing in single spacing, it is usual to turn up two single spaces between paragraphs. However, if double spacing is used, an extra space or spaces should be left between paragraphs, ie turn up three single or two double spaces.

Indented paragraphs

When using indented paragraphs, the first line of each paragraph is indented from the left margin, usually five spaces. This indentation is made by setting a tab stop five spaces to the right of the point fixed for the left margin. When using indented paragraphs, two single or one double space is turned up between paragraphs when typing in single or double spacing.

Hanging paragraphs

When using hanging paragraphs, the second and subsequent lines of each paragraph are usually inset two spaces to the right of the first line. This type of paragraph may be used to draw particular attention to certain points. (See page 138; enumerated items i, ii, iii and iv in exercise 4.)

Headings centred in the typing line

Main and subheadings may be centred in the typing line when using any of the above paragraphs, although it is more usual to block headings when using blocked paragraphs and centre headings when using indented paragraphs. To centre headings in the typing line, find the centre point by adding the two margins together and dividing by two. Then backspace from this point, one space for every two characters and spaces in the heading.
Examples: Margins set at

12 pitch 22–82	22 + 82 = 104 ÷ 2 = 52	(centre point)
10 pitch 12–72	12 + 72 = 84 ÷ 2 − 42	(centre point)
12 pitch 13–63	13 + 63 = 76 ÷ 2 = 38	(centre point)

1   Key in the following in double spacing with indented paragraphs. Centre the main heading and subheading. Suggested margins: 12 pitch 22–82, 10 pitch 12–72.

Indent the first line of ea para 13 mm (0.5")

ROVING   ROBOTS

COMPUTER-CONTROLLED

Robots have been developed that will be capable of performing mundane tasks in the home and office. A robot in the home will not be capable of cooking a meal but it will be able to take it from the kitchen to the dining room, as well as doing the cleaning. In the office, robots will be able to perform simple tasks such as distributing the mail.

Robots are already in use in at least 40 Japanese hospitals (and in some hospitals in the UK) reading bar codes on test tubes containing blood samples:

this tells them wh tests to apply to specific samples.

It is said, that by the year 2000, robots will become more commonplace in the UK as they should be no more expensive to buy than a PC today.

Credit notes

1 Used to cancel an incorrect invoice.
2 Used for crediting goods or packing cases returned.
3 A supplier who credits a customer for goods/services relating to taxable supplies, must issue a VAT credit note, which should give: VAT registration number, amount credited for each item, rate and amount of VAT credited, etc.
4 See also information about **window envelopes** on page 197.

8 Type the details from the credit note below on to a suitable form. (An original form is available from the publishers.)

CREDIT NOTE   NO 2487

MAGNET OFFICE EQUIPMENT PLC
33 Magnet Buildings
ENNISKILLEN   Co Fermanagh   BT74 6DX

Telephone (01365) 23480
VAT registration No 008 3765 87

Fax (01365) 25879

Date 13 June 1996

T MacMannus & Co Ltd
2 Dowell Lane
ENNISKILLEN
Co Fermanagh
BT74 7AA

Original tax invoice No 8301
Date of invoice 5 June 1996

Reason for credit	Quantity	Description	Total	
			£	
Damaged in transit	1	Roller blind cupboard	178	99
		Total Credit	178	99
		Plus VAT	31	32
		TOTAL	210	31

E & OE

VAT SUMMARY
Code % Goods Tax
1   17½ £178.99 £31.32

6 (20 mins)

Send a memo to Jos Higginson in our Advertising Dept, please.
Insert all the usual info — my name, date, ref, subject hdg —
HANDBOOK, & take a copy.

Wd you check the ~~contents~~ Contents page of our Handbook, please; I
think some of the following items hv bn ommitted.

Pages

	Pages		
Energy Conservation	1-2	Exhaust System	65
Introduction	3-4	Chassis "	66
Instruments	5-24	Brakes	67
Body Features	25-36	Wheels & Tyres	68-70
Safety	37-38	Problems	76-80
Lighting	39-44	Service & Maintenance	81-86
Windows & sun roof	45-46	Vehicle Care	87-88
Driving Hints	55-58	Engineering Features	89-92
Fuels	59-61	Technical Data	93-100
Catalytic Converter	62-64		

I think we shd also add something abt our European service
along the following lines.

"To obtain the benefits of our European service, you shd either
tel our Reservations Dept on 0171 969 9696, or complete
the registration form.
MAKE CERTAIN th yr registration form is sent by post at
least 12 days before yr intended departure date, or that you
tel not less than 6 working days prior to departure ···"

(working)

Some of the items in this list are missing. You wl
find them in the Data Files (filename CON) on
page 173. Insert them in correct page order, please.

KEYBOARDING SKILLS

Before proceeding to the exercises below, you should type the following skill buildings exercises:

proofreading No 6, page 150.   **techniques and reviews** No 6, page 157.

skill measurement No 23, page 159.   **record your progress** No 18, page 165.

PRODUCTION DEVELOPMENT

- *Special signs, symbols and marks*—See **data store**, page 193.

- *Constructing special signs, symbols and marks*—See **data store**, page 193.

1   Type each of the following lines three times. Use double spacing.

$$\underline{/756} \div 12 = 63\underline{/} \quad \underline{/12} \times 5 = 60\underline{/} \quad \underline{/200} \div 2 = 100\underline{/} \quad \underline{/10} + 15 = 25\underline{/}$$

$$\underline{/20} + 6 \div 2 = 13\underline{/} \quad \underline{/200} \times 2 \div 4 + 30 = 130\underline{/} \quad \underline{/40} + 6 \div 2 = 23\underline{/}$$

Superscripts (*superior or raised characters*)

A superscript is a character that is typed half a space above the line of typing. To type a superscript, turn the paper down half a space and type the character(s) to be raised; then return to the original typing line. If your machine does not have half spacing, use the interliner. In the exercise below, notice the degree sign. On its own it is typed immediately after the figure, but when followed by C (Centigrade/ Celsius) or F (Fahrenheit), there is a space between the figurès and the degree sign but no space between the degree sign and the letter C or F. Use lower case o for the degree sign, unless your keyboard has a degree sign on it, eg 10 °C. Superscripts are used for typing degrees and mathematical formulae, eg $a^2 - b^2$.

Subscripts (*inferior or lowered characters*)

A subscript is a character that is typed half a space below the line of typing. To type a subscript, turn the paper up half a space and type the character(s) to be lowered; then return to the original typing line. If your machine does not have half spacing, use the interliner, eg H_2O, $C_{12}H_{22}O_{11}$. Subscripts are used for typing chemical formulae.

2   Type the following lines three times each. (a) A5 landscape paper. (b) Double spacing.

Subscripts are used in typing H_2SO_4, $CaCO_3$, N_2O and CO_2.

Superscripts are used for typing the degree sign 4 °C.

A right angle equals 90°; 1° equals 60', and 1' equals 60".

At 10 am the temperature was 4 °C; at 2 pm it was 20 °C.

$ax + b^2 = a^2 - bx$. $a^2 (a - x) + abx = b^2 (a - b)$. $x^2 - a^2$.

3   Turn to page 193 and practise typing the special signs, symbols and marks.

(5) (20 mins)

Type an original on our letterhead paper, plus 2 copies, please — one for Justin McDowell & the other for the file.

Ref CJW/(Your initials)

Ms Karen Bebbington 24 Edinburgh Ave CASTLE DOUGLAS Kirkcudbrightshire DG7 1LU

Dr Ms B ——

SAPPHIRE CAR

I wld like to thank you once again for choosing to buy yr new Sapphire car from our Co. We are committed to customer satisfaction, & our dedication to customer needs does not diminish with the completion of sale. // I give below the specifications of yr Sapphire 4/5 door car.

(Inset 25mm (1"))

Max length — 4036 mm (13.25 ft)
Overall width — 1692 mm (5.50 ft)
Max height — 1395 mm (4.50')
Wheelbase — 2525 mm (8.25')
Track — Front 1440 mm (4.75 ft)
 Rear 1439 mm (4.75 ft)

(Double spacing for inset position.)

(exciting)

We are proud to be associated with the current range of Sapphire cars, & we are confident you wl enjoy a comfortable & trouble free use of yr new car. If, however, a problem occurs with yr new vehicle, I wd like you to contact me immed. // May I wish you many years of safe driving.

Yrs sinc

CALLUM J W ——
Sales Director

PS For yr extra convenience, we are now open on Sundays from 10.00 am to 4.00 pm.

(If you experience difficulty in obtaining a satis solution to th problem,)

Accents

When a typewriter is used for a great deal of foreign correspondence, the keys are usually fitted with the necessary accents. However, when accents are used only occasionally, the following are put in by hand in the same coloured ink as the ribbon.

Usually typed as special characters are:
diaeresis and umlaut = quotation marks typed over letter, eg Düsseldorf
cedilla—letter c, backspace and comma, eg Alençon

    ´   \   ^   ~
acute grave circumflex tilde

4   Type the following on A5 landscape paper. Use double spacing.

Heinz Schmüde, 18 Münchnerstrasse, Düsseldorf, West Germany.

Mme P Sené, 10 Boulevard Dalez, Alençon, France.

Señor Pedro Quijote, Carret del Legs, Bejar, Salamanca, Spain.

Most word processors and word processing software have special symbols, such as accent marks, that can be inserted during typing.

5   Type each of the following lines three times on A5 landscape paper. Double spacing.

From afar there came to our ears the call "Cuckoo! Cuckoo!"
They had spent $300 on presents and came home with only 90¢.
The asterisk (*) is used for a reference mark in a footnote.
250 ÷ 5 + 50 ÷ 4 = 25; 25 x 5 - 15 ÷ 2 = 55; $125 ÷ 5 = $25.

Ornamental borders—see also data store, page 177.

Information displayed in the form of a notice, menu, etc, may be given more emphasis, and made more eye-catching, by the use of an ornamental border—as in exercise 6 below.

Brace

The brace is used by printers for joining up two or more lines. To represent the brace in typing, use continuous brackets as shown in exercises 6 and 7.

6   Display the following on A5 portrait paper. (a) Follow the line spacing shown. (b) Type an ornamental border as shown.

```
* - * - * - * - * - * - * - * - * - *
-                                   -
*     MARTOCK AND PROCTORS          *
-                                   -
*     Opening Times from 1 May 1996 *
-                                   -
*                                   *
-     Monday          0915-1715 hours   -
*                                   *
-     Tuesday   )     0900-1800 hours   -
*     Wednesday)                    *
-     Thursday  )                   -
*                                   *
-     Friday    )     0845-1900 hours   -
*     Saturday  )                   *
-                                   -
*     Sunday          0930-1300 hours   *
-                                   -
* - * - * - * - * - * - * - * - * - *
```

CAR RENTAL TARIFF[1]

<u>All rates are quoted inclusive of VAT,</u>
<u>collision waiver</u> AND unlimited mileage

Model	Daily £	Weekly £	Weekend[2] £
Astra 1.4i – Saloon/Hatch	32.00	174.00	62.00
Cavalier 2.0i – Saloon/Hatch	43.00	215.00	84.00
Carlton 2.0i – " "	50.00	234.00	93.00
Calibra – Carlton Estate	98.00	435.00	174.00
Cavalier 1.6 – Auto – Saloon/Hatch	43.00	215.00	84.00
Corsa 1.2i – Saloon/Hatch	30.00	140.00	54.00
Senator	453.00	90.00	173.00

1 <u>Vehicle Availability</u> While every effort is made to provide
the vehicle req'd, it may be nec, because of unforseen circs,
to substitute an alternative ~~vehicle~~ car.

2 <u>Times</u> From Sat @ 8.30 am to Mon @ 8.30 am.

Send a letter to Casper Laxby thanking him for his
enquiry abt renting a saloon car for 2 wks next month. Tell
him th we hv 2 cars available at th time – a Cavalier 2.0i
Saloon or Hatchback at a rental of £ __ ,
(enter the cost here from the table above; remember it is for 2 wks)
or a Cavalier 1.6 Auto – Saloon or Hatchback at the same
rental of £ (quote price again). Ask Mr Laxby to contact us,
stating wh vehicle he prefers, by the end of next wk at
the latest.
Insert tomorrow's date, our ref (my initials followed by yr own)
& Mr Laxby's address wh you wl find in the Data Files
(filename RENT) on page 174. Oh, & insert a heading – CAR
RENTAL. Thank you.

This has to be replaced by the round brackets, used in exercise 6, on the previous page. Where lines of unequal length are bracketed together, the brackets are typed immediately after the last characters in the longest line. All brackets in any one group are typed at the same scale point.

7 Type the following on A5 landscape paper. (a) Use the same linespacing as in the exercise. (b) Leave five spaces between the columns. (c) Replace the handwritten brackets with round brackets.

```
SPACING BEFORE AND AFTER PUNCTUATION

Full stop            Two spaces at end of sentence.

Comma          ⎫
Semicolon      ⎬     No space before, one space after.
Colon          ⎭

Dash                 One space before and one space after.

Hyphen               No space before and no space after.

Exclamation sign⎫    No space before, 2 spaces after at end
Question mark   ⎬    of sentence.
```

NOTE: It is permissible to type the single-line text against any of the lines to which it refers.

• *Proofreaders' marks*—See **data store**, page 191.

8 Display the following on A4 paper. (a) Make all the necessary corrections. (b) Suggested margins: 12 pitch 22–82, 10 pitch 12–72. (c) Double spacing.

```
Videophones  ⟵ ― up caps

A videophone looks like, and has all the features of,
an push-button ordinary phone. //It has the re-dial
button, the hands-free button and the memory button,
as well as a call-timer button so you know how long
you have been on the phone.

The big difference is the addition of a 3 in x 4 in
pop-up colour screen with a built-in video camera
which enables you to see - and be seen by - your
caller, in colour.
```

✓ It is easy to use with a simple on/off video button.

Calls cost the same as ordinary phone calls, & if the power goes off the phone wl keep working even though the screen goes blank.

✓ The other important button is the self-view button, a useful feature wh allows you to practice yr smile & body language before you make a call!

CAR RENTAL TARIFF - RENTAL INFORMATION

UK in full throughout. Do not key in paras D or E.

Damage Waiver

In the event of accidental damage to the insured vehicle, the hirer is responsible for the following costs:

Two columns as shown

Mainland - UK

The first £250 cost of damage to the insured vehicle or £400 where the driver is between the ages of 21 and 29 years inclusive (excluding windscreen breakage).

Northern Ireland

The first £450 of damage to the insured vehicle or £600 where the driver is between the ages of 21 and 19 years inclusive (excluding windscreen breakage).

A Driver Qualification

except for minibuses where the min age is 25 yrs

Drivers must be between the ages of 21 and 70 years inclusive. A full valid driving licence is required at commencement of rental and must have been held for at least one year for drivers 21 and 22 years of age. A satisfactory driving record and a clean driving licence are required although certain endorsements may be acceptable at the Company's discretion. Valid licences for non-UK residents are acceptable at the Company's discretion when accompanied by a current passport.

C
B Payment Terms

£250/£400

Prepayment of the estimated charges, including the Cost of Damage Waiver (CDW) charges of £300/£450 (mainland of the UK) insurance excess deposit, together with a security deposit, to include provision for fuel supplied at commencement of rental, is required.

B
C Insurance

All vehicles are insured for comprehensive risk in accordance with the provisions of the Insurance Policy, a copy of which is available for inspection upon request. Drivers between the ages of 21 and 24 years inclusive, are requested to pay an insurance surcharge of £10.00 (including VAT) per day or part thereof.

D Extension of Rental Period

The rental may only be extended *by prior arrangement* before the initial rental period expires and with the Company's approval when a further prepayment will be required. It may be that failure to comply with this requirement will render void the insurance cover provided.

E Continental Rental

Vehicles may not be taken outside the United Kingdom without prior written authority. Special rates, documentation and insurance requirements apply.

Payment by cash or by cheque up to £50, supported by a bank cheque card or by certain credit cards, is accepted. Please check on precise amt & procedure at the time of booking.

- *Footnotes*—See **data store**, page 186.

Standard margins

In the following and subsequent exercises fewer instructions will be given about margins and layout of documents. If you are not given any instructions, you should decide what you consider to be the most suitable margins for the length of document and type of display. One point to remember is that, as far as possible, the document should be balanced horizontally on the page, ie approximately equal margins on either side, unless you are given special instructions to the contrary. If you are given specific measurements (millimetres/inches) for margins—say 25 mm (1 inch) on the left and 13 mm ($\frac{1}{2}$ inch) on the right—it is wise to measure and mark the paper, in pencil, before inserting it into the machine.

- See **data store**, page 188, for further information about **margins**.

9   Type the following on A4 paper. (a) Double spacing, except for the footnotes which must be typed in single spacing with double between each one. (b) Suggested margins: left 38 mm (1$\frac{1}{2}$ inches), right 25 mm (1 inch).

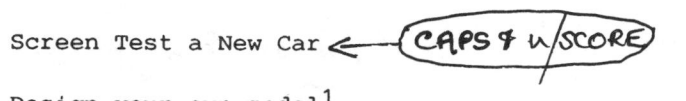

Screen Test a New Car ⟵ CAPS & u/SCORE

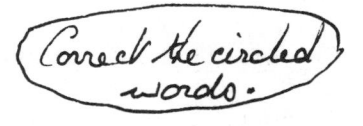

Correct the circled words.

Design your own model[1]

Car buyers can now help to design the model of car they would like, on a showroom computor. This system allows customers to add extras to a basic model, then press a button *to* or order it. //Soon[2] the car a buyer choses will actually appear - as a life-size, 3-dimensional hologram.

The customer will be able to view it from all angles - everything but get in it and drive it.

Press a button, and the ~~interior~~ *inside* seating, dashboard, engine and boot compartments can be viewed. The idea is to allow customers to sit in comfort and tell a computer the extra features they want in there cars.

---

[1]   Research has revealed that 68% of potential buyers hate walking into showrooms and being pressured by salesmen.

[2]   By the end of 1995.

10

A4 paper & double spacing. Margins as in ex 9.

TEXT EDITING A DOCUMENT

You may wish to make alterations to a document you hv already created & stored on disk. // The method used to recall the document wl depend on the ~~prom~~ program you are using. *

You wl then be able to edit using the cursor movement keys ** (usually marked with directional arrows) together with the ~~various different~~ functions available to you in yr wp program.

In full please

---

* On some systems it is rec to press the appropriate command key, ~~bring up the menu~~, & enter the name of the file you wish to edit.

** Or mouse.

Driving a motor vehicle ← ⟨Highlight⟩   ⟨Double spacing between ea numbered item. please.⟩

I   Duration of a Licence

For driving a car (category B) the duration of your licence is normally until your seventieth birthday - it is then renewable every 3 years. The Large Goods Vehicle (LGV) and Passenger Carrying Vehicle (PCV) licences (categories C and D) last until your forty-fifth birthday and, thereafter, for 5 years until the age of 65 when the license is issued for one year only.[1]

II   If you have an accident

⟨injury to someone else or⟩

If you have an accident in your car which results in damage to a vehicle, property or animal, the law in the UK says you must:

⟨In full⟩

1   stop;

2 give your address and name and the registration mark of your car to anyone who has reasonable grounds for requiring the information;

3 produce your Certificate of Motor Insurance to the police or to anyone who has reasonable grounds for requiring you to produce it;

4 obtain

4.1   the name and address of the driver, and the registration mark of each vehicle involved;

4.2   the name and address of the owner of each vehicle if different from the driver; . . .

III   Disqualification - it could happen to you!

Each year 1.3 million licences are endorsed.[2] Enforceable restrictions and tougher penalties should encourage safer driving.

⟨Inset 25mm (1")⟩

Offence ← ⟨Highlight⟩	Number of points
Speeding	3-6
Failing to comply with traffic light signals or road signs	3

⟨You will find the remaining offences in the Data Files (filename FAIL) on page 173.⟩

[1] Licences may be restricted if a driver suffers from certain medical conditions, eg, diabetes.

[2] This figure is set to rise now photographic evidence is admissible.

⟨If, after stopping, you do not give yr name & address or are not able to produce yr Cert of Motor Ins as req'd, you MUST report the accident to the police asap, & in any case within 24 hrs of the accident.⟩

KEYBOARDING SKILLS

Before proceeding to the exercises below, you should type the following skill building exercises:

improve your spelling Nos 13 and 14, page 155.   **alphabetic sentence** No 7, page 156.
skill measurement No 24, page 159.   **record your progress** No 19, page 166.

PRODUCTION DEVELOPMENT

- *Additional copies*—See **data store**, page 179 (4.14).

- *Photocopying*—See **data store**, page 179 (4.14.5).

- *Printing additional copies*—See **data store**, page 179 (4.15)

Simple display in fully-blocked letters

Emphasis may be given to important facts in a letter by displaying these so that they catch the eye of the reader. In fully-blocked style, this display may start at the left margin, with one clear space being left above and below, as in the specimen letter that follows.

1   Type the following letter from Leys Enterprises on A4 letterhead paper. Take one copy and type an envelope of suitable size.

NOTE The date has been typed on the same line as the reference and ends level with the right margin. To do this, backspace once for every character and space in the date, from the right margin, or use the right-aligned tab stop if you have one. A number of organizations prefer to have the date typed in this position. Follow house style or layout of input from which you are copying.

Our ref PD/FG/2075   28 June 1996

Mr S B Stanley
26 Grove Avenue
Biggar
Lanarkshire   ML12 6JJ

Dear Mr Stanley

SUBSCRIPTIONS

After very considerable thought, it has been decided that a subscription increase is now essential to keep pace with rising costs and increasing demands on our resources.

The full list of the new subscription rates agreed by us is as follows:

Single: £15.00
Joint: £20.00
Under 25: £10.00
Local Organization   £17.00

> TYPIST – Please check the figures in the Data Files (filename SUBS) & if necessary, alter accordingly.

The new rates will not come into effect until January 1997.

Yours sincerely

PADDY DONNOLLY
Chairman

BRADY & SONS LTD

OFFICE SERVICES—REQUEST FORM

This sheet contains instructions that must be complied with when typing the documents. Read the information carefully before starting, and refer back to it frequently.

Typist's Log Sheet

Originator **Callum J Williamson**   Designation **Sales Director**   Date **Tomorrow's**   Ext No **4**

Typists operating a word processor, or electronic typewriter with appropriate function keys, should apply the following automatic facilities: top margin; carrier return; line-end hyphenation; underline OR bold print (embolden); error correction, centring; any other relevant applications.

Remember to (a) complete the details required at the bottom of the form; (b) enter typing time per document in the appropriate column; and (c) before submitting this **Log Sheet** and your completed work, enter TOTAL TYPING TIME in the last column so that the typist's time may be charged to the originator.

Docu-ment No	Type of document and instructions	Copies— Original plus	Input form[1]	Typing time per document	Total typing time ¥
①	Driving a motor vehicle	1 original	AT		
②	Car rental tarrif information sheet	1 original	Printed		
③	Car rental rates	1 original	MS		
④	letter from brief notes	1 original	MS		
⑤	2-page letter to Karen Bebbington (+ envelope)	1 + 2	MS		
*⑥	Memo	1 + 1	MS		

TYPIST—please complete:

Typist's name: Date received: Date completed:

                                   Time received: Time completed:

If the typed documents cannot be returned within 24 hours, the office services supervisor should inform the originator. Any item that is urgent should be marked with an asterisk(*).

¶T = Typescript   AT = Amended Typescript   MS = Manuscript   SD = Shorthand Dictation   AD = Audio Dictation
¥ to be charged to the originator's department   AP = Amended Print.

Column display in fully-blocked letters

When the matter is to be displayed in columns, three spaces should be left between the longest line of one column and the start of the next. The first column may start at the left margin and tab stops are set for each of the other columns, as explained on page 45.

2 Type the following letter from Leys Enterprises on A4 letterhead paper. Take a copy and create an envelope. Mark the letter and envelope PRIVATE.

Ref   AG/OW   12 April 1996

Ms Mandy Treslake-Roper
The Hollow
Camomile Lane
FOLKESTONE
Kent   CT20 4JL

Dear Ms Treslake-Roper   (END-OF-SEASON SALE)

As summer is just around the corner we shall be bringing out our new brochure next month, showing our styles and designs for the holiday season. (Spring)

In the meantime, we have reduced our stock by up to 50% as shown in the enclosed leaflet. This amazing offer is open to our valued customers until the end of May.

Examples of our fantastic savings are given below.

	Sale Price	Catalogue Price
	£	£
Fashionable cotton leggings	14.59	24.50
Shawl collar blouses	19.50	42.50
Long length jerseys	29.50	49.50

We look forward to receiving your order. very soon

Yrs sinc

ALAN GALLOWAY
Sales Promotions Manager

3 Key in document 2 (filename SALE) for 10-point printout. Use the decimal tab key when typing the sums of money. Embolden the word PRIVATE and the subject heading. When you have completed this task, save under filename SAVE and print out an original and one copy. Recall the document and follow the instructions for text editing on page 171.

3 Please type the same letter to MRS JACQUIE FREEMAN who lives at 8 Stanley Road, Folkestone, Kent, CT20 1AL. Add one extra item example of our savings to her letter as follows —
Luxurious pure silk blouses £29.50 £55.00

4 Type this exercise in single spacing, following the display given as an example at the foot of the page. Display the items in alphabetical order.

DATA BANK*

Tailpiece

This is an illustration or ornamental motif at the end of a page, unit or chapter and is made up by combining characters, such as hyphen, colon, etc.

```
:-:-:-:-:-:-:
 -:-:-:-:-:-
   :-:-:-:-
    -:-:-
     :-:
      -
```

Time

1   Twenty-four hour clock

As international travel has become more popular, we are all more aware of the 24-hour clock. It always consists of four figures with no full stops /; *for example:*

0001 hours (one minute after midnight) 0700 hours (7.00 am) *1200 hours* → 1300 hours *(1.00 pm)* 1800 hours (6.00 pm) 2359 hours (11.59 pm). Midnight is always represented by the word 'midnight'. *noon*

2   am/pm and o'clock

Words or figures may be used with o'clock: one o'clock, 9 o'clock. Use *am* and *pm* with figures with no space between the two letters; see examples above. *There is a full stop after ea letter when using full punctuation, e g   4.00 p.m.*

Proportional spacing

With proportional spacing, the characters do not all take up the same amount of space. As in printing, each character is given its natural width. For example, an n is wider than an i, an m is wider than an n and a capital M is wider than a lower-case m. The characters are not measured in spaces but in terms of units. One of the outstanding features of proportional spacing is that the typed copy appears to be printed rather than typed.

Bibliography

A bibliography is a list of books, magazines, or newspaper articles, included in footnotes at the end of a chapter or book to show the source from which the information has been taken, or as a reading list for people who want to go further into the subject. The items are listed alphabetically according to the author's last name which is typed in upper and lower case. The author's name is typed first followed by the forename(s) or initials. With full punctuation, use the comma and full stops as follows:

Drummond, A. M. and Coles-Mogford, A., *Typing First Course, First Course, Stanley Thornes: 1993.*

With blocked style, it is usual to block all lines although the second and subsequent lines for any one item may be inset five to ten spaces. The titles of the books are typed in upper and lower case and underlined, or in sloping type, because the printer will set them in italic.

Hyphen

This is used to replace the word 'to' in certain instances. Examples:

The firm's address was 19–23 North Street. He lived from 1901–1976. This date could also be typed 1901–76, but you must be careful if the dates spread over two centuries, eg 1707–1806 (NOT 1707–06). The dash is also used to replace 'to'.

House style

An organization may decide that letters, memos, reports, etc should be displayed according to certain conventions or style. This would mean that all letters sent to customers and clients would have the same layout. If the organization you work for has a particular house style which differs from your training or preference, you **must** conform to it without deviation.

* Taken fr Applied Typing, sixth edition, Archie Drummond and Anne-Coles-Mogford, published by Stanley Thornes.

EXAMPLE:

```
D A T A   B A N K*

BIBLIOGRAPHY

A bibliography is a list of books, magazines, or newspaper articles, included
  in footnotes at the end of a chapter or book to show the source from which the
```

Postscripts

Sometimes a postscript has to be typed at the foot of a letter, either because the writer has omitted something he wished to say in the body of the letter, or because he wishes to draw special attention to a certain point. The postscript should be started two single-line spaces below the last line of the complete letter (but before the enclosure notation, if there is one) and should be in single spacing. Leave two character spaces after the abbreviation PS, which has no punctuation with open punctuation, but a full stop after the S with full punctuation.

4 Type the following letter on A4 letterhead paper. Take a copy and create an envelope. Use suitable margins.

NH/ *(Yr initials)*   *(Insert to-day's date)*

URGENT

Grimely & Grimely Associates
23 City Road
HENLEY ON THAMES   *(Correct the 2 circled errors.)*
Oxfordshire
RG9 7VP

Dear Sirs *SOLAR HEATING*

I am sure that you are very concerned about helping to save
our environment. If doing so means reducing your fuel bills,
I think you will wish to find time to read the enclosed
leaflet which gives details of our Solar Heating System. *very popular*

✓ The advantages of *(instaling)* solar heating are ~~many:~~

   1 Solar energy is available even when there is no direct
      sunlight.

   2   Sunlight is a free and everlasting source of energy.
   3

   3   Of course, if you use *(soler)* energy, you are also helping
   2   to save our environment because it is a non-polluting   *For this information*
       method of heating.   *see Data Files (filename)*
                                                                   HEAT, page 173

We would welcome an opportunity to visit you to discuss our
proposals. This service is completely free and without obligation.
                                    (, by appointment,)

Yours faithfully

NICK HOLLIER
Operations Director

PS We are currently subsidizing selected installations in your
    area, so it is important to act now.

Enc

 Key in document 4 (filename HEAT) for 12-point printout. Embolden the word URGENT and the subject heading. When you have completed this task, save under filename HEAT and print out an original and one copy. Recall the document and follow the instructions for text editing on page 171.

Forms of address with full punctuation—addressing envelopes

The guide to the addressing of envelopes, given on page 42, applies with the exception of inserting punctuation after abbreviations and at line-ends. It should be noted that Miss is not an abbreviation and, therefore, does not require a full stop.

Examples:

Mr. M. James   Dr. O. Coleman   Messrs. W. O. Horne & Sons   Ms N. Gray

```
Mrs. W. Fallon,              E. P. Freeman, Esq., M.A., B.Sc.,
24 St. John's Street,       T. R. Beach & Co. Ltd.,
BOSTON,                     2 Herne Bay Road,
Lincs.                      BANBURY,
PE21 6AA                    Oxon.        OX16 8LB
```

Points to note:

1 Full stop after an initial, followed by one clear space.
2 Comma at the end of each line except for the last line before the postcode, which is followed by a full stop.
3 NO punctuation in postcode.

4 Comma after surname, followed by one space before Esq.
5 Full stop and NO space between the letters of a degree, but a comma and space between each group of letters.
6 Notice recognized abbreviation for Oxfordshire.

Preparing documents from print

Today, most firms keep on hand a wide variety of fonts for use in typing documents of all kinds and especially for preparing camera-ready copy (CRC). Each font is a complete set of type of one particular face. The increasing use of electronic keyboards and other sophisticated machines now available for desktop publishing, means that many organizations print thier own circulars, leaflets and catalogues. If you are using an ordinary typewriter and are copying from previously printed matter, make good use of the following in order to make your work more eye-catching.

1 Where a word(s) is in italic print, underline the word(s) when typing, or print in italic if it is available to you.
2 Where a word(s) needs to be emphasized, use bold type, underline (but not if you are already using the underscore for italic print), spaced or closed capitals.

Horizontal centring—all lines centred

Follow the points given for horizontal centring on page 34, but do not set a left margin and centre EACH line, not just the longest one.

● **Vertical centring**—See **data store**, page 183 (Display).

3 Type the following on A5 landscape paper. Set a tab stop at the horizontal centre point of the page, eg 12 pitch 50, 10 pitch 41. Centre each line horizontally and the whole notice vertically. Create an ornamental border.

```
*-*-*-*-*-*-*-*-*-*-*-*-*-*-*-*-*-*-*-*-*-*
-                                         -
*           DOGS ARE OUR BUSINESS         *
-                                         -
*               *-*-*-*-*                 *
-                                         -
*         Boarding - dogs and cats        *
-                  Feeding                 -
*                 Training                 *
-                 Grooming                 -
*         Well bred puppies for sale       *
-                                         -
*               *-*-*-*-*                 *
-                                         -
*           B A R K I N G   K E N N E L S  *
-       Frogmore Lane  Bingley  West Yorkshire  -
*           Telephone: 01274 509761       *
-                                         -
*-*-*-*-*-*-*-*-*-*-*-*-*-*-*-*-*-*-*-*-*-*
```

INTEGRATED PRODUCTION PROJECTS

These simulated office tasks are preceded by a **typist's log sheet**. Refer to the log sheet for instructions and relevant details before and during the preparation of the documents.

Timing

Today, because of the number of automatic functions on certain electronic keyboards (as compared with, say a manual typewriter), it is impossible to set an average timing for any one document. In some examinations you should complete all questions; therefore we suggest that your objective is to finish the **integrated production projects** in the 2 or $2\frac{1}{2}$ hours allowed, and, to help you judge just how much **time you can afford to spend on each task**, we have allocated the maximum number of minutes you should devote to any one task in order to finish the paper within the stipulated time. This time includes proofreading the typed page before removing it from the machine and making corrections where necessary, or if you are using a computer, proofreading on screen and then printing out the document.

Reading the manuscript or typescript through to see that you understand the contents (which is of paramount importance), deciding on linespacing and margins, reading and following instructions, are all essential techniques that require immediate decisions and must be carried out speedily and accurately. Therefore, within the timing of 2 or $2\frac{1}{2}$ hours, we have left 15 minutes unused so that you can spend the first 10 minutes reading through the complete script, marking the special points to watch for and corrections to be made, deciding on what paper to use, what margins to set, where copies are required, etc, and another five minutes for a final check to see that each task has been attempted and each instruction followed. Of course, it may be that you will take less time than that stated, and this is good as you will then have time in reserve.

Any writer, when preparing a draft or editing a script, may unwittingly make a mistake—it may be a word spelt incorrectly; an apostrophe in the wrong place or no apostrophe at all when there should be one; it may be that the verb does not agree with the subject. You have to correct these mistakes. In practice exercises we draw your attention to the words by circling them; in all but the first **integrated production project** we do not circle them: you have to watch for the errors and correct them, just as you would do in business.

Folders

Keep the completed documents in a folder marked FOR SIGNATURE, and the folder (with the tasks in document number order, together with the **log sheet**) should be handed to your tutor when you are sure that all the documents (in any one group) are MAILABLE and ready for approval and signature where appropriate. Also, keep a separate folder for the documents that have been approved/signed—file the documents under the **log sheet** number and in document number order.

Mailable documents

The contents must make sense; no omissions (you could have a serious omission and the document may still make sense); no uncorrected errors (misspellings, incorrect punctuation, keyboarding errors, etc); no careless corrections (if part of the wrong letter(s) is showing, the correction is not acceptable); no smudges; no creases. Consistency in spelling, in format, in displaying sums of money, etc, is vital. Occasionally, your tutor may return a document marked C & M (correct and mail). This means that there is an error that will not be difficult to correct, and after a correction the document may be mailed. Remember to correct any additional copies.

Typist's log sheet

The information in the **typist's log sheet** will follow a pattern: name of employer will be at the top; the name of the originator and the department (where appropriate) will be handwritten; the date may or may not be given, but letters and memos must have a date unless there are instructions to the contrary. If you have access to a word processor, a text-editing electronic typewriter or a correction only electronic typewriter, follow the general instructions given on the **log sheet** against the symbol ▆ and enter your name, date and starting time near the bottom of the sheet. When all the documents have been completed and are ready for approval/signature, calculate and enter the TOTAL TYPING TIME at the bottom of the last column, and also record the date and time of completion.

Urgent

Note that any input marked with an asterisk (*) is urgent and should be dealt with first. Type the word URGENT at the top of the document, and see that it is ready for approval/signature within 40 minutes of your starting time.

Stationery requisition

Before starting the **integrated production project**, you should read it through and decide on the quantity and kind of stationery you will require for all the tasks, and then fill in a **stationery requisition form** which you should hand to your tutor for approval. You will need headed paper for business letters and memoranda; bond white paper for top copies of other documents; bank paper for carbon copies; carbon paper, envelopes, cards, labels, etc. You may allow yourself a few sheets more than you require, but you should in no circumstances give yourself unlimited supplies. Most employers keep a strict control over the use of stationery. In an examination, your supply of typing paper will be limited. Of course, you will have readily available some means for correction of errors, ruler, pen, pencil, dictionary, etc.

KEYBOARDING SKILLS

Before proceeding to the exercises below, you should type the following skill building exercises:

use of apostrophe Nos 5–8, page 155.   **alphabetic sentence** No 12, page 156.
skill measurement Nos 34 and 35, page 162.   **record your progress** No 29, page 168.

PRODUCTION DEVELOPMENT

Open punctuation

Up to this point in the book all the exercises have been displayed with open punctuation. This means that full stops have not been inserted after abbreviations, and business and personal letters have been typed with the omission of commas after each line of the address, and after the salutation and complimentary close. The modern trend is to omit punctuation in those cases as it simplifies and speeds up the work of the typist. However, punctuation is always inserted in sentences, so that the grammatical sense is clear.

Full punctuation

It is also acceptable to insert punctuation after abbreviations and after each line of an address as well as after the salutation and complimentary close. Grammatical punctuation is always inserted. Open and full punctuation must NEVER be mixed: a document must be typed in either open or full punctuation.

● *Abbreviations*—See **data store**, page 175.

1   Type the following sentences, using open punctuation. Note the use of abbreviations.

Mr & Mrs P R Fielding were told to see Dr M Grant-Phillips at St Paul's
Hospital at 4.30 pm and not 10.30 am.

The lorries, motor cycles, coaches, etc, were all parked in a small area which
measured only 800 sq ft.

Tyler & Royston plc is a large company, but A C Grosvenor & Co Ltd is more well
known, although employing fewer staff.

Leave a top margin of 25 mm (1 in), a left margin of 38 mm (1½ in) and a right
margin of 13 mm (½ in), when typing the report for Ms D Carpenter BSc.

2   Type the following sentences, using full punctuation. Compare the sentences with those in exercise 1,
     noting the differences in the use of the full stop after abbreviations.

NOTE: One space after a full stop at the end of an abbreviation, unless it occurs at the end of a sentence when
you leave two spaces. No space after a medial full stop within an abbreviation.

Mr. & Mrs. P. R. Fielding were told to see Dr. M. Grant-Phillips at St. Paul's
Hospital at 4.30 p.m. and not 10.30 a.m.

The lorries, motor cycles, coaches, etc., were all parked in a small area which
measured only 800 sq. ft.

Tyler & Royston p.l.c. is a large company, but A. C. Grosvenor & Co. Ltd. is more
well known, although employing fewer staff.

Leave a top margin of 25 mm (1 in.), a left margin of 38 mm (1½ in.) and a right
margin of 13 mm (½ in.), when typing the report for Ms. D. Carpenter, B.Sc.

Distractions

As an office worker, it is a necessity of life that you should be able to cope with interruptions and distractions which are a normal part of the office scene. Your boss may ask you to make alterations to a script (already in your possession) while you are engrossed in preparing an urgent or complicated document; you may be interrupted by the telephone; a client may call to see your boss, etc. You should be sufficiently accomplished to be able to return to your work unaffected by these distractions. To simulate office conditions your tutor may interrupt you while you are working on the **integrated production projects** and give you alterations to an exercise, or hand you an additional task. Examining bodies may incorporate this form of distraction during an examination.

Dates

A business document is of very little use unless it is dated and has a reference as to its origin. Documents, other than letters and memos, are usually dated at the bottom of the last page with the reference either before or after the date. When you are at business, follow the house style. Examiners for certain boards will penalize you if you date any document (unless there are instructions to do so) apart from letters and memos.

Superfluous wording

If you add a word(s) not in the script, eg a reference in a letter when it is not given, then you may be penalized by the examiner. Similarly, if you insert a line before a footnote and there is no line in the script, then you may be penalized.

Check very carefully to ascertain what the examiner does and does not accept.

Because you still need a great deal of practice on conventions and display, deciding on margin settings etc, we have supplied much more detail in this first integrated production project than we have in the later projects.

5 Type the travel itinerary, following the display indicated. Retain ditto marks.

> *Please leave one space clear at the points marked X and 2 spaces clear at the points marked XX*

```
Itinerary
X
Jon Bromley's visit to Bristol
```
> *Highlight the first 4 lines*

```
X  19,20    21        1996
20, 21 and 22 November 1995
XX    19
Tuesday 20 November
X
```
> *I think these days are incorrect throughout. Please check them in the Data Files (filename ITIN) p 173, & change if nec.*

```
1325 hours    Taxi from office to New Street Station, Birmingham.
1405 "        Depart from Platform 7.
1620 "        Arrive Bristol (Temple Meads).
```
Accom booked for 1 night at the Grand Hotel, Broad St - tel 01272 216453.
Dinner @ Grand Hotel with Ben Goldsmith.

```
XX
```
Wed 20 Nov ← *Highlight as above*
```
X
```
1000 hours   Town Clerk's office, Council House - tel 01272 217154. Discussion abt new factory. Correspondence in file No1.

1130 "   Appt with Frederick Manson, Manager, Secure Bldg Society, 7 Temple Gate - tel 01272 217091.

> *Please check address in Data Files (filename ITIN) p 173.*

Correspondence in file No 2.

1700 "   Depart Grand Hotel. Ben G—— wl collect yr luggage + drive you to Weston-Super-Mare.

1745 "   Arrive at W—S—M—. *Atlantic*
Accom booked @ Grand Hotel, Beach Rd - telephone 01934 654321.
Dinner @ Grand Atlantic Hotel with Peter & Joan Salmon & B—— G——.

```
XX
```
Thur 21 Nov ← *Highlight as above*
```
X
```
0930 hours   Depart Weston-Super-Mare.
Dining car on train.
1222 "   Arrive New St, Birmingham.

Key in document 5 (filename ITIN) for 9-point printout. Embolden any words that need to be highlighted. When you have completed this task, save under filename ITIN and print one original. Recall the document and follow the instructions for text editing on page 172.

SCOTNEY and Sons Limited
OFFICE SERVICES – REQUEST FORM

Typist's log sheet

Originator GRAHAM SCOTNEY Managing Director   Department —   Date Today's   Ext No 424

> Typists operating a word processor, or electronic typewriter with appropriate function keys, should apply the following automatic facilities: top margin; carrier return; line-end hyphenation; underline OR bold print (embolden); error correction; centring; any other relevant applications.

Remember to (a) complete the details required at the bottom of the form; (b) enter typing time per document in the appropriate column; and (c) before submitting this **log sheet** and your completed work, enter TOTAL TYPING TIME in the last column so that the typist's time may be charged to the originator.

Document No	Type of document and instructions	Copies – Original plus	Input form¶	Typing time per document	Total typing time ⅌
1	Memo to Amos Turle	1 + 1	MS		
2	List of sizes & prices of garden sheds, etc	1 top	AT		
3	Letter & envelope to Mr & Mrs McLennon	1 + 1	MS		
4	Credit note (I will let you have the form shortly)	1 top	Printed		
*5	Notice about working with VDUs	1 top	AT		
6	Personal letter to Alec Simmonds	1 + 1	MS		
				TOTAL TYPING TIME	

TYPIST – please complete:

Typist's name: Date received: Date completed:
                    Time received: Time completed:

> If the typed documents cannot be returned within 24 hours, the office services supervisor should inform the originator. Any item that is urgent should be marked with an asterisk (*).

¶ T = Typescript   AT = Amended Typescript   MS = Manuscript   SD = Shorthand Dictation   AD = Audio Dictation
⅌ To be charged to the originator's department.

3 Display the following exercise on paper of a suitable size. Use double spacing.

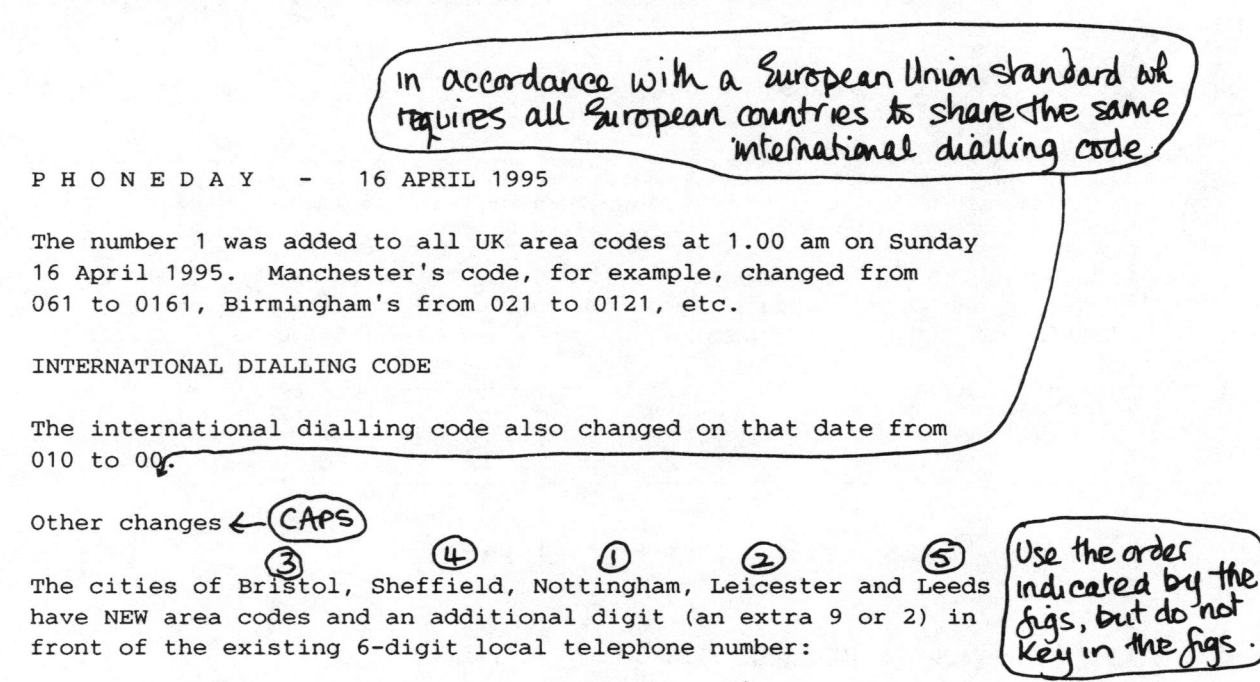

P H O N E D A Y - 16 APRIL 1995

The number 1 was added to all UK area codes at 1.00 am on Sunday
16 April 1995. Manchester's code, for example, changed from
061 to 0161, Birmingham's from 021 to 0121, etc.

INTERNATIONAL DIALLING CODE

The international dialling code also changed on that date from
010 to 00.

Other changes ← (CAPS)

The cities of Bristol, Sheffield, Nottingham, Leicester and Leeds
have NEW area codes and an additional digit (an extra 9 or 2) in
front of the existing 6-digit local telephone number:

* The City of Nottingham - 0602 becomes 0115 9
* "   "   " Leicester - 0533 "   0116 2
* "   "   " Bristol   - 0272 "   0117 9
* "   "   " Sheffield - 0742 "   0114 2
* "   "   " Leeds   - 0532 "   0131 2

Itinerary

If your employer has appointments outside the office, an itinerary may have to be prepared for him which will enable him to know exactly where he should be at any given time. If short, the schedule may be typed on a card, or paper of any convenient size. The display varies, but it makes the listing clearer if you use side headings for the times of the appointments as in the example below.

4 Display the following itinerary on a card.

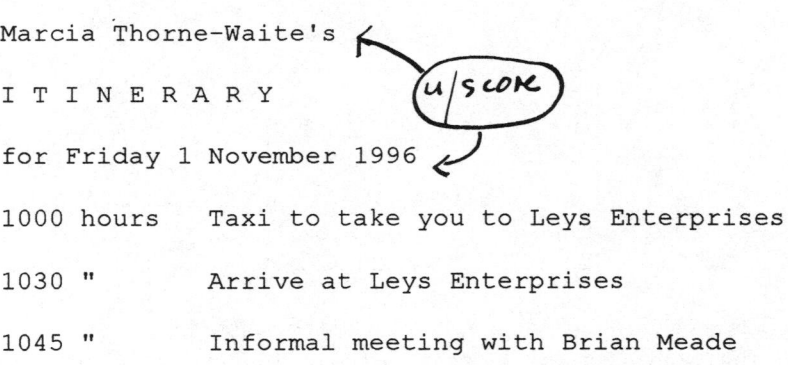

    Marcia Thorne-Waite's

    I T I N E R A R Y

    for Friday 1 November 1996

    1000 hours   Taxi to take you to Leys Enterprises

    1030 "   Arrive at Leys Enterprises

    1045 "   Informal meeting with Brian Meade

    1230 "   Lunch with Directors
    1345 "   Taxi for your return visit to the office
    1500 "   Interviews in Board room (3 applicants
                   for the post of General Manager)

(1) (10 mins) (The original on headed memo paper and one copy, please.)

FROM: (Insert my name + designation here.)

TO: Amos Turtle Advertising Executive

DATE:

NEW CATALOGUE

It is time we reprinted our catalogue + brought it up to date, for the new season, ie, for the beginning of (insert month here — 2 months from now). [I have made some suggestions on the enclosed sheet, + I shd like yr comments together with any other ideas you may hv.

We must either affix a self-adhesive label to the front cover, or insert a loose-leaf page, advertising the fact th we are giving a 10% discount to new customers.

GS/ (Yr initials)   (, with the revised prices,)

[Please let me hv yr ideas by the end of next week.)

(2) GARDEN SHEDS, WORKSHOPS AND   (10 mins)
     GENERAL GARDEN BUILDINGS*

Name	Size	Price**
	mm	£
Cotswold workshop	2 690 x 1 790	510.95
Houndslow shed	2 090 x 1 190	399.00
The Hunter (general purpose)	2 980 x 2 390	490.00
Prism garden building	2 390 x 2 390	515.99
The Sportsman (for gardeners) gardening enthusiasts	1 790 x 1 190	358.00

**   Including VAT.

*   All buildings sold untreated.

2   Display the following income and expenditure account.

```
J C PRITCHARD (1971) CO LTD

Income and Expenditure Account for the Year ended 31 December 1996

                                                      1995      1996

                                                       £         £

EXPENDITURE

Fees ..............................................     867     1 010
Stationery ........................................   7 391     9 137
Meetings ..........................................   1 300     1 187
Delegations .......................................     682       940
Hire of halls .....................................   4 634     4 650
Groups ............................................   4 300     4 134
Printing and publications .........................   1 153       880
Events ............................................   2 037     3 103
Films and equipment ...............................     140        71
Donations .........................................      19       140
```

Please check the total figures for ea yr.   22 623   25 252

Income ← (CAPS)

(Insert leader lines)

Grant   10 500
Interest   4
Halls   11 357
Groups   751
Publications   3
Events   193
Films   118
Excess expenditure over income   2 326

You wl find the '95 figures in the
Data Files (filename EXPEN) page 173.
Please insert them here.

(Insert total figure)

 Key in document 2 (filename EXPEN) for 10-point printout. Embolden the main heading and use the automatic underline feature and the decimal tab key. When you have completed this task, save under filename EXPEN and print out an original. Recall the document and follow the instructions for text editing on page 172.

③ (20 mins)

GS/(Yr initials)/4605   (An original & one copy, please.)

(Date)

Mr & Mrs L P McLennon

(You wl find their address in the Data Files (filename SHED) page 174.)

Garden Sheds ← (CAPS)

Thank you for yr tel call enquiring abt a̶ shed for yr garden. (an all-purpose) I understand th, as you hv only a small garden you wd like to utilize the shed for storage of garden tools as well as having some space for propogating plants from seeds & growing 1 or 2 tomato plants & maybe some courgettes. ~~As the space you have available~~ [I wd ~~particularly~~ recom our PRISM garden bldg wh has windows all round to let in the max amt of light, & is within the size for the space you hv available.

	Size mm	Price £
Houndslow shed		
The Hunter		
Prism garden bldg		

(Copy details from the previous page here.)

[I am enclosing our catalogue & wd draw yr attention to pp 4 & 5 showing the following bldgs. Provided you hv the foundations laid, we will erect the bldg free of charge.

Yrs sinc

GRAHAM SCOTNEY
Managing Director

PS As you are a new customer you wl be eligible for our 10% discount.

④ (15 mins)

Please send a credit note to Ms Fiona Simmons. All the details are in the Data Files (filename SHED) on page 174.

KEYBOARDING SKILLS

Before proceeding to the exercises below, you should type the following skill building exercises;

proofreading No 11, page 153.   **techniques and reviews** No 11, page 157.
skill measurement No 33, page 161.   **record your progress** No 28, page 168.

PRODUCTION DEVELOPMENT

● *Financial statements*—See **data store**, page 185.

1   Display the following balance sheet.

```
CRANLEIGH & COOPER

Balance Sheet - 31 December 1996

Liabilities and Reserves              Assets

                      £'000                              £'000

Shares ..........     4 951 718    Mortgages .....      4 901 332

Deposits and loans      760 792    Investments and
                                     cash ........     1 096 113
Taxation and other
   liabilities ....      89,8885    Fixed assets ..        75 104

General reserve ..      238 8787    Other assets ..        2 0282

Deferred tax .....        6 299
                      _____                         _____
                      6 047 571                         6 047 674
                      _____                         _____
```

(Please check the totals - they should be the same)

Key in document 1 (filename SHEET) for 12-point printout. Embolden the main heading and use the automatic underline feature, the vertical line key and the decimal tab. When you have completed this task, save under filename SHEET and print out an original. Recall the document and follow the instructions for text editing on page 172.

(A4 paper)

WORKING WITH VDUs

<u>The Health and Safety at Work Act</u>

All computer and word processor operaters should be aware of the requirements of the current safety and health legislation, and take careful note of the points set out below.

1   Plan your daily activities so that you have periodic breaks during the working day, with a change of routine.

2   Make sure that you take advantage of the free eyetests at regular intervals and that, if you need to wear glasses, they are suitable for working at a VDU. Yr normal reading glasses are not appropriate.

Renumber

3   If you find the lighting unsuitable in your office, please report it to the appropriate department.

4   Footstools is available for your use. Contact your head of department if you need one.

The electrical wiring is checked quarterly in your offices, but if you see any loose wiring, or have reason to feel their is a problem caused by static electricity, contact the appropriate department immediately. ← CAPS

3 It is important to keep the screen smear-free & dust-free. Use the anti-static cleaning fluid for this purpose.

Send a letter to Alec Simmonds, Simmonds Motor Co Ltd, Portland House, Willen, Milton Keynes, MK15 9JW.

As you already know, we wish to phase out our present fleet of co cars over the next 2 yrs & replace the 15 vehicles with 10 smaller models. // Please let me hv details of any reliable makes you feel wd be suitable for our purpose & within a price range of £13 000 to £18 000. // Do hope you & yr family are well.

Very best wishes.

Insert our ref GS/ followed by yr initials, today's date & Alec's name & address, but leave abt 8 single spaces after that & I wl write the salutation. Also do NOT insert my name or designation at the end of the letter.

5 — (10 mins)

(Display the following attractively on a card.)

F R E E

V A L U A T I O N   S E R V I C E

Lester Kelly's remain independent Estate Agents
who have specialized in residential property for
many years.
For advice on marketing & valuation, call on our
expertise now.
THE LESTER KELLY PARTNERSHIP
(Insert address & telephone no here, please.)

---

6 — (20 mins)

(Send a letter to Mme Chantal Deveraux enclosing
details of the cottage at 4 Mill Street. Her address
is on page 107. The ref is — my initials, an oblique
& yr initials. Don't forget the date — & also type
an envelope, please.)

4 MILL STREET
I am enclosing details of the cottage at 4 Mill Street,
Amersham.
This desirable property has been the subject of considerable
(Complete this paragraph from the details of the property
on page 115, up to . . . . of woodwork renewed.)
If you wish to view this property when you are in this
country, the keys may be obtained from our office in
South Street, Amersham.
Yrs sinc
(My name & designation here)

PRODUCTION DEVELOPMENT

● *Roman numerals*—See **data store**, page 191.

1   Type the following on A5 paper. Use double spacing.

> Refer to Section IX, Chapter II, Page 340, Paragraph 2(iii).
> Read parts XVI, XVII, and XVIII, subsections ii, vi, and ix.
> The boys in Forms VI and IX will take Stages I, II, and III.
> Charles II, Henry VIII, George IV, James VI, and Edward III.

Enumerations using roman numerals

When roman numerals are used for enumerations, they may
be blocked at the left, eg

(i)[4]   Title of book   Leave four spaces after right bracket.
(ii)[3] Name of author   Leave three spaces after right bracket.
(iii)[2] Publisher   Always leave two spaces after right bracket in *longest* number.

2   Type the following in single spacing on A4 paper. The coloured arabic figures indicate the number of spaces
   to be left after the roman numeral and are not to be typed.

> SPECIAL BT NUMBERS
>
> Every day thousands of people use the very wide range
> of services offered by businesses and organizations
> using BT lines. These can include free and low-cost
> calls.
>
> I[4]   If the number begins with 0800
>
> This means that you can ring the ~~company~~ business or organization
> free from anywhere in the UK.
>
> II[3]   Local call rate
>
> If you are ringing a number which begins with 0345 you
> will be charged only at the local rate, no matter where
> in the country you are phoning from.
>
> III[2] Information and entertainment
>
> Numbers which begin with 0891 or 0882 offer information
> or entertainment. Calls are charged at a premium rate,
> which is higher than the standard call rate.

You will find item IV in the Data Files (filename PHONE) page 174. Please enter it here.

(FRONT COVER)

THE LESTER KELLY PARTNERSHIP

E S T A T E   A G E N T S

108 South Street
Amersham
Bucks
HP6 5AP
Telephone: (01203) 332232

(INSIDE LEFT)

A U C T I O N

Friday 15.11.96
Commencing at 9.30am

ANTIQUE AND other FURNITURE

TOYS, DOLLS, MODELS
and effects

(INSIDE RIGHT)

To be held at

THE CORN EXCHANGE

High Street
AMERSHAM

Viewing: Thurs 14.11.96.
from 10.30am to 8.0 pm

---

4) — (20 mins)

(Display the following as a folded leaflet.)

● *Draft copies*—See **data store**, page 184.

3

DRAFT

SELF-CHILLING CANS

THE CAN THAT NEEDS NO FRIDGE ← *Small letters u/scored with initial caps*

A4 paper

A revolutionary, self-chilling can, perfected by a British

inventor, could be on supermarket shelves by the end of 195~~9~~.

The 'inbuilt fridge' works in the following way.

I   At the bottom of the can is a small capsule of compressed

    carbon dioxide gas which works as a cooling device.

II   When the sealed can is opened, *by pulling a tab,* ~~pressure~~ is released and

    the gas is pushed out of the capsule.

III   The carbon dioxide swirls rapidly around, forcing heavier

    cold molecules to separate from lighter warm ones.

Roman numeral please → 4   *This cools the capsule, then the liquid around it, until the entire drink is cooled. This shd take abt 30 secs.*

[The UK* is already the ~~biggest~~ largest user of canned drinks in Europe, with a 35% share of the market, compared with the German's share of 23%, Spain's share of 10% and France's share of 6%.

* Recent figures show Britons buy 16 million cans a yr, with the soft drinks market rising to 3.9 billion items a yr over the last 12 yrs.

It is inexpensive to produce & the can wl be fully recyclable.

[5] Key in document 3 (filename CAN) for 12-point printout. Use the word wraparound function and type the main heading in bold. When you have completed this task, save under filename CAN and print an original. Retrieve the document and follow the instructions for text editing on page 171.

3 — (25 mins)

(Please rearrange the table so that the 'size' column comes before 'accommodation'.)

'Riverside'
Luxury Flats ← (Use any method to emphasize these 2 lines.)

'Riverside' is a unique development, with landscaping to a high standard & offering a wide range of accom. The flats, from a studio type to a large, 2-bedroomed penthouse, each hv their own allocated parking space, whilst those above the ground floor also hv balconies.

Flat No	Accommodation	Size
Flat No1, 3* & 5 (Studio)	Living room	17' 0" x 12' 3"
	Kitchen	7' 8" x 7' 7"
Flat No 2, 4 & 6* (One-bedroomed)	Living room	12' 8" x 12' 4"
	Kitchen	(I will check the size of the kitchen & give it to you shortly.)
	Bedroom	14' 0" x 10' 7"
Flat No 7*, 9 & 11 (Two-bedroomed)	Living room	14' 5" x 13' 2"
	Kitchen	8' 11" x 8' 1"
	Dining area	8' 11" x 6' 3"
	Bedroom 1	12' 10" x 8' 10"
	Bedroom 2	12' 10" x 8' 11"

* Already sold.

(Do not rule.)

Modification and rearrangement of material

In an office, your employer may give you specific or general instructions about altering the layout of a document, and these instructions should be followed very carefully.

If in an examination you are directed to modify or alter the layout of an exercise, these instructions MUST be followed, otherwise marks will be lost. Before starting to type, carefully read through the task and mark the script clearly in ink where any alterations have to be made. For example, if items have to be rearranged in date order, write 1, 2, 3, 4, etc, against the items in the order in which they should be typed. Time spent in preparation, will lead to greater accuracy and speed in typing.

4   Type the following on A4 paper in double spacing.

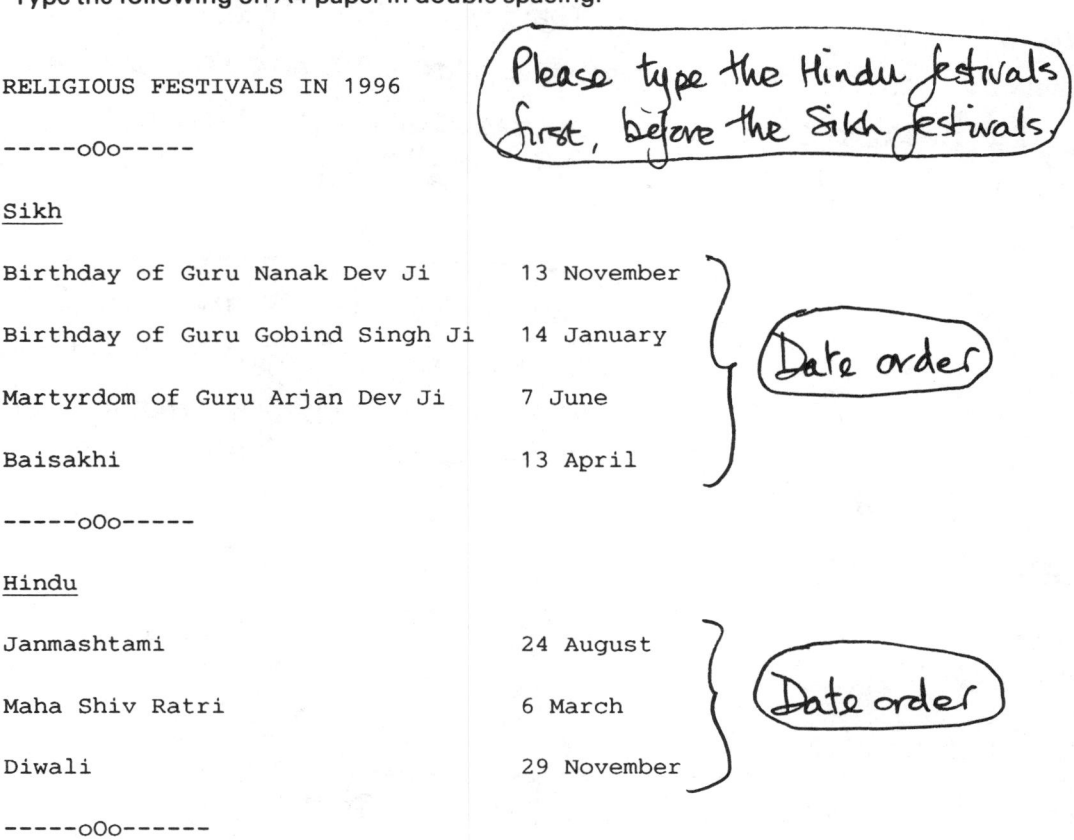

```
RELIGIOUS FESTIVALS IN 1996

-----oOo-----

Sikh

Birthday of Guru Nanak Dev Ji        13 November

Birthday of Guru Gobind Singh Ji     14 January

Martyrdom of Guru Arjan Dev Ji       7 June

Baisakhi                             13 April

-----oOo-----

Hindu

Janmashtami                          24 August

Maha Shiv Ratri                      6 March

Diwali                               29 November

-----oOo------
```

Please type the Hindu festivals first, before the Sikh festivals.

Date order

Date order

5   Type the following on A5 landscape paper in double spacing.

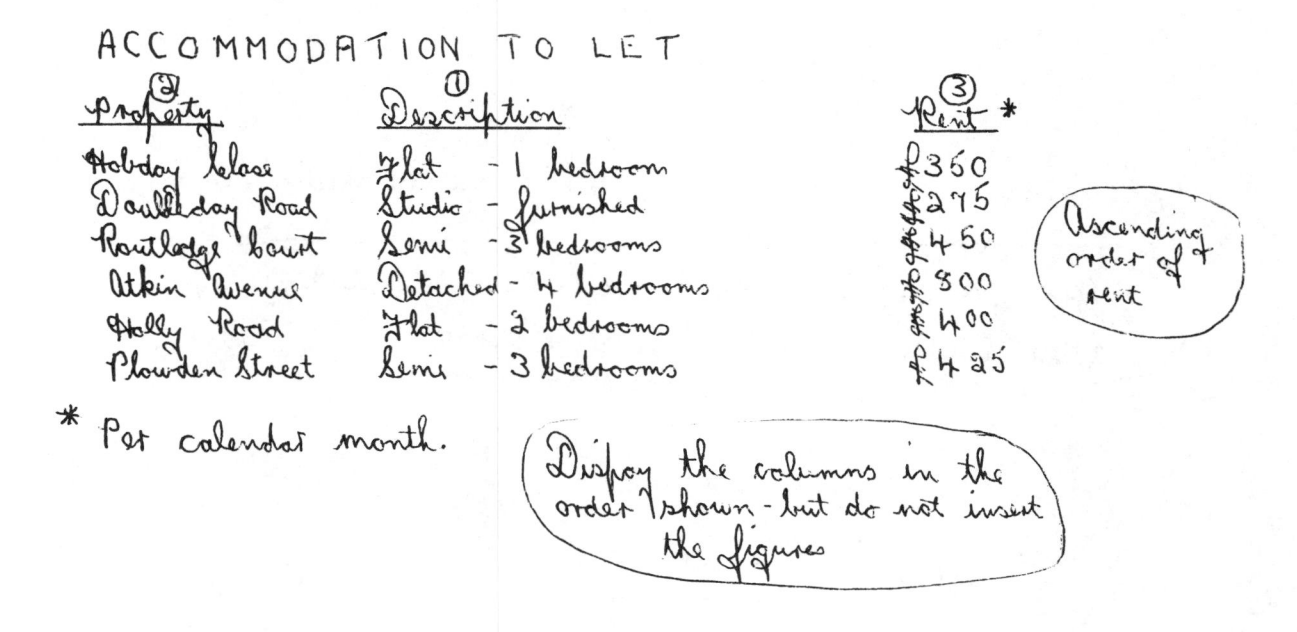

ACCOMMODATION TO LET

② Property	① Description	③ Rent *
Hobday Close	Flat – 1 bedroom	£360
Doubleday Road	Studio – furnished	£275
Routledge Court	Semi – 3 bedrooms	450
Atkin Avenue	Detached – 4 bedrooms	800
Holly Road	Flat – 2 bedrooms	400
Plowden Street	Semi – 3 bedrooms	£425

* Per calendar month.

Ascending order of rent

Display the columns in the order shown – but do not insert the figures

(Inset) { structural defect. It should be stressed that the likelihood of any serious problem arising is very remote, but you hv peace of mind knowing you are protected. ←

The exterior masonry surfaces of yr property hv been specially coated with a protective application wh wl guard against dampness, corrosion & the need for constant redecorating i should be glad if you would complete the attached slip & forward it to the builders so that they hv yr details on file.

Yrs sinc

> Our houses are sound and, as our many customers will readily confirm, reliable & trouble free.

Betti Goddard
SALES DIRECTOR

- -

Please forward to:
Devlin Developments

> Insert address here. You will find it on page 107

NAME . . . .
ADDRESS . . . .
. . . .
Postcode . . . . Telephone number . . . .

> Type an envelope to Mr & Mrs Greene & a label to Gavin Matthews, please.

Side headings

These headings are typed to the left of the set left margin. Side headings are usually typed in closed capitals with or without the underscore, but lower case may also be used. The following steps should be taken:

1 First decide on left and right margins.
2 Set right margin.
3 Set a tab stop at the point where you intended to set the left margin.
4 From the tab stop set in point 3, tap in once for each character and space in the longest line of the side headings, plus three extra spaces.
5 Set the left margin at this point.
6 To type the side headings, use the margin release and bring typing point to tab stop set in point 3.

Indent margins

If you are using an electronic keyboard you may the facility for setting a second left margin (often referred to as an **indent margin**) instead of using the tabular mechanism.

6 Type the following on A4 paper in single spacing. Set a tab stop at 12 pitch 18, 10 pitch 15, for the side heading. Margins: 12 pitch 31–88; 10 pitch 28–72.

TOYS SAFETY REGULATIONS

Examinations are carried out by bodies approved by the *European* Community ~~governments~~ to check and certify that a model of a toy meets the essential safety requirements.

CE MARK*   Products meeting the European standards carry the CE
                  conformity mark.

PHYSICAL   Toys must be so designed |and| constructed as to minimise
INJURY   the risk of physical injury which could be caused by the
                  movement of parts.

✓ FUNCTIONAL   Functional toys, ~~or~~ *and* their packaging, must bear the marking
  TOYS   'WARNING: to be used under the direct supervision of an adult'.

  Age (CAPS)   Toys which may be dangerous for a child under a certain
                  age must bear a warning. For example: 'Not suitable
                  for children under 36 months'.

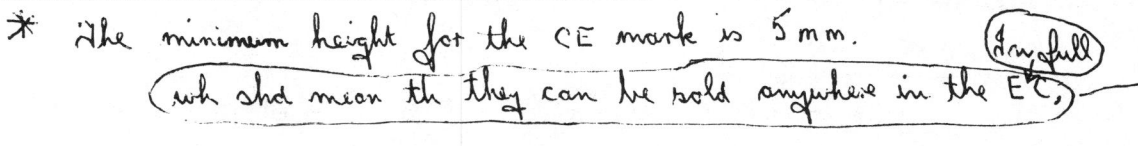

*   The minimum height for the CE mark is 5mm.   (In full)
     (wh shd mean th they can be sold anywhere in the EC.)

7 Type the following on A4 paper in the order indicated, but do NOT type the figures. Retain the side headings.

(In full) BEAT THE THIEF
In the UK more than 1·5 million vehicles are broken into |or| stolen every yr - that's one every 20 secs.

(2) RADIOS   Radio theft is a major cause of vehicle crime. It is wise to hv yr radio cassette player protected by a security code.

(4) WINDOW   hv yr vehicle registration no etched into the window glass.
    ETCHING

(1) CAR ALARM   An electronic car alarm is one of the most effective deterrents.

(3) FUEL   Make sure you hv a lockable filler cap to stop the thief siphoning petrol. (As a safeguard,)

2 — (30 mins)

Two carbon copies, please — one for the file & one for Gavin Matthews at Devlin Development. Mark the letter PRIVATE.

Our ref BG/Sales/4061P/(Yr initials)

Mr & Mrs W Greene
6 Daroby Court
Camomile Green
Amersham
Bucks HP6 5AP

Change 'house/s' to 'home/s' throughout.

Dr Mr & Mrs G——————

GUARANTEED STANDARDS — TEN-YEAR WARRANTY

You wl be pleased to know that yr house has bn thoroughly checked during construction & that it complies with guaranteed standards. This means that the builders hv ensured that it wl be as trouble free as poss.

The ten-yr warranty wl protect you in the un likely event of any major defect arising.

The ten-yr warranty ← (CAPS, no u/score)

(a) The first two yrs
The builders hv undertaken to put right almost any problems ~~that~~ may arise during the first two yrs of the life of yr house. This does not include 'shrinkage cracks' wh often ~~occur~~ appear in new houses, or ~~for~~ electrical fittings.

(b) The remaining yrs
Please contact yr builder if you hv any major

Inset 13 mm (½") both sides

KEYBOARDING SKILLS

Before proceeding to the exercises below, you should type the following skill building exercises:

improve your spelling Nos 15 and 16, page 155.   **alphabetic sentence** No 8, page 156.
skill measurement No 26, page 160.   **record your progress** No 21, page 166.

PRODUCTION DEVELOPMENT

● *Circular letters*—See **data store**, page 181.

1   Type the following on A4 letterhead paper. As the name and address of the addressee is not being typed, turn up two single spaces after typing 'Date as postmark' and type the salutation.

```
HD/frl                                        Date as postmark

Dear Student

Remission of course fees  (Highlight)

I am writing to let you know that, although assistance can be
given with course fees, your income is above the scale set  for
remission to be given.

Unfortunately you will be required to pay the full course fee.
It may help you to pay your fee in 3 (installments,) payable as
follows:

September                Inset
January                  5 spaces for left margin
April

If this still causes you difficulty I suggest you get in touch
with the Course (Tuter) who may be able to suggest another course
but with less hours and a considerably reduced fee.
                                      , asap,
Would you please let me know which course of action you wish to
take.
follow
Yours faithfully

HARRY DICKSON                    I am encl an up to-
                                 date brochure for
Assistant Registrar              yr info.

Enc
```

BEDROOM 1 — 13' x 8' 6" with double radiator, window overlooking the front.

BEDROOM 2 — 14' x 9' with radiator, window overlooking the front.

BEDROOM 3 — 15' 2" x 6' 6" with radiator, 2 windows overlooking the rear, fitted cupboard.

BATHROOM — with coloured suite of panelled bath, pedestal wash-basin, low-level WC, radiator.

(leave 3 single lines clear)

Outside ← (spaced)

(Double spacing here) There is no garden at the front of the property, but at the side there is parking space with a delightfully landscaped little garden with a small area of lawn surrounded by flower & shrub borders, wood panel fencing ensuring privacy & a concrete path. . . .

(leave 3 single lines clear)

RATEABLE VALUE — ←

SERVICES — All main services connected.

PRICE — ←

(These figures are in the Data files (filename PROP) on page 174. Please insert them.)

(Insert the month & year here, please.)

2   Type the following on A4 letterhead paper and take a copy. Turn up 10 single spaces after typing the reference, so that the date and the name and address of the addressee may be inserted before the letter is sent out.

GEG/23/95/tp

Dear Sir/Madam   _Home Bldgs Insurance_

As you know, we have experienced very severe weather/ _conditions_ in this country over the last few years.

I am sure you will appreciate that the knock-on affect of such conditions has been a very large increase in both the number and cost of the claims being dealt with by all insurers, which have led to heavy trading losses.// As a result, we have to announce significant rate increases, but our rate of increase will still be very competitive when compared with most insurance cos. _in full_

The rate can be reduced if you is willing to accept an additional claims excess on your Policy. Our currant discounts are -

(a) 10% for a £50 excess;
(b) 20% for a £100 excess.   _Inset 5 spaces fr left margin & use double spacing_

We will endeavour to maintain a high standard of service to you as one of our valued clients.

Yours faithfully
LEYS INDUSTRIES

I am attaching a leaflet giving full details of these increases.

Geoffrey E Goodwood
Deputy General Manager

Att(1)

3   _Send the original of the above letter to Dr Jeremy Brooker. You will find his address on page 42. Insert today's date, & address an envelope. Don't forget to delete the oblique & the word 'Madam' in the salutation._
Send the copy to Ms Thelma Bradley, 12 The Links, Great Missenden, Bucks HP6 0RY. Date it for tomorrow & alter the salutation. Thank you.

(Headed paper for the first sheet, plain bond for the second. Keep to the linespacing shown.)

Ref: 1218

A B S O L U T E L Y   I M M A C U L A T E

┌─────────────────────────┐
│ Draw a rectangle here   │
│ 51 mm × 38 mm   │
│ (2" × 1½")   │
└─────────────────────────┘

TOWN CENTRE COTTAGE

4 Mill Street

Amersham Bucks

(Leave 3 single lines clear)

This desirable property has been the subject of considerable expenditure

in recent years, and offer a beautifully presented, 3-bedroomed home.

The cottage is constructed of brick and stone sermounted by a slate roof,

and has recently been rewired, replumbed and had a considerable amount

of woodwork renewed. // The decor is in pristine condition and the fittings

in both the kitchen and bathroom are lovely modern units. Outside there

is parking space and also a small, but beautifully landscaped garden

which provides an ideal sitting-out area.

(Leave 3 single lines clear)

A c c o m m o d a t i o n

① COVERED PORCH - with steps to entrance door.

④ DINING ROOM   - 14' x 8' 8" with window overlooking the front, telephone
                   point, double radiator.

③ SITTING ROOM   - 13' 4" x 13' with window overlooking the front, TV point,
                   window to side, double radiator, built-in cupboards.

② KITCHEN   - 14' 8" x 6' fitted with an excellent range of modern
            ∅ ~~units comprising~~ electric cooker point, plumbing for
                   automatic washing machine, flourescent striplight,
                   double raditor, half-glazed, hardwood door to side.

⑤ LANDING   - with hatch to roof space.

(TYPIST - Type the above items in numerical order, but do not type the figures.)

Sometimes a letter will have a tear-off portion at the foot, so that a customer can fill in certain details and return the tear-off portion to the sender.

After typing the complimentary close leave a minimum of four clear spaces, ie turn up five single spaces and then type, from edge to edge of the paper, continuous hyphens or continuous dots; then turn up two single spaces and type the information on the tear-off portion.

When blank spaces are left on the tear-off portion for details to be filled in, use continuous dots or the underscore and double spacing. Remember to leave one clear space after the last character typed before starting the dots or underscore and one clear space at the end of the dots or the underscore before the next typed character if there is one, eg

```
      (space)              (space)             (space)
        ↓                    ↓                   ↓
Surname .....................  Christian names ....................
```

4   Type the following personal business letter on A4 paper. It is not necessary to leave space for the name and address of the addressee.

Backspace the longest line in the address from right margin & start all lines at this point.

31 Forge Lane
Headington
OXFORD
OX3 7LD

July 1996

Dear

It has been decided to arrange a dinner for our Association on Friday 6 Sept 1996 at the Beaufort Arms in Oxford. Tickets will be £14.00 per head - wine not included.

The evening will start with drinks at 7.30 pm and dinner will follow at 8.00 pm. // There will be a choice from the following selections. *shown on the attached menu* Places will be limited so please book early by completing the slip below.

// *I hope you wl be able to attend. It shd be an enjoyable evening.*

Sincerely

Camilla Russell
Secretary

Att(1)

NAME ....

ADDRESS ....

.... Tel No ....

No of tickets required ....

Cheque enclosed for £......................................

Please change times to 24-hour clock; abbreviations in full.

THE LESTER KELLY PARTNERSHIP

This sheet contains instructions that must be complied with when typing the documents. Read the information carefully before starting, and refer back to it frequently.

OFFICE SERVICES – REQUEST FORM

Typist's log sheet

Originator BETTI GODDARD Sales Director   Department Sales   Date 18.10.96.   Ext No 29

	Typists operating a word processor, or electronic typewriter with appropriate function keys, should apply the following automatic facilities: top margin; carrier return; line-end hyphenation; underline OR bold print (embolden); error correction; centring; any other relevant applications.

Remember to (a) complete the details required at the bottom of the form; (b) enter typing time per document in the appropriate column; and (c) before submitting this **log sheet** and your completed work, enter TOTAL TYPING TIME in the last column so that the typist's time may be charged to the originator.

Docu-ment No	Type of document and instructions	Copies – Original plus	Input form¶	Typing time per document	Total-typing time ¥
1	Details of cottage (2-page)	1 + 1	AT		
2	Letter with tear-off to Mr & Mrs Greene (plus envelope + label)	1 + 2	MS		
3	Table of accommodation at 'Riverside'	1 top	MS		
4	Display, on a card	1 top	MS		
5	Letter from brief notes (plus envelope)	1 top	MS		
* 6	Folded leaflet (I would like the leaflet before I go out, please. I should be back in approx 2½ hrs – leave the other typing on my desk for me, please.)	1 top	MS		

TYPIST – please complete:

Typist's name:	Date received:	Date completed:
	Time received:	Time completed:

If the typed documents cannot be returned within 24 hours, the office services supervisor should inform the originator. Any item that is urgent should be marked with an asterisk (*).

¶ T = Typescript   AT = Amended Typescript   MS = Manuscript   SD = Shorthand Dictation   AD = Audio Dictation
¥ To be charged to the originator's department.

5

One original on A4 letterhead paper, & one copy, please. Insert a subject heading:

NOTIFICATION OF PROPOSED CHANGES

GD/508822.1/AF

Leave sufficient space here for the date & address of addressee.

Dear Sir/Madam

Because of increased postal charges we are now ~~extremely~~ *very* concerned about the cost of distributing information each month, to over ↑ members in our region. *Insert the no of members here. You wl find the fig in the Data Files (filename NEWS) p.173*

It is our intention in the future, therefore, to send out only 2 notifications each year. The next will be the Annual General Meeting where the business for the year will be discussed. ←

In view of the proposed change, will you please return the attached slip, giving your opinion of these proposals. If you (do not) return *CAPS* the slip it will be assumed that you do not wish to be circulated other than for the AGM. ← *in full*

You wl, of course, still obtain much info fr the Newsletter wh wl continue to be sent to you.

Yrs sinc

GINNY DAYES
Secretary

If you attend, you will get most of the info at that time.

- -

Double spacing here

NAME ....

ADDRESS ....

(Please tick in the appropriate space)

I agree with the proposed change ....

I disagree with the proposed change ...... *Leave 4 single lines clear.*

Signature .... Date ....

6 Key in document 5 (filename NEWS) for 10-point printout. Use the word wraparound function and embolden all words in capitals. When you have completed this task, save under filename NEWS and print one original and one copy. Retrieve the document and follow the instructions for text editing on page 171.

6

Now complete the details. Date the letter for last month & this year, & address it to yourself. Amend the salutation. Imagine tht you hv just received this letter & complete the tear-off portion by inserting yr name & address & today's date. Then, in ink, insert a tick saying whether or not you agree w the changes, & sign the slip.

2
~~Date~~
Kate F—— Office Supervisor

is not always the fastest option & is probably not the best way to send a report of more than 3 or four A4 pages. Bear in mind th it costs recipients money to download, so it is important not (too) send long messages just for the sake of it. We might ~~think abt~~ consider sending lengthy reports on disk through the post, or by courier, as we do at present.

3 Urgent messages. It may not be appropriate to send messages th require immed action since you cannot be sure when ~~it~~ they wl be read.

(leave the same space as previously, here please)

Have you heard of Smilies? (Apparently) they are used to help to convey the mood of an electronic mail message. E-mail is often used instead of a phone call, or saying something face to face, but you cannot convey th extra meaning to an electronic message — a laugh, a change of tone, etc — so, Smilies are used instead. They (is) created by typing a set of characters to form a face sideways on; for example

(You wl find the Smilies in The Data Files (filename EMAIL) on page 173. Please insert them here.)

Let me hv yr thoughts on the points I hv raised asap, please, & we can then call a mtg of key staff.

BF/ (Yr initials)

DISTRIBUTE TO: Joanna C-S

(An initial phone call, followed by an electronic mail message on Internet, may be nec.)

 Key in document 2 (filename EMAIL) for 10-point printout. When you have completed this task, save under filename EMAIL and print an original and two copies. Retrieve the document and follow the instructions for text editing on page 172.

KEYBOARDING SKILLS

Before proceeding to the exercises below, you should type the following skill building exercises:

proofreading No 8, page 151.   **techniques and reviews** No 8, page 157.
skill measurement No 27, page 160.   **record your progress** No 22, page 166.

PRODUCTION DEVELOPMENT

- *Blocked tabulation with single-line column headings*—Refer to unit 28, page 45, for the method to be used when arranging items in columns.

- *Footnotes*—See **data store**, page 186.

NOTE: It is not usual to type a line above the footnote when it occurs after a table.

1 Use A5 paper. Follow the linespacing used in the exercise.

YOUR HOLIDAY WEATHER*

The following table shows the average daily maximum
temperatures and monthly rainfall.

City	Country	Temperature	Rainfall
Orlando)	United States	91°F	Nil
Los Angeles)		72°F	6"
Bali	Indonesia	87°F	2"
Cape Town	South Africa	65°F	3"
Durban		73°F	1"
Johannesburg		62°F	Nil
Bombay	India	89°F	19"
Delhi		102°F	3"

(handwritten note: Display in alphabetical order of countries)

* In the month of June.

- *Leader dots*—See **data store**, page 196.

2 Display the following on A5 paper. Insert leader dots.

HOLIDAY BROCHURE ← *(Sp caps)*

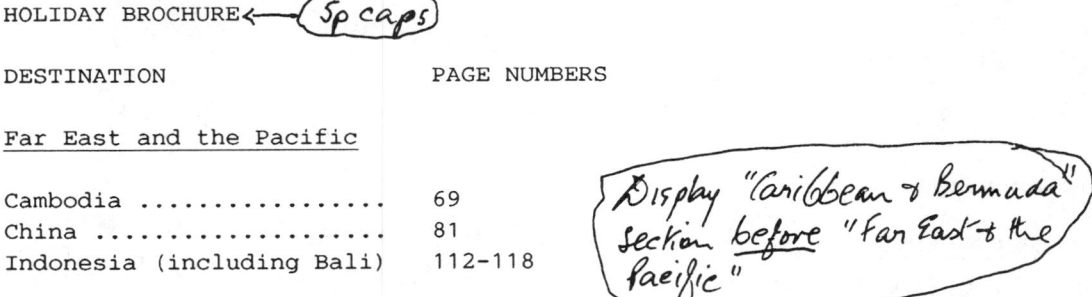

DESTINATION	PAGE NUMBERS
Far East and the Pacific	
Cambodia	69
China	81
Indonesia (including Bali)	112-118

(handwritten note: Display "Caribbean & Bermuda" section before "Far East & the Pacific")

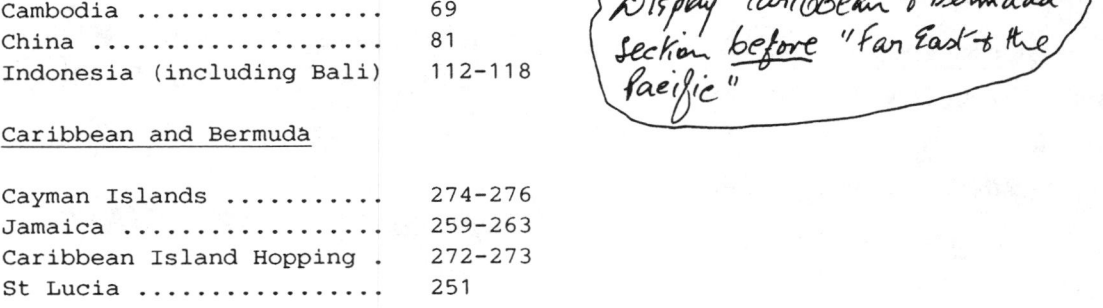

Caribbean and Bermuda	
Cayman Islands	274-276
Jamaica	259-263
Caribbean Island Hopping .	272-273
St Lucia	251

Quotation marks

When two or more paragraphs are quoted, the quotation marks are placed at the beginning of each paragraph and at the end of the last paragraph only.

With ellipsis, there is a space after the initial quotation mark and before the first dot, and a space after the third dot and before the final quotation mark.

2   Type the following two-page memo taking an original and two copies, one for Joanna Crighton-Smythe and the other for the file. Prepare two labels, one for Kate Flynn and the other for Mrs Crighton-Smythe.

CONFIDENTIAL

TO   Kate Flynn   Office Supervisor

Highlight all headings in some way, please.

FROM   Barry Filkins   Marketing Director

DATE   *(Insert next Monday's date here.)*

E-MAIL

As our business is fast expanding I feel we should definitely consider sub-scribing to Internet and using electronic mail.   I shall need some discussion with you, but I give below certain of the advantages and disadvantages for you to consider before we meet.

Advantages   *(Change electronic mail to e-mail from this point on.)*

One manufacturer gives the following advantages:

"1   For most users, when they have joined Internet, sending e-mail costs merely the price of a local phone call.

"2   Electronic mail is fast - just compose your message, affix the electronic address of the recipient and press the send key. In seconds your missive can be in the correct mailbox on the other side of the world.

"3   Messages are unlikely to ~~go astray~~ *get lost*, but if they do not get through, you will probably be informed of the failed delivery on your screen.

"4   It is possible to send the same message to groups of people simultaneously This would be excellent for our use when we wish to announce new products or prices to our customers.

"5   Electronic mail is not restricted to text.   You can attach all sorts of other files to your messages, including photographic images, graphics, soft-ware and video."

(Leave a space here - approx 38 mm (1½") please)

Disadvantages

1 Junk mail. Once our electronic address becomes (widley) known we cld become the recipients of electronic junk mail. The problem is then tht it can become more difficult to spot the important messages among the junk.

2 Lengthy reports. Despite (it's) apparent speed, electronic mail is not/

3

Environmental Efforts ← (Unspaced caps) (A4 Paper)

PERCENTAGES PUBLISHED IN 1992 ← (Initial caps, underlined)

Do you?	Regularly	Sometimes	Not at all
	%	%	%
③ ② ①			
(Double Spacing) Buy produce grown organically[1] ...	7.8	38.3	25.8
Return empties for recycling[2]	32.4	30.8	36.3
Cut back on driving	12.1	18.2	35.4
Buy products not tested on animals	32.1	34.0	29.5
Refuse unnecessary packaging	17.4	32.4	49.3

[1] Farming without the use of synthetic fertilizers.

[2] Processing of industrial and household waste (such as paper, glass and some metals and plastics).

(Please check these figs from Data Files (Filename Prod). p.174 and alter if necessary.)

4

BICENTENARIES + CENTENARIES OF 1995

Born | Date
King George VI .... | 14 December 1895
Rudolf Valentino, film actor | 6 May 1895
John Keats, poet .... | 31 October 1795
Buster Keaton, film comedian* | 4 Oct 1895

(Leave 3 single spaces here)

Died
Josiah Wedgwood, potter | 3 Jan 1795
James Boswell, writer | 19 May 1795
Louis Pasteur, chemist** | 28 Sept 1895

* American
** French

---

7. Key in document 4 (filename DATE) for 12-point printout. Embolden all words in capitals. When you have completed this task, save under filename DATE and print one copy. Retrieve the document and follow the instructions for text editing on page 171.

2

6 September 199~~5~~ 6

Mr Alec Tranter

In this respect, you can rest assured th

Your quotation is based on the information you gave us, and I would urge you to check that you are taking full advantage of the **EXTRA DISCOUNTS** available. There are 4:

Inset 13 mm (½")

1   fully retired - save up to 15 per cent
2   drive less than 3 000 miles a year - save up to 10 per cent
3   overnight garaging - save up to 10 per cent
4   car over 5 years old - save up to 20% (In full)

I would emphasize that these discounts are in addition to the usual low-cost premiums that we ~~usually~~ offer. We keep these premiums down because you are not subsidizing younger drivers - we only accept principal drivers aged 55. Such drivers present a lower risk to ~~l~~ (& over) our under writers because they tend to be more (carefull) and honest. // We have arranged our plan through the **Savings Insurance Company (UK) Ltd**, a member of the International Group, & one of the largest Ins Groups in the world with assets in excess of £5 billion. // When deciding on wh co to choose, you shd bear in mind th, while the amt you pay for ins is important, the quality of cover & the service factors are well worth considering. ↙ The Brady Car Insurance Plan is almost impossible to better. Special features include:

Inset as above

1   no upper age limit or medical examination
2   prompt & polite claims service
3   free windscreen etching   (4 protected no claims bonus.)

We also offer a wide choice of types of cover, not only comprehensive but any driver over 50 with emergency driver cover. This wl

Display as above

1   permit any driver over 50 to drive yr car; or
2   (Items 2 & 3 are in the Data Files (filename CAR) p 173.)

To start yr cover simply complete all details on the enclosed proposal form & enclose the amt shown on yr personal quotation. Make yr (check) payable to BRADY CAR INSURANCE. // If you hv any questions, or if you need cover immed, please tel us free on ↑ 23601.

Yrs sinc   (Please find the BRISTOL code from the tel directory & insert it here.)

MARION GOLDSMITH (Gen Man)

PS ~~Do~~ remember, (their) is no upper age limit or medical examination req'd with this policy.

COPY FOR —
Belinda Goodhall, Marketing Manager
File

 Key in document 1 (filename CAR) for 10-point printout. Embolden the subject heading and use the wraparound function. When you have completed this task, save under filename CAR and print an original and two copies. Retrieve the document and follow the instructions for text editing on page 172.

Blocked tabulation—horizontal ruling

A neat and pleasing appearance may be given to column work by ruling in ink or by the use of the underscore key. An 'open' table has no ruled lines. A 'ruled' table has the column headings separated from the column items by horizontal lines above and below the headings, and below the last line in the table. When typing a ruled table, proceed as follows:

1 Decide on a suitable top margin.
2 Set the left margin in the usual way.
3 It will be necessary to set a right margin at the point where the typed horizontal lines will end. To do this, from the last tab stop, tap space bar once for each character and space in the longest line of the last column and set the right margin at the point reached.

4 Type main heading and subheading (if there is one) at the left margin. Turn up TWO single spaces and type the underscore from margin to margin.
5 Turn up TWO single spaces and type the column headings and then ONE single space and type the underscore again from margin to margin.
NB Remember to turn up ONCE before and TWICE after each horizontal line (in single spacing).

If you are using a word processing package, you may be able to use the program to create tables automatically.

5 Display the following on A5 landscape paper.

Turn up

2 spaces

WILD HERBS USED FOR HEALING

2 spaces

_____

Herb	Parts used	Healing uses

1 space
2 spaces

_____

Agrimony	Leaves	Coughs, colds, arthritis
Chickweed	Whole herb	Chilblains, skin diseases
Elder	Flowers	Colds, influenza, toothache

1 space

_____

NOTE: Column headings are not usually underlined when the table is ruled.

Blocked tabulation with columns of figures

When columns in a table contain figures, care must be taken to see that units come under units, tens under tens, etc. Where there are four or more figures, these are grouped in threes starting from the unit figure, a space being left, or a comma inserted, between each group. When typing blocked tabulation, the £ or % symbol, or the abbreviations m, ft, in, etc, are placed above the first figure in the longest line ie, blocked at the tab stop.

6 Type the following on A5 landscape paper in double spacing.

Turn up

LONGEST BRIDGES IN THE UK ← *In full*

2 spaces

2 spaces

_____

Name of bridge	Completed	Length	Length

1 space
2 spaces

_____

		m	ft
Humber	1980	1 410	4 626
Forth Road ...	1964	1 006	3 300
Severn	1966	988	3 240
Firth of Forth	1890	521	1 710

Double spacing

1 space

_____

KEYBOARDING SKILLS

Before proceeding to the exercises below, you should type the following skill building exercises:

use of apostrophe Nos 1–4, page 155.   **alphabetic sentence** No 11, page 156.
skill measurement No 32, page 161.   **record your progress** No 27, page 167.

PRODUCTION DEVELOPMENT

Continuation sheets for letters and memos

When a letter or memo extends to extra pages, these continuation sheets are typed on plain paper, which must be the same size, colour and quality (ie bond paper) as the first sheet. It is usual to type the following details at the top of the second and subsequent pages, starting on the fourth single-line space from the top of the paper.

No of page	It is preferable to type this information in double spacing. Turn up a minimum of three single spaces and continue with the remainder of the letter.
Date	
Name of addressee	

When a continuation sheet is needed, the letter must be so arranged that at least three or four lines are carried over to the continuation page. On no account must the continuation page contain only the complimentary close and the name of the writer. Do NOT divide a word from one page to the next. Leave approximately 25 mm (1 inch) clear at the bottom of the page before continuing on to the extra sheet. It is a good idea to mark the sheet lightly in pencil at 38 mm ($1\frac{1}{2}$ inches) up from the bottom to remind you, or, if a backing sheet is used and no carbon copy, you may wish to draw a heavy line on the backing sheet, so that it will show through as an indication to you that you are nearing the bottom of the paper. The word CONTINUED or PTO or a CATCHWORD may be used. (The first word or two that appear on the continuation page are typed in the bottom margin on the previous sheet and are known as catchwords.)

Additional copies

It is quite often necessary to make more than one copy of a document as well as the original copy. These extra copies are for the information of others concerned. If this is the case, the name(s) of these people is (are) typed either:
1 in the top right or left corner, or
2 at the foot of the letter or memo.

The names are usually typed one under the other and preceded by the words 'Copy for . . .', 'Distribute to . . .' or 'cc . . .'. When the completed letter is removed from the machine, the individual names are ticked or underlined. A copy should also be taken for the file. See page 183 for further information about distribution lists.

eg

1st copy	2nd copy	3rd copy
cc J Atkinson ✓	cc J Atkinson	cc J Atkinson
Mrs A Farmer	Mrs A Farmer ✓	Mrs A Farmer
File	File	File ✓

1 Type the following two-page letter on A4 paper. Mark the letter URGENT. As well as the original take two copies, one for the file and the other for Belinda Goodhill, Marketing Department. Prepare an envelope.

```
Our ref   MG/Ins/                                      6 September 1996

Mr Alec Tranter
45 Halberton Avenue
BRISTOL
Avon
BS1 1BW     Dr Mr T

BRADY CAR INSURANCE PLAN WITH EXTRA DISCOUNTS
                                    our
Thank you for your enquiry about/car insurance plan.

I am pleased to enclose your (personnal) quotation which I hope will meet
meet with your full approval.
                                          Your quotation/
```

In addition to the horizontal lines, a boxed table has vertical lines and the left and right sides may or may not be closed in by vertical lines. The vertical lines between the columns must be ruled exactly in the middle of each blank space. It is therefore advisable to leave an odd number of spaces between the columns—one for the vertical ruling and an equal number on either side of the ruling. If the outside verticals are to be ruled, the horizontal lines must extend (usually two spaces) to the left and right of the typed matter. To rule the vertical lines, take the following steps:

1   First set left margin and tab stops.
2   From the last tab stop, tap space bar once for each character and space in the longest line of the last column plus two spaces (if you are allowing three spaces between the columns) and set right margin at point reached.
3   After typing main heading and subheading (if there is one), turn up two single spaces and return to left margin.
4   Press margin release key and backspace two (if you are allowing three spaces between the columns). This gives you the starting point for the horizontal lines which will extend to the right margin.
5   Move to first tab stop and backspace two (if you are allowing three spaces between the columns); at this point make a pencil mark for the first vertical line.

6   Move to the next tab stop and backspace two; at this point make a pencil mark for the second vertical line.
7   Continue in the same way for any additional columns.
8   When you have typed the last horizontal line, mark the bottom of each of the vertical lines.
9   Horizontal lines may be ruled by underscore and the vertical lines in matching colour ink; all lines may be ruled by using the underscore, or all lines may be ruled in ink. If you are using an electronic keyboard, you may have the facility for setting out the columns and inserting the vertical lines. Refer to the user's handbook.
10 Do not allow the vertical lines to extend above or below the horizontal lines. They must meet precisely.

NOTE: When marking the top of the vertical lines, make a note of the scale points at which they have to be drawn so that when you have typed the bottom horizontal line, you will know exactly where to make the pencil marks.

7   Type the following table on A4 paper. Rule the lines carefully.

HOLLYBUSH COURT

Estimated costs per month

	Rose	Jonquil	Daisy
	£	£	£
Service charge	20.50	19.50	17.95
Ground rent	11.00	10.00	9.00
Water rate	9.87	9.87	9.87
Management services	15.45	14.45	13.45
Warden's salary ...	11.75	11.75	11.75
TOTAL			

Please calculate and insert the column totals

Margins on pages 2 & 3 — Top 38 mm (1½")
Left & right 25 mm (1")

PAGE 2

SPECIAL COLLECTIONS ← *Sp caps*

Domestic waste can be disposed of at
Recycling and Waste Reception Centres / *free of charge*

If you are not able to reach these
Centres the District Council can arrange
a special collection. There may be a
small charge for this service.

Some areas are now trying out a pilot
scheme to collect recyclable materials.
You will be informed if you live in one
of these areas.

The following items can be disposed of
at the Waste Reception Centres shown
on the following page of this leaflet -

glass	newspapers and magazines
scrap metal	textiles
cans	green garden waste

Arrange items in 2 columns, as shown

Highlight the names of the reception centres in some way.

PAGE 3

Quarry Pit
Mondays to Saturdays   8.30 am to 4.00 pm

Align times with right margin in ea case

Heath Fields
Mondays to Sundays   9.00 am to dusk

Poachers Wood
Mondays to Sundays   Dawn to dusk
                    (Check times in local press)

Gresham Corner
Mondays to Saturdays
(October to March)
(April to September)

You wl find the times in the Data Files (filename WALK) on page 174.

 Key in document 3 (filename WASTE) for 12-point printout. Use the 'flush right' facility for page 3 and
embolden all words that require emphasis. When you have completed this task, save under filename WASTE
and print an original. Retrieve the document and follow the instructions for text editing on page 172.

- *Multiple-line headings*—See **data store**, page 195.

NOTE: If an item in the descriptive column takes up more than one line, type the figures against the last line of the item, as shown in exercise 8, below.

8

OFFICE SUPPLIES

Price Buster Sale

Display the items under the hdg 'Office Sundries' in the order indicated — but do NOT insert the figures.

The following items, and many more, are on offer in our incredible Price Buster Sale.

ITEM	ORIGINAL PRICE	SALE PRICE
	£	£
Office Sundries		
③ Electronic stapler (supplied with foot/control)	412.00	350.00
① Rotary trimmer A4; light, portable	29.97	25.50
② Board clips (packs of 12)	27.66	25.00
Office Machines		
Facsimile (12-month guarantee)	595.00	545.50
Telephone answering m/c* (stylish design - - - - · ·	99.95	95.00

pedal (against Electronic stapler foot/control)

* C60 micro cassette provided.

** 16-line LCD display.

Personal word processor**   437.33   399.00

Key in document 8 (filename SALE) for 10-point printout. Embolden the column headings. When you have completed this task, save under filename SALE and print an original. Retrieve the document and follow the instructions for text editing on page 171.

Folded leaflets

The contents and display of folded leaflets varies enormously; it is therefore important to follow the layout given and any instructions very carefully. Brief details are usually typed on the front cover and further information on the inside pages 2 and 3. Occasionally, some brief details may be typed on the back cover. The paper may be folded and then fed into the machine, but unless great care is taken, it may crease. If possible, insert the paper lengthwise but, before doing so, mark the page numbers clearly in pencil as a guide. The following diagram will help:

FRONT SIDE OF PAPER (UNFOLDED)

fold

back page	front page

REVERSE SIDE OF PAPER (UNFOLDED)

fold

page 2	page 3

3   Type the following folded leaflet, displaying the information according to the instructions given and the display shown.

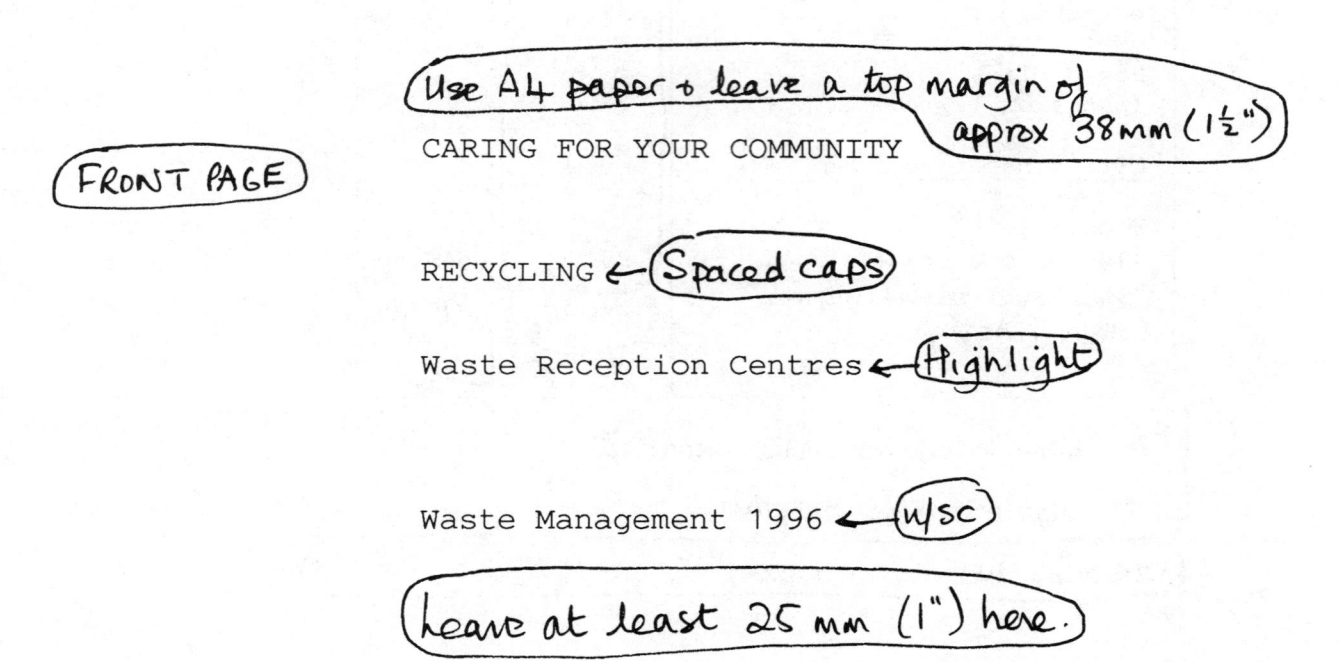

Use A4 paper + leave a top margin of approx 38mm (1½")

CARING FOR YOUR COMMUNITY

FRONT PAGE

RECYCLING ← *Spaced caps*

Waste Reception Centres ← *Highlight*

Waste Management 1996 ← *w/sc*

Leave at least 25 mm (1") here.

```
Further recycling information
can be obtained from -
01865 296715
```

THE NEWTOWN BUILDING SOCIETY

This sheet contains instructions that must be complied with when typing the documents. Read the information carefully before starting, and refer back to it frequently.

OFFICE SERVICES – REQUEST FORM

Typist's log sheet

Originator *Sally Peterson Chief Executive* .Department *Admin*   Date *Today's*   Ext No *31*

> Typists operating a word processor, or electronic typewriter with appropriate function keys, should apply the following automatic facilities: top margin; carrier return; line-end hyphenation; underline OR bold print (embolden); error correction, centring; any other relevant applications.

Remember to (a) complete the details required at the bottom of the form; (b) enter typing time per document in the appropriate column; and (c) before submitting this **log sheet** and your completed work, enter TOTAL TYPING TIME in the last column so that the typist's time may be charged to the originator.

Docu- ment No	Type of document and instructions	Copies – Original plus	Input form¶	Typing time per document	Total typing time ¥
1	"Make the most of yr money"	1 original	AT		
2	Memo	1 + 1	MS		
3	Ruled table	1 original	AT		
4	Banker's order form	1 original	MS		
5	Letter to Ann Dunbar	1 + 1	MS.		
6	"Change in invest- ment statement"	1 original	MS		
	(You wl need headed paper for the letter + the memo.)				
			TOTAL	TYPING TIME	

TYPIST – please complete:

Typist's name: Date received: Date completed:
                 Time received: Time completed:

> If the typed documents cannot be returned within 24 hours, the office services supervisor should inform the originator. Any item that is urgent should be marked with an asterisk (*).

¶ T = Typescript   AT = Amended Typescript   MS = Manuscript   SD = Shorthand Dictation   AD = Audio Dictation
¥ To be charged to the originator's department.

KEYBOARDING SKILLS

Before proceeding to the exercises below, you should type the following skill building exercises:

proofreading No 10, page 153. **techniques and reviews** No 10, page 157.
skill measurement No 31, page 161. **record your progress** No 26, page 167.

PRODUCTION DEVELOPMENT

- *Aligned right margin*—See **data store**, page 176.

Example in open punctuation

```
BROWN, A J, 46 Thomas Street, Leeds, LS2 9JT .....................      01532 21376
FISHER, L, & Co Ltd, 20 Clitton Road, Northampton, NN1 5BQ .......      01604 6868
```

1 Type the following telephone index in double spacing. Put names in alphabetical order according to surname (if a personal name) or the first word of name (if an impersonal name). Margins: 13 mm ($\frac{1}{2}$ inch) on either side. Align (block) right margin.

```
Akmal Ramzan & Son, 6 Crown Drive, Bedworth, Warwicks, CV12 8QR ...      01203 316890
Liam Kennedy Car Sales Ltd, 12 New Street, Dublin 8 ..............   00 3531 4648440
McBride (Sports) Ltd, 6 Park Street, Rosyth, Fife, KY11 2JL .......      01383 215585
Jones Bros, 13 Carmarthen Road, Swansea, West Glamorgan, SA5 7BL ..      01792 687141
Devlin Developments, PO Box 26, Cambridge, CB1 2JT ...............       01223 66510
P F Simcox & Co Ltd, 2 Mill Street, Nottingham, NG1 6BW ...........      01602 414014
Frau Inge Schneider, Kapellenstrasse 8, Geissberg, Wiesbaden 6200,
   Hesse, West Germany ...........................................  00 49 611 06121341201
Mme Chantal Deveraux, 25 rue de Paris, 0300 Moulins, Bourbonnaise,
   France .......................................................   00 33 (70) 44 00 58
```

Brief notes

You may be asked, in the office or in an examination, to type a letter or memo from brief notes. The following procedure should be adopted:

1 It is often wise to type a rough draft, making sure you get the points in the correct order, usually in the order they are given in the brief notes.
2 Avoid short, disconnected sentences and decide where to paragraph.
3 There is no need to correct typing errors if you make a rough draft as it will waste time, but verify dates, people's names, etc, and type them accurately.
4 Remove the paper with the rough draft from the machine and read carefully what you have typed, making any further amendments that may be necessary.
5 Insert a fresh sheet of paper, with appropriate carbon copies, if needed, and type a final copy ready for despatch.

2 Send a letter to Frau Inge Schneider, please & say how very much I am looking forward to seeing her again. Tell her that I wl meet her at Heathrow Airport next Friday (put date in please) at 1715 hrs. Say it is only an hour and a half's drive to my home, & my husband wl hv a meal waiting for us. He is an excellent chef! Finish the letter — Very best wishes. By the way, the salutation wl be — My very dear Inge. Date the letter for today & put her address (wh you wl find it in Ex 1 above) after mine, which is — Holly House, 4 Long Lane, Witney, Oxon, OX8 7AW.

MAKE THE MOST OF YOUR MONEY

Our new Fasset investment account is one of a whole range of ideas

to help you make the most of your money. // After you have studied

the following facts we are sure you will wish to complete the

enclosed
~~attached~~ form and return it to us.

3. Means you can start investing w. just £500.

The Fasset Investment Account -

1   Pays a top rate of interest; the more you save the higher the
    interest earned.   *on balances under*
2   Allows 2 penalty-free withdrawals each year.   *£10 000*
3   Allows additions to be made at any time.
4   Is an ideal way to invest large sums of money.
        Please change numbers

See how our interest rates compare with those of other accounts,

particularly if you have sums of over £10 000 to invest.

Copy the table shown overleaf, here, but omit the main heading, the initial paras & any ruling.

---

② (10 mins)

TO   Bill Longden
FROM   (Insert my name here - no designation)
DATE   (Insert)   *Use as a heading, please*
                                          a
*I hv bn asked to give a talk to/mtg of retired/people in our
town. The main theme is to be "Tips to Save Cash". As
well as giving them/ advice /abt saving w. a bldg society, I   ↳ l.c.
wanted to give them some practical hints such as —*

• *see if big bills can be pd in instalments;*
• *cancel subscriptions to clubs & publications you no longer
  make use of or need;*
• *buy in bulk those items you use every day;*
• *search thro' yr attic or wardrobe for those things
  you no longer need, & sell them - perhaps @ a car
  boot sale.*

*Have you any more ideas? If you hv, perhaps you cd let
me know by Fri of next week. Many thanks.*

SP *(Your initials)*   *Use 2 asterisks ** if you cannot form
                         a bullet mark.*

3 Type the following information on a postcard.

PENTAGON INDUSTRIES LTD ← (Highlight)
Langdon Estate   Station Road   CAMBRIDGE   CB12 1FY

Ref   LP/Wp.5/rt   14 August 1996

Thank you for your letter applying for the post
of word processor operator.

We now have 2 vacancies, one in the Accounts
Section and the other in Maintenance.   Your
application is being considered for the vacancy
in Accounts as you already have had experience
in this department.   I will contact you again
after the closing date for applications.

(Address the reverse side to Miss Nicola Tranter.
Her address is on the ~~previous~~ ~~page~~.)

4   *ARTHUR S FOLLETT   Opticians*
      Tranter House   Range Road   Glencaple   Dumfries   DG2 4RE
      Telephone: 01387 43219   Fax: 03 24 56 50 87

JFR/4890.26
According to our records it is now 2 yrs since yr
last eye test.
                              ,therefore,
~~If you wish~~ We suggest/th yr call in, or tel,
to arrange an appt, in the near future.
                    (,with Mr Follett,)   (Address the reverse
                                            side to yourself.)

Today's date
                    _____

5 LEYS ENTERPRISES
   (Insert address, tel & fax nos from p 39.)

Ref JP/ (Yr initials)   (Today's date)

If you like our merchandise, you may wish to recommend us
to others. If so, please call us with their details on
(enter phone no here from the hdg) & we wl forward a catalogue
to them immediately.
If they place an order with us we wl send you, free of charge,
(leave one clear line space & enter the details from
the Data Files (filename LEYS) on ~~page~~ 173.)

Fassett Investment Account ← *Caps not u/scored*

The minimum investment is £500; additions to this amount may be made at any time. The interest is paid annually.

Investment	Gross [1] per annum %	Net [1] per annum %	Gross [2] per annum %	Net [2] per annum %
£500 - £2 999	4.00	3.00	3.25	2.44
£3 000 - £9 999	4.55	3.41	3.80	2.58
£10 000 or more	*5.00*	*3.75*	*4.25*	*3.19*

[1] Including bonus, which will be earned for 3 or less withdrawals in a year.

2. *Excluding bonus.*

(4) (15 mins)

BANKER'S ORDER

Title of bank _____

Address of bank _____

Postcode _____

Please pay on the _____ day of _____ 19 _
to the Newtown Building Society the sum of
£ _____ (in figures) _____ (amount in words)
& a similar amt thereafter on the _____ day of ea
mth until I give notice in writing to the contrary.
(leave 1" (25 mm) clear here)

SIGNATURE _____ DATE _____

NAME _____

ADDRESS _____

Postcode _____

BANK ACCOUNT NUMBER _____

A4 paper & double spacing, unless otherwise stated.

2   Type the following letter of application from Nicola Tranter, on plain paper with a copy on bank paper.

7 Welcombe Close
CAMBRIDGE
CB4 2SE

Your ref LP/Wp.5/rt

9 August 1995 [6 inserted above, changing to 1996]

Mr Lionel Pardoe
(Personal) Officer
(Please take address from CV)

Dear Sir   (APPLICATION FOR WORD PROCESSOR OPERATOR)

I wish to apply for the post that was advertised in the Evening
Post yesterday, for a word processor (operater.)

While at Cams College of Technical Training I undertook my work
experience with Pentagon Industries Ltd where I ~~undertook a~~ was employed in a
[office ^] variety of/duties.

I have since gained an NVQ in Business Administration, as well as external
examinations in both Word Processing and Typewriting and as I
found working with Pentagon so enjoyable and interesting I feel
I am now qualified to apply for the position advertised.

I am enrolling for a further evening/course at Cams College in the autumn
when I shall be taking NVQ Level 3 in Bus Admin. // As I hv
bn away for a holiday this yr, I shall be available for an
interview at any time. (My CV is enclosed.)

Yrs ffy

NICOLA T———

Postcards

Many firms send postcards [A6—148 mm × 105 mm (5$\frac{7}{8}$ inches × 4$\frac{1}{8}$ inches)] in acknowledgement of letters and orders. These formal acknowledgements are typed like memos without a salutation or complimentary close. Note the following:

1   The firm's name may be printed, typed at the left margin or centred, usually about four single spaces from the top of the card.
2   Margins: 13 mm ($\frac{1}{2}$ inch) on either side is preferable.

3   Use single spacing with double between paragraphs which may be blocked or indented.
4   After typing the firm's name and address, it is usual to turn up two single spaces and type the reference at the left margin with the date backspaced from the right margin on the same line.
5   Turn up two single spaces and type the main body of the postcard.
6   The name and address of the addressee is typed on the reverse side, parallel to the longest edge.

(5) (25 mins)

Send the following letter to Ann Dunbar. You wl find
her address & account no. in our Data Files (filename
ACCO) p.173. I wd like one copy as well as the original
+ an envelope, please. Don't forget to mark the letter
PERSONAL.

Our ref SP/(Miss Dunbar's a/c no)/(Yr initials)
Dr Miss D _____
Account Number - (type in caps + enter no. fr Data Files)
I am pleased to tell you th the above-numbered a/c wl
mature on (insert date here - 1st Mon of next month). Its
value wl be in the region of £27 083. 14. // Since you
opened the a/c their hv been many changes in the
Society's range of investment opportunities. The following
rates are on offer until the end of (insert month - 3 mths
today), on selected a/cs.

	Interest rates	
£25 000	5.00%	These rates wl increase
£35 000 + over	5.75%	over a 5-yr period

As you know, our society is comitted to providing
impartial + independant advice. W. this in mind,
I wd welcome the opportunity of discussing yr future
investment requirements, + shd be grateful if you wd
contact me to arrange a mutually convenient time to do so.
// I look forward to hearing fr you.

    Yrs sinc

    SALLY P _____
    (Designation here)

PS I am enclosing details of our latest FASSET Investment a/c
    for yr info.

(6)   (10 mins)

CHANGES IN INVESTMENT STATEMENT
(Leave 2" (51 mm) here before inserting the following para & then
the table wh you will find in the Data Files (filename
ACCO) p.173.

On yr statement we wl now show both gross interest
earned and any tax deducted. Where tax has bn deducted,
we wl also show net interest earned. In future we wl be
sending out the Investment Statement AFTER the last
payment in ea of interest in ea/yr rather than in Jan/ tax
of ea yr. The following table is a guide as to when
to expect a statement.

KEYBOARDING SKILLS

Before proceeding to the exercises below, you should type the following skill building exercises:

improve your spelling Nos 19 and 20, page 155.   **alphabetic sentence** No 10, page 156.
skill measurement No 30, page 160.   **record your progress** No 25, page 167.

PRODUCTION DEVELOPMENT

- *Curriculum vitae* (*cv*)—See **data store**, page 182.

1 Type the following exercise on A4 paper. Suggested left and right margins 25 mm (1 inch).

```
C U R R I C U L U M   V I T A E

PERSONAL DETAILS
```

Highlight the words in bold type in some way.

```
Nichola Tranter                    Date of birth: 15 June 1978
7 Welcombe Close
CAMBRIDGE   CB4 2SE                Telephone: 01223 4708
```

```
EDUCATION AND TRAINING

1989 - 1994     Highcrest Comprehensive School, Cambridge
1994 - 1995     Cams College of Technical Training
```

```
QUALIFICATIONS
```
RSA Stage II in Typewriting Skills & Word Processing

```
GCSE            Grade A in Typewriting
                Grade B in English, Maths and Geography
                Grade C in History
NVQ             Levels 1, 2 and 3 in Business Administration
```

```
WORK EXPERIENCE

Pentagon Industries Ltd, Cambridge.
While there I undertook general typing, as well as reseptionist
duties where I had to liaise with customers.  I also dealt with
the mail and undertook some petty cash and invoice processing.
```

```
PERSONAL INTERESTS

Guides, cycling and climbing.  I am also doing the Duke of
Edinburghs Award Scheme.  I have been awarded a bronze medal
and am now working towards a silver.
```

```
REFEREES
```
Insert the name & address of the 2nd referee here, please. You wl find the details in the Data Files (filename CV) page 173.

```
Mr R F Clayton BA
Head
Highcrest Comprensive School
Highcrest Rd                          Telephone: 01223 67093
Cambridge   CB6 4TR
```
In full

PRODUCTION DEVELOPMENT

Allocating space

In examinations and in business, you may be given instructions that will require you to leave a certain amount of blank space in a typewritten document for the insertion, at a later date, of further information. For example, you may be asked to leave room for the name and address of the addressee in a circular letter, to leave a specified top margin of, say, 51 mm (2 inches), or to leave a certain amount of space in the middle of a document for the later insertion of a diagram, photograph, etc.

In an examination, you will be told how much space to leave, either as a measurement, eg leave 25 mm (one inch), or as a number of linespaces, eg leave seven single lines clear.

It is important to remember that if an instruction states 'leave seven single lines *clear*', you must turn up *one extra space*, ie turn up eight single spaces and type on the eighth line, so leaving seven clear. If the instructions ask for a space of '*at least* 51 mm (2 inches)', it is wise to leave a little extra space rather than risk not leaving sufficient space. If the words 'at least' are not used, then the amount of space left must be exact. However, if you have to *insert lines* and use the *underscore* for the horizontals, you would turn up the exact number of lines. For example, if you had to draw a square 51 mm (2 inches) deep, and you were using the underscore for the horizontal lines, you would type the first horizontal line, turn up 12 (*twelve*) and type the second horizontal line.

1   Type the following on A4 paper in single spacing.

leave a top margin of at least 51 mm (2 inches)

TWO SIDES TO A FAX

The problem of faxing a two-sided document has now bn overcome. [A m/c is ~~now~~ on the market wh scans both sides of a document at the same time, so saving the operator the time & cost of photocopying both sides of a paper on 2 (Seperate) sheets.

leave 38 mm (1½ inches) here for the later insertion of a photograph of ~~the~~ machine.

NOTE: The m/c stores the second side in its memory for transmission later. Up to 50 pages can be (handeled) in this way.
The m/cs are not cheap. The cost is in the region of £3 000.   (Please correct the circled errors)

Decimalized enumeration

In addition to the methods of enumeration already introduced, it is modern practice to use the decimal point, followed by a figure, for the subdivisions. For example, 4(a) and 4(b) would become 4.1 and 4.2, and 4(a)i and 4(a)ii would become 4.1.1 and 4.1.2. This method of enumeration is often used when numbering minutes. When using open punctuation, the decimal point must be inserted. Leave two clear character spaces after the final figure, not a full stop.

4 Type the following exercise on A4 paper. Suggested left and right margins: 25 mm (1 inch).

LEYS ENTERPRISES

Insert address here. You wl find it on p 39.

Minutes of a meeting of sales representatives for the south-west region held in the main building in Druce Road, on Tuesday, 3 September 1996 at 2.30 pm. *Change to 24-hr clock*

PRESENT: Alan Cox *(Chairman)*

Jo Steinberg, Bob Anderson, Glyn Watts, Brenda Abbotts, Bill Julyan, René Grant, Ivan Parojcic

22.1   APOLOGIES FOR ABSENCE

Inset 6 spaces

22.1.1   An apology was recieved from Geoffrey Raynor who was in Germany on business for the company.

22.1.2   An apology was also received from Patricia Fowler who was in hospital recovering from a major operation. Best wishes were sent for her speedy return to good health.

22.2   MINUTES OF THE LAST MEETING

The minutes of the mtg held on 2 July '96 had already bn circulated & were taken as read. They were approved & signed by the Chairman.

22.3   MATTERS ARISING

There were no matters arising from the minutes.

22.4   REPORTS

22.4.1 Glyn Watts, Brenda A — & Bob A — gave full & comprehensive reports for their particular areas.

22.4.2 Bob Anderson was commended for his excellent efforts in his first 4 mths with the co.

22.5   CELLULAR TELEPHONES

The Chairman reported th cellular telephones are to be fitted in all cars used by senior managment & sales staff as from the end of Oct.

22.6   AOB *(In full)*

The Chairman said th he had rec'd a report from Geoffrey R — who was in Düsseldorf, & his visit was proving most successfull.

22.7   DATE OF NEXT MTG

Wed 23 Oct '96 @ 1430 hrs.

Chairman . . . . DATE . . . .
(Caps)

2

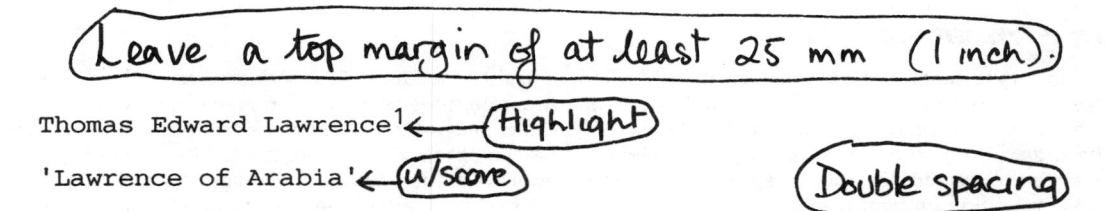
Leave a top margin of at least 25 mm (1 inch).

Thomas Edward Lawrence[1] ← (Highlight)

'Lawrence of Arabia' ← (u/score)

(Double spacing)

← 51mm (2") →

51mm (2")

Rule a box here
51 mm x 51 mm
(2" x 2")
for the later
insertion of a
photograph.

T E Lawrence[2] was born at Tremadoc, North Wales on 15 August 1888. He was educated at Oxford High School and Jesus College, Oxford, where he obtained a first in modern history in 1910. He then travelled in the Middle East where he learnt to live like an Arab.

In 1916 he became adviser to Prince Faisal who was then uniting the Arabs in revolt against their Turkish rulers. Winning the Arabs' confidence lawrence joined the campaign of guerrilla raids from/ helping to defeat the Turks. It was/then he became known as 'lawrence of Arabia', + remains a legend to this day. // lawrence enjoyed the excitement of speed + was killed, in a motorcycle accident in Dorset, where he had bn living at th time.

[1] 1888 – 1935

[2] T E L ——— wrote various books, his most important being The Seven Pillars of Wisdom ← (u/sc the title.)

, at the age of 47,

Key in document 2 (filename ARAB) for 10-point printout. Use the word wraparound facility. When you have completed this task, save under filename ARAB and print an original. Retrieve the document and follow the instructions for text editing on page 171.

Minutes of meetings

Details of any decisions, resolutions or business discussed at a meeting, are recorded and preserved. These are known as minutes. Each minute is usually numbered as this facilitates indexing. The order in which the minutes are typed always follows the order in which the items appeared on the agenda. As well as being numbered, each minute will have a heading which may be typed as a side heading or as a shoulder heading. A description of the meeting, including the date, time and place appears first together with a list of those present with the chairman's name first followed by the names of the officers/members. After the minutes have been approved, the chairman will sign them; a space may be left for signature when the minutes are being prepared together with a space for the date on which the minutes are signed.

3 Type the following minutes on A4 paper. Suggested left and right margins: 25 mm (1 inch). Set a tab stop or second margin a minimum of three character spaces after the longest side heading for the matter following the side headings.

THE LEYS SOCIAL CLUB

Minutes of a committee meeting held in the Club Room, Sports Pavillion, Highfield Lane, on Tuesday ↑ at ↗
Insert date and time here from Ex 1, p100

Present

Rosa Payne (Chair)
✓ (Secretary) *Insert sec's name from Ex 1, p100*
Isobel Brett (Treasurer)
Cherry Dixon ⎫ (Committee members)
Maisie Baron ⎪ *Names of cttee in alphabetical order, please.*
George Plowden ⎬
Ray Hudson ⎪
Liz Tarrant ⎭

1 APOLOGIES FOR ABSENCE — Apologies were received from Garry Little, Madge Springett and Trevor Philpot.

2 MINUTES OF MEETING HELD ON ↑ *Insert date here from Ex 1, p100* — These were accepted as (bieng) a true record of the proceedings and signed by Rosa Payne, Chair.

3 MATTERS ARISING — Maisie Baron had looked into the possibility of hiring caterers for the monthly social events and gave the committee details of costs. It was agreed to discuss this fully at the next meeting.

4 CORRESPONDENCE — There was no correspondence.

5 ANNUAL CLUB OUTING — Ray H— agreed to book the coach for the outing. It was agreed th a full time-table of the (days) events be sent to those members going. ~~word~~ This was unanimously agreed.

6 CHANGE OF VENUE FOR MONTHLY SOCIAL EVENTS — Cherry D— said she had booked a room in The Manor for all future mtgs. She stated th the hiring charges were £2.00 a mtg less than the present venue. This news was welcomed by the cttee.

7 AOB — There was no further business.

8 DATE OF NEXT MTG — *Insert first Tues of next mth*

CHAIR . . . . DATE . . . .

Continuation sheets

In a long document that extends to more than one sheet of paper, it will be necessary to note the following points:

1. To ensure that you do not continue to type too low down on the paper put a light pencil mark at least 25 mm (1 inch) from the bottom edge of the paper, before inserting it into the machine, and do not type below this mark. Or, rule a heavy line on a backing sheet across the complete width, at least 25 mm (1 inch) from the bottom edge of the sheet, so that it will show through your typing paper, and do not type past this line.
2. **Pagination (the numbering of pages)** The first page is not generally numbered; second and subsequent pages are usually numbered in arabic figures, approximately 13 mm ($\frac{1}{2}$ inch) from the top edge of the paper. The number may be blocked at the left or right margin, or centred on the typing line. In some documents, the pages may be numbered at the bottom.
3. **Catchwords** Sometimes the typist may be required to type the first word or two that appear on a continuation sheet at the foot of the preceding page. These words are known as catchwords. They are typed below the last line and are aligned at the right margin. CONTINUED or PTO may be used instead of the catchwords, but not the number of the next page.
4. **Reverse of paper** If a continuation sheet is typed on the reverse of the paper and the margins are not equal, the margin settings should also be reversed.

Ellipsis (*the omission of words*)

Words are sometimes deliberately omitted at the beginning, end or in the middle of a sentence. Such omission is indicated by the use of three spaced full stops with a space either side, as follows . . . When quotation marks come before the ellipsis, there is a space between the mark and the first full stop. There is also a space before the final quotation mark, eg " . . . "

3 Type the following exercise on A4 paper in double spacing.

Change word operator(s) to typists throughout, please.

Repetitive Strain Injury (RSI)   *in full*

(An extract from TYPING FIRST COURSE, Sixth Ed, HANDBOOK, SOLUTIONS, and RESOURCE MATERIAL, by Archie Drummmond and Anne Coles-Mogford, published by Stanley Thornes.)

Ever since our first publication in 1963, we have advocated and emphasized the need for correct posture at the keyboard. For many years RSI has been a common ailment in industrial jobs, but only recently have office workers, particularly word processor operators, complaned.

This affliction can be minimized by correct positioning of the hands . . . perfecting of typing techniques and rest periods away from the keyboard. //Employers who introduce equipment and furniture without planning how and where it will be used are letting themselves in for employee complaints that range from eye strain, blurred vision . . . and workers' compensation claims increase while productivity drops. *highlight*

PTO

2 Type the following notice of meeting and chairman's agenda on A4 paper. Suggested margins: left and right 25 mm (1 inch). Tab stop for 'Notes' column: 12 pitch 52, 10 pitch 43.

LEYS ENTERPRISES

(Please type the address here, on one line. You wl find it on page 59.)

A meeting of sales representatives for the south-west region will be held in the conference room of the main building in Druce Road, on Tuesday, 3 September 1996 at 2.30 pm.

A G E N D A	N O T E S
1 Apologies for absence. (Geoffrey Raynor will be in Germany on business.)	1
2 Minutes of the last meeting of sales representatives held on Tuesday, 2 July, 1996.	2
3 Matters arising.	3
4 Recieve reports from Glyn Watts, Brenda Abbotts, Bob Anderson. (Bob Anderson has recently joined the company.)	4
5 Cellular telephones. (They are to be instaled in all cars by the end of next month.)	5
6 Any other business. (Mr Raynors visit to Germany and Ms Grant's impending visit next month.)	6
7 *Date of next mtg. (Some time towards the end of Oct.)*	7

VDU Screen

This should be ~~be~~ at /a suitable angle and at a comfortable distance from the

operator.   Wherever possible:

1   the body should be positioned so that the operator is looking
    straight /at the VDU - not looking at the screen sidways; /ahead

2   the operator should bend forward /and not bend the shoulders;
    fr the hips

3 there shd be adequate lighting - no glare on
   the screen fr daylight or artificial light;

4 a document holder can be very helpful +
   it shd be ~~positioned~~ _placed_ so th the text book ⊃
   (or source document) is at the same level +
   distance [so as to reduce the amount of head,

6 neck + eye movement; (as the VDU display,)

7 the eyes shd be level w the top of the screen
   + btwn 400 - 760 mm (16-30 inches) fr the screen;

5 the screen shd be positioned at a suitable
   distance, shd be adjustable + at an acceptable
   angle;

7 noise, (temprctures) + humidity shd be regulated.

Many repetitive strain injuries hv bn linked /U.C.
to the poor ~~posture of the~~ _unsuitability of the_ operator because
of the [chair, desk, + poor typing techniques;

Lighting ← (Highlight)

Adequate lighting can reduce glare on display
screens + help to avoid operator eyestrain +
fatigue.) [+ strained/ more easily +, when the eyes are tired
Eyestrain wl tire the operator / there wl be more
mistakes. || Ideally, to be as readable as possible,
the screen shd be 3 to four times brighter
than the lighting in the room.
A difficulty arises when one needs to illuminate
the paper copy and [avoid screen glare. [, at the same
~~time,~~
Where possible, the (ceiling) lights shd be dim
+ replaced by a desk lamp with a bowl-
shaped reflector.
Some vendors recommend th a screen shield
(a mesh or glass device w a special coating
of conductive material) shd be placed . . .

 Key in document 3 (filename SAFE) for 12-point printout. Use the word wraparound function. When you have completed this task, save under filename SAFE and print an original. Retrieve the document and follow the instructions for text editing on page 171.

KEYBOARDING SKILLS

Before proceeding to the exercises below, you should type the following skill building exercises:

proofreading No 9, page 152.   **techniques and reviews** No 9, page 157.
skill measurement No 29, page 160.   **record your progress** No 24, page 166.

PRODUCTION DEVELOPMENT

Notice of a meeting

The notice should contain details of the date, time and place
of the meeting and is usually incorporated with the agenda.

Agenda

An agenda contains a list of items to be discussed at a
meeting. These items are usually listed in a certain order and
numbered for easy reference, as follows:

1 Apologies
2 Minutes of last meeting
3 Matters arising out of the minutes
4 Correspondence
5 Reports
6 Any special points for discussion
7 Any other business
8 Date of next meeting

Agendas may be displayed in a variety of different ways. It is
wise to follow the display indicated in the exercise being
copied, or to use the house style when typing agendas in the
office. The CHAIRMAN'S AGENDA may contain more
information than the agenda for the other members of the
committee, the right side of the page being left blank so that
notes can be made by the chairman of any decisions
reached, etc. The word NOTES is usually typed above the
blank space to the right of the listed items, and the item
numbers may be retyped for ease of reference.

1 Type the following notice of meeting and agenda on A4 paper. Suggested margins: Left 38 mm (1½ inches),
   right 25 mm (1 inch).

THE LEYS SOCIAL CLUB   *Insert date - first Tues of this month for the mtg.*

A committee meeting of The Leys Social Club is to be
held in the Club Room, the Sports Pavillion, Highfield
Lane, Crewe, on Tuesday   at 7.30 pm.

change to 24-hr clock

A G E N D A

1 Apologies for absence

2 Minutes of the meeting held on *Tues*

   Insert date - first Tues of last mth

3 Matters arising

4 Annual club outing

5 Correspondence

6 Change of venue for monthly social events

7 Any other business

8 Date of next meeting

SIMON O'DELL
Honorary Secretary